Opposing Currents

Opposing Currents

The Politics of Water and Gender in Latin America

Edited by Vivienne Bennett,

Sonia Dávila-Poblete,

and María Nieves Rico

University of Pittsburgh Press

For the women in Latin America whose struggle for water
is an example of their strength.

For the men of tomorrow, especially the ones we are raising:
Adin and Sebastian.
VB and MNR

For Sergio, an understanding and supportive compañero.
MNR

In memory of my parents and especially my grandmother Pepita,
whom I admired for their strength in moments
of hopeless despair and loss.
SDP

Published by the University of Pittsburgh Press, Pittsburgh, Pa., 15260
Copyright © 2005, University of Pittsburgh Press
All rights reserved
Manufactured in the United States of America
Printed on acid-free paper
10 9 8 7 6 5 4 3 2 1

Library of Congress Cataloging-in-Publication Data

Opposing currents : the politics of water and gender in Latin America /
edited by Vivienne Bennett, Sonia Dávila-Poblete, and María Nieves
Rico.
    p. cm.— (Pitt Latin American series)
Includes bibliographical references and index.
ISBN 0-8229-5854-6 (alk. paper)
1. Water-supply--Government policy—Latin America. 2. Water-
supply—Social aspects—Latin America. 3. Women in development—
Latin America. I. Bennett, Vivienne, 1953- II. Dávila-Poblete,
Sonia. III. Rico, Nieves. IV. Series.
HD1696.5.L37O66 2004
333.91'0098—dc22

2004015716

Contents

v

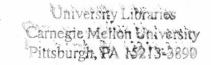

Tables and Map

Preface

This book is the result of a fortuitous meeting. The book's coeditors—Vivienne (an American living in San Diego, California), Sonia (a Bolivian living in Mexico), and Nieves (an Argentinean living in Chile)—met in Mexico City at a conference on women and water management in Latin America in May 1998. The conference made it clear that the discussion on women and water was in its infancy and that gender equity in the water sector was being confused with gender equality. Whereas equity means justice and fairness, equality means aiming for sameness. The three of us (with a handful of conference attendees) argued for the need to work toward equity while others responded by arguing that equality had already been achieved.

Later that year, in August, coincidentally, Vivienne and Nieves presented their work at the Stockholm Water Symposium, again finding considerable agreement in perspectives. The conversations we had over the course of the week in Sweden led to the idea for a book. At the Mexico City conference, we both felt that we were swimming against the current, a current that was enabling a status quo set on ignoring the very tangible benefits from incorporating a gender perspective. In Stockholm, we conceived of a book that would continue this journey against the current by demonstrating that a gender perspective is not only possible but essential for effective water management.

In September 1998, Sonia and Vivienne met again at the Latin American Studies Association (LASA) Congress in Chicago. We began sketching out concepts for the book in between sessions, and that led to the three of us creating a panel on gender and water for the LASA 2000 Congress that brought together researchers and practitioners working with women on water projects in different Latin American countries.

We moved from concept to book during the spring of 2001 when Vivienne was on a six-month sabbatical in Querétaro, Mexico. Through an active transcontinental networking process, we invited as many people as possible to submit case studies. We received thirteen abstracts from eight countries, eventually netting the eight case studies in this book. In early 2002, we sent the case study authors conceptual questions to guide their analysis and provide unifying threads that would run through the book. In August 2002, the three of us (Vivienne, Sonia, and Nieves) met in Cuernavaca, Mexico, to read and discuss each of the case study chapters and to sketch out the remainder of the book.

We have been extremely fortunate to work with twelve extraordinary contributors, who approached the book with great enthusiasm. They persevered in writing their chapters, most of them doing so under very stressful circumstances, demonstrating how social upheaval increasingly bisects our work. Norma Giarraca and Norma Del Pozo wrote their chapter on Tucumán, Argentina, in January and February 2002 when the Argentine economy collapsed, the banking system closed down nationwide, and street protests were going on outside the authors' window. The Cochabamba, Bolivia, chapter was written during the 2002 presidential elections, which were fraught with tension when an indigenous peasant leader nearly upset the status quo. Stephanie Buechler wrote her chapter on Mexico while working in India during the nuclear war scare between India and Pakistan; in the middle of writing she and her family were evacuated to Sri Lanka, where she picked up the thread of her writing. Two authors suffered very serious health problems in the middle of writing their chapters—both managed to complete their writing despite physical obstacles. Another author wrote during a transcontinental move, one wrote while nursing a newborn, while yet another wrote while taking her doctoral exams.

The life stories of our authors point to the increasing globalization of our communities—an American writing about Mexico from India, an Argentinean working on gender in Chile, a Bolivian involved in a water project in Mexico, two Americans studying water in Mexico, a Dutch woman writing about women and water in Mexico and Bolivia while studying in the United States, a Peruvian writing about women and water in Peru while studying in Holland, an Ecuadorian writing about women and water in Ecuador while living in the United States. They also point to the increasing challenges of everyday life, where we have all become adept at managing multiple complex situations simultaneously (nuclear war threats, having babies, childcare, long-distance moves, health problems, and work commitments).

We feel privileged to have had the opportunity to collaborate with our contributing authors, and we thank them very deeply for their unswerving commitment to their work with women and water and for their commitment to this book. They were cheerful in the face of multiple revisions of their chapters, and we learned much from working with them and their case material so closely.

Collectively, the three of us would also like to thank the following people: David Barkin; Soledad Gutiérrez; Larry Herzog; Patricia Rosas; Herzonia Yáñez-Chávez; Aníbal Yáñez-Chávez; Margreet Zwarteveen, and members of the Red de Investigadores Sociales sobre el Agua in Mexico. We also thank Nathan MacBrien, acquisitions editor at the University of Pittsburgh Press, for his ongoing support and enthusiasm for this project; the two anonymous reviewers who read our prospectus, gave the University of Pittsburgh the thumbs up, and sent us very helpful comments and suggestions; Steve Humme and the anonymous reveiwer who read the completed manuscript; Linda Farthing, who signed on to edit a couple of chapters and stayed on to help revise the entire manuscript; and the copyeditor for the press, Kathleen Paparchontis, for her excellent tightening of the writing.

Vivienne would like to thank her nine-year-old son, Adin Herzog, who endured Mom working on this book early mornings, late evenings, and during a big part of every weekend. I would also like to deeply thank my co-authors, Sonia Dávila-Poblete and María Nieves Rico. To make this book happen, we met on two continents, in three countries, and six cities; we traveled not only the world together but the mind and the spirit. Without their expertise and insights in the areas of water (Sonia) and gender (Nieves) this book would not have been possible. Working on this book with them has been one of the great experiences of my life, and for that I thank them.

Sonia would like to thank Vivienne Bennett because without her this book never would have seen the light of day. I particularly appreciate her perseverance, her meticulous commentaries that always hit the nail on the head, her encouragement to continue along the lengthy and torturous process of writing, her generosity with her time and her knowledge, and most invaluable of all, the friendship that we have developed. I thank Nieves Rico for being patient during our interminable discussions about the material in chapter three during which I had to rethink many of the assumptions inherent to my profession. The friendship that developed with Vivienne and Nieves as we worked on the book, and the wonderful shared moments, were a gift for which I will always be grateful. I thank my "paisana," Soledad, who had to put up with all the ups and downs that accompany the writing of a book, for her patience, and for the support she offered continuously, consistently, and selflessly. I thank all my friends who gave me encouragement and who had to tolerate my ramblings and digressions as well my anxieties stemming from the extensive reading I did to better understand the socio-economic situation facing our beloved Latin America.

Nieves would like to thank the two people who daily were witness to the effort that it took to write this book: Sergio, my life companion, and Sebastián, my six-year-old son, who both showed great patience with my absences due to professional travel and with seeing their companion and mother seated at the computer, sometimes happy with how the chapters were going and sometimes anguished. I would especially like to thank my coeditors, Viv and Sonia, from whom I learned so much and felt so much support and respect. I thank Sonia because the experience of coauthoring a chapter was a very rich one that enabled me to grow professionally as it forced me to rethink many of my ideas and to develop my ability to dialogue about the gender perspective with professionals from other arenas. I thank Viv because without her, without her efforts, enthusiasm, and her on-target commentaries and contributions, this book would never have been possible. She is the one who kept our spirits up each time it seemed that we would never reach the end, and she is the one who assumed the responsibility of coordinating between us and maintaining open and continuous communication with all of the contributors to the book. I thank Viv and Sonia for having given me the opportunity for two new and very close friendships, despite the distance from Santiago de Chile to Mexico and to the United States, friendships that go far beyond the confines of this book.

Opposing Currents

UNITED STATES

ATLANTIC OCEAN

MEXICO

□ *Comarca Lagunera*

□ *Irapuato*

Mexico City □*La Purificación Tepetitla*

CUBA HAITI

DOMINICAN REPUBLIC

BELIZE

HONDURAS

GUATEMALA NICARAGUA

COSTA RICA

EL SALVADOR PANAMA

Heredia Province

San José

GUYANA

VENEZUELA

FRENCH GUIANA

COLOMBIA

SURINAME

Carchi

★

Quito

ECUADOR

PERU

BRAZIL

Lima ★

Llullucha □

BOLIVIA

La Paz

★ □ *Cochabamba*

Sucre ★

PARAGUAY

PACIFIC OCEAN

CHILE

San Miguel de Tucumán □

ARGENTINA

URUGUAY

Buenos Aires ★

□ Case study site

★ National capital

| 0 | | 500 miles |

| 0 | 400 | 800 kilometers |

Latin America, Showing Case Study Sites

Vivienne Bennett

1 Introduction

The 1992 Dublin Conference on Water and the Environment was a watershed event in the world of water policy because of the adoption of the four "Dublin principles" that have guided decision making ever since. The principles state:

1. Fresh water is a finite and vulnerable resource, essential to sustain life, development, and the environment.

2. Water development and management should be based on a participatory approach, involving users, planners, and policy makers at all levels.

3. Women play a central role in the provision, management, and safeguarding of water.

4. Water has an economic value in all its competing uses and should be recognized as an economic good (United Nations 1992a).

The first principle has focused worldwide attention on the importance of sustainable development, the second on mainstreaming a participatory approach in development projects, and the fourth has led to a conceptual shift from water as a basic right to water as a commodity. But for the third principle, we have only deafening silence. Although the first, second, and fourth Dublin principles have shaped a revolution in water policy, the third principle—no less revolutionary—has been marginalized. Despite variations on the third principle that appear in every global policy statement on water (Global Water Partnership Technical Advisory Committee 2000; Sitarz 1993), with rare exception, it is not spelled out, mainstreamed, or implemented (for exceptions, see the work of the Netherlands Development Assistance [1997] and the Swedish International Development Cooperation Agency [no date]).

Yet translating the third principle into action would be quite straightforward as it recognizes an important reality: not that women *should become* central to water management but that they *already are*. What are the implications of this reality? It is simply that women already know about water management. Why is this powerful? Because if women already know about water management, then their knowledge, experiences, and priorities will enrich policy and planning in the water sector. Bringing in women's knowledge, experiences, and priorities regarding water use alongside men's *is* to implement a gendered perspective in water management. The connection between gender and water is actually as visible as the connection between water and sustainable development, but the mainstream current of global policymaking until now has tended not to look at it.

Our objectives are threefold: (1) to examine the evolution and implementation of water and gender policies with a focus on Latin America and explore how they intersect, (2) to present case studies of women involved in urban and rural water resources management in Latin America, (3) to demonstrate that a gendered perspective is essential for successful water resources management.[1]

In almost every region of the world today, water looms as a crisis because of overexploitation of groundwater and contamination of surface water. All world cities face inadequate water supplies, and in many rural areas, water for production and consumption is insufficient. Chronic water shortages afflict more than eighty nations, and at least 40 percent of the world's population lives with insufficient water (Dávila-Poblete 2002, 248). Demand is constantly increasing because of population growth and the consequent increased need for food. Often the local demand for water outstrips supply. As a result, local supplies of water are exhausted, water is diverted from distant watersheds, and dams are built to store water, all of which cause environmental damage and ecosystem disturbances. Across the globe, domestic, industrial, and agricultural waste products pollute water supplies, further depleting the available supply of usable water.

In region upon region, poor water management, characterized by top down, fragmented, and sectoral approaches, exacerbate these problems (Global Water Partnership Technical Advisory Committee 2000, 9). Often groundwater extraction is either not regulated, or regulations are not enforced, thus aquifers become depleted as water demand increases. Similarly, surface water (rivers, streams, lakes) allocation is subject to the influence of powerful lobbies and interest groups that have short-term gain rather than

Table 1.1   Population without Water Service in Latin America

	Urban (%)	Rural (%)	Total (%)
Brazil	N/A	N/A	28
Ecuador	19	49	29
Peru	13	49	23
Argentina	15	70	21
Bolivia	7	45	21
Venezuela	12	42	16
Chile	1	34	6

Source: United Nations 2001
   Note: Population without water service is defined as population without access to water from home connections, public standposts, wells, or spring water. Without access to these services, urban populations receive water primarily from water truck deliveries, and rural populations carry water from rivers or streams.

long-term resource sustainability in mind. Industry and agriculture have both caused widespread contamination of surface water, a problem that is not only extremely costly to mitigate but also has a lasting influence on community health and related health sector costs. Clean up of heavily contaminated rivers has been achieved in Europe and the United States but not to date in low-income countries.

In Latin America, 16 percent of the total population lives without water service (8 percent of the urban population and 32 percent of the rural population; United Nations 2001). Table 1.1 details the extent of the problem.

Among the rural poor, many have to walk as long as fifteen minutes to reach a source of water. This is true for 59 percent of the population in Bolivia, 92 percent in Brazil, and 74 percent in Colombia (Ayad et al. 1997). The lack of home water service severely affects the health of the population and thus health care expenditures and financing. According to the Economic Commission for Latin America and the Caribbean (ECLAC 1994), contaminated water causes 80 percent of all illness, and more than one third of the region's mortality. Furthermore, on average, water-related illnesses cause the loss of one-tenth of the productive time of each individual.

In many places in the world, a vicious cycle exists whereby water misuse has put enormous pressure on existing water resources, and this water stress has led to further misuse. As water has increasingly become a resource in crisis, it also has become a strategic resource, the control of which is a source of power and therefore contention. Regions within countries as well as sovereign nations contend (sometimes quite strenuously) for the right to water from common watersheds, water that is often critical to economic development and social welfare.

Sustainable management of water resources is now seen as essential to the survival of humankind (Asmal 1999; Dávila-Poblete 2001; van Wijk-Sjebesma 1998, 1). As Dávila-Poblete and Rico discuss in chapter three, a series of international conferences have led to significant shifts in global water resource management policies, accompanied by the creation of new worldwide organizations charged with developing policy guidelines and frameworks for action (Asmal 1999; Green and Baden 1995; van Wijk-Sjebesma 1998). Both the International Conference on Water and the Environment in Dublin in 1992 and the UN Conference on Environment and Development (the "Earth Summit") held in Rio de Janeiro later the same year agreed to the four principles cited at the beginning of this chapter.

One significant feature of new global water policies is that the management unit is no longer the city, the municipality, or the state—but the watershed (even when watersheds spread across political boundaries, which they inevitably do)—so that all uses of water within a watershed are factored into water management policies and practices, using participatory planning that includes all stakeholders. The definition of stakeholder is as broad as possible, including not only all water users within a watershed but also the environment itself as a stakeholder (represented by environmental organizations). Appropriate watershed management is now seen as integrating the needs of all stakeholders into a plan for sustainable water use.[2] Water resource management at its best is seen to be location specific and must be based on understanding local culture, customary uses of water, and relationships between local residents (Global Water Partnership Technical Advisory Committee 2000, 6; Mollinga and Straaten 1996, 250, cited in van Wijk-Sjebesma 1998, 28).

Needless to say, a huge gap exists between international policy formulations and local level implementation. Although global water policies sound good in principle, their implementation often involves crafting and passing new national water laws, creating new government institutions and new watershed agencies, developing new procedures for water management that take into account regional and subregional differentiation, and researching the realities of water usage at the watershed level and the interdependence of contiguous watersheds. These steps involve complex political maneuvering as well as long-term financial commitments and have been carried out to very different degrees in different places.

In general, global policies set broad goals and individual countries take on as much as they choose or are able to. Nowhere have the global policies been fully implemented or anything even remotely close to that. And, of the four pillars of the new global policy—sustainable development, a participatory approach, incorporating women, and the commodification of water—the least understood, and therefore the most ignored, has been the principle recognizing that women and men already have differentiated experiences in water use and differentiated knowledge about domestic and irrigation water management. Yet this principle sets the stage for as significant and powerful a shift in water resource management as do the other three. That this principle has to be stated at all stems from the imbalance and inequality in access to, use of, and control over water between men and women and that women's distinct knowledge bases and experiences have been left out of water policy and planning. While redressing this imbalance and inequality would bring significant improvements, to date, paying lip service to the third principle has been mistaken for policy formulation itself.

In the late 1970s and 1980s, activists began urging policy makers, planners, nongovernmental organizations (NGOs), and bilateral/multilateral agencies to consider women's needs and women's roles during policymaking, planning, and implementation processes. Most agencies responded by adding on "offices of women's affairs," where women's issues were then promptly marginalized and ignored (Barrig 2001, 32; Levy 1992). In the 1990s, the conceptual shift from "women's issues" to a "gender perspective" placed women's issues into larger contexts. The gendered approach does not consider women in isolation, rather it focuses on men *and* women, on their differentiated responsibilities, knowledge, and priorities, and on the relationships between them in different settings (in the household, in the community, in the workplace). As Zwarteveen and Bennett show, a planning process based only on men's knowledge is incomplete and reproduces existing gender inequalities in the water sector as well as severely limiting the effectiveness of policies that improve water management.

In most rural societies, almost all the work in the home and in the fields involves water. Women's and men's access to water, use of water, and understanding of the principles of water management within their spheres of life can differ markedly. Though women are usually responsible for water management within the home, both women and men are involved in the fields.

In Mexico and Ecuador, as shown in the case studies by Buechler and Bastidas, entire regions have seen massive male out-migration, as men move to find waged labor, leaving women and children to manage the fields. In many regions, women are able to pick up the ball because they have been working alongside men since childhood—though calling them "helpers" often diminishes their work. Yet despite their abilities, women often face serious barriers when left to manage irrigation water on their own. Cultural constraints prevent them either from attending water-user meetings that the men of the household attend or from speaking at such meetings if they do. They are not always allowed to irrigate when and where the men can. They are not included in development projects that focus on community or irrigation water management (see the case studies by Vera and Aguilar). As the case studies in this book amply demonstrate, however, in the absence of men, women develop their own mechanisms for assuring that their fields are irrigated and that they get the water they need.

When only the men in a given community or region participate in water management and planning, valuable opportunities to design the most effective community water systems are lost. For example, when the leaders of a community water project in Ecuador asked about priorities, the women of the community stated that irrigation water would help them in their tasks of washing clothes and bathing children, would nurture nearby greenery and make their work of gathering firewood easier, and would serve as drinking water (when purified by boiling), saving them hours of walking to distant water sources. For these reasons, the women favored an irrigation design with continuous water flows during the day, with side canals bringing water closer to their homes. The men (who did not take into account any of the household burdens the women face), however, preferred a rotational scheme whereby they did not get water every day, but when it was their turn for water, the flow was heavier, and they could irrigate in a shorter period. Clearly, the men and women both had compelling reasons for their preferences regarding irrigation system design. Taking into account both sets of preferences would lead to an irrigation system that was most effective for the community as a whole (Arroyo and Boelens 1998, 410).

Within the categories of end users, men and women have different interests and resources. Hence the categories of end users cannot be treated as one and the same. Distinctions are needed between what either category knows, does, and decides, and the effects for them, their families, and the community. Balanced attention to all actor categories both optimizes social and economic development and reduces competition and conflicts over water. Water resources practices that have a negative effect on women also have a deleterious effect on development (van Wijk-Sijbesma 1998, 3).

Incorporating a gender perspective into water management means taking into account local cultural conventions that condition men's and women's place and voice within the family, in the workplace, and in the local community; the differentiated power and control that women and men have over water; other differences that affect water use and knowledge of local water management including age, ethnicity, and income; the differences in how women and men use water in various settings; the differentiated knowledge that men and women have regarding water management; and the way gender roles and relations change as a result of other events such as migration, the implementation of new laws, the opening up of new roads, and other features of accelerating economic development (van Wijk-Sijbesma 1998, 3–4). Fundamental for incorporating a gendered perspective in water management is creating an enabling environment that actively and effectively addresses all the above. Without such an environment, talking about a gendered perspective will remain just that—talk.

Although a gender perspective is becoming more visible in the policy statements emanating from international policy-setting conferences, the translation of global water policies that claim to include all stakeholders into national policies and their application in the real world is highly sporadic and localized at best (Green and Baden 1995, 94; van Wijk-Sijbesma 1998, 5). While the Dublin statement discusses the implications of three of the four principles at length, nowhere in the action agenda or the report on the conference is there any further mention of the third principle, its objectives, or prescriptions for its implementation. Thus the global policies developed in the 1990s include a gendered approach only in the most superficial, simplistic, and dismissive manner, without the critical steps of spelling out what such an approach actually means (Global Water Partnership Technical Advisory Committee 2000, 18).

Given the dire statistics on the population without water services in Latin America, a lot of work clearly lies ahead. This book contributes to that process by focusing on women as stakeholders in water resources management, making the contributions of women visible, explaining why doing so is essential for effective public policy and planning in the water sector, and providing guidelines for planning and project implementation.

The book is divided into four parts. The first presents the book's conceptual framework. Zwarteveen and Bennett discuss the social right to water, explore the connections between gender and water in the contexts of household and irrigation water management, and lay out differences between urban and rural issues of water management. Dávila-Poblete and Rico then examine the evolution of global water policies and global gender policies since the early 1990s, look for the links between the two, and discuss their implementation in Latin America.

The book's second part includes three case studies. Ahlers provides a theoretical exploration of neoliberal water policy and its gender dimensions, with attention to the experience in Mexico and Bolivia. Bustamante, Peredo, and Udaeta analyze the Cochabamba (Bolivia) "Water War" of 2001 in the context of privatization of water services and the commodification of water under neoliberalism. Giarraca and Del Pozo examine the consequences of the privatization of water services in Tucumán, Argentina. Both the Cochabamba and the Tucumán cases demonstrate the devastating social effects of neoliberal water policies as well as the organizing capacity of women and their skills at active resistance.

In part three, Vera Delgado examines what happened in the Andean village of Llullucha when a development team arrived to implement water projects using the participatory approach and included only the men of the village as project participants. She explores the response of the women in the village and their ability to bypass the project's parameters and find alternate pathways to participation. Aguilar reports on a community water development project in the province of Heredia, Costa Rica, that a team of specialists from outside the region who had no understanding of women's roles in water management in the village initiated. Her chapter explains how, over the course of many years of involvement with the village, the team developed a significant repertoire of strategies for incorporating an effective gender perspective into project design and implementation.

The book's fourth part begins with an examination by Ennis-McMillan of the evolution of women's roles in water management in La Purificación Tepetitla, a town in a periurban area not far from Mexico City. Bastidas explores the changing responsibilities of women in water management in two rural communities in the province of Carchi, Ecuador, and analyzes obstacles to participation. Buechler analyzes how Mexico's 1992 water reform, as implemented in a Guanajuato irrigation district where there has been a massive exodus of men in search of waged labor, affected women's access to water rights and their participation in rural water management.

The final chapter of the book, by Bennett, Dávila-Poblete, and Rico, provides analytical conclusions for each of the four sections by bringing together the key issues developed by the authors of the case studies in each section. Furthermore, the concluding chapter weaves the conceptual framework with the material from the case study chapters. We explore what can be learned about gender and water management from the case studies to provide guidelines for integrating a gendered perspective into water policy, water management, and water projects. Implementation of a gendered approach in the water sector will take extensive commitment from individual nations at the federal, state, and local levels. Bringing women in can upset the apple cart, so to speak, and affect traditional roles and relationships between women and men, thus the process must be carried out thoughtfully and from the bottom up. This book takes the third Dublin principle seriously, challenging the prevailing attitude of ignoring it and demonstrating why it is crucial and how it can be applied.

Understanding Water and Gender

The connection between water and gender is not apparent at first glance, unless you have been out in the fields of the Latin American countryside, in the impoverished neighborhoods of Latin American cities, or in the conference rooms of international agencies. The two chapters in part one provide the framework for discussion by conceptualizing the connection between water and gender at the community level as well as at the international policy-setting level. First the differentiated rights, responsibilities, knowledge bases, and priorities of women and men regarding water in everyday life are explored. Then the evolution of global water management policies and global gender policies since the early 1990s are discussed, and their points of intersection are analyzed.

2 The Connection between Gender and Water Management

What is the connection between gender and water? In the world of gender policies, water is almost never mentioned. Few cases of women organizing around water issues are known. And in the world of water policies, lip service is paid to gender, without depth or consequences for water management practices. Yet this book's premise is that important connections exist between gender and water, and when these relationships are made explicit, more effective and equitable water resource management results. Within the contexts of household (domestic) water use and irrigation, we demonstrate how water and gender are linked.[1]

The worlds of domestic water and irrigation water policy, planning, and management are very different. Domestic water issues are framed in contexts of social rights and welfare, health and hygiene, and basic needs, and irrigation is framed in terms of production and economic efficiency. These differences shape the possibilities for recognizing and addressing gender concerns. The "basic needs/social welfare" approach to domestic water recognizes women's needs for water, which in itself does not guarantee that they will have the right to a voice in water management, but it at least establishes that women have a legitimate place on drinking water and sanitation policy agendas.

This approach is in contrast to irrigation policy, which focuses on production and where women are invisible. In much of Latin America, farming and irrigation are strongly associated with masculinity and identified as male jobs. Though many women farm and irrigate, they are seldom seen as farmers by water management agency staff (or even by their own communities) and, as a consequence, they are seldom endowed with the associated rights and resources. For these reasons, the irrigation policy discourse and professional culture is more resistant to recognizing women's roles in and differentiated knowledge of water management than the domestic water sector (Lynch 1993). For such recognition to happen, deeply embedded stereotypes and cultural norms about gendered patterns of labor and behavior need to be challenged.

Gender bias refers both to unequal access to resources (land, water, credit, knowledge, new technologies, etc.) and to gender-differentiated access to the process of making and implementing decisions. What is important is not "who does what," but the exclusiveness of role distribution and its implications for resource allocation and the distribution of power. Women may be prohibited from certain roles—some that are critical for survival. In the rural water world, this situation is most evident in the effects of male out-migration. When men migrate, as is more and more often the case, they leave behind their wives, mothers, and children to manage the land. In communities where only men attend water-user assemblies and the men of a household migrate, then that household has just lost its voice in communal water decisions, and household survival may become precarious. Similar problems arise with credit (more easily available to men than to women), with irrigation (schedules that work for men do not always work for women who must juggle childcare and housework), and even with driving (more men drive than women).

The dichotomies between water for household use (which is considered part of the "private, domestic" sphere) and water for irrigation (which is recognized as located in the "public, productive" sphere) have led to a division of the water world into more or less neatly gendered halves. Because the domestic water/productive water dichotomy is to some extent pragmatically and strategically justifiable on the grounds that different agencies, with different professional discourses and cultures frequently manage domestic water and irrigation water, it perpetuates a division of the world into a "woman's world" and a "man's world." It also renders invisible the different priorities that men and women assign to water within each sphere as well as their different knowledge bases regarding water use that could be applied to water project design. Furthermore, as this chapter shows, this division is overly simplistic as it obscures the many interconnections between the varied uses and users of water and leads to distortions in planning.

Planners often claim that the cost of implementing a gender perspective during policy and project development is too high. Yet the failure to do so means that policies are based on incomplete information (drawing primarily, or only, on men's experiences, needs, and priorities) and are unable to address the full needs and priorities of the whole population. Most important, the reluctance to deeply incorporate gendered perspectives is based on a failure to recognize that substantial gains accrue if poor women and children spend less time on the household water supply process *and* if water service improvements take into account women's knowledge.

The Right to Water

The focus of this book speaks to an inherent social right of all human beings: the right to water. Social rights can be defined as the right to a minimum standard of living and well-being according to the prevailing values of one's society (Bustelo 2001, 4–5). A key element is easy access to a consistently sufficient supply of water of adequate quality to sustain the health and hygiene of all members of a community. Over the last twenty-five years, water for domestic uses has come to be treated and seen as a social right while water for irrigation has not. In most irrigation policy narratives, irrigation water is more likely to be treated as a production input and sometimes as a property right (i.e., as an economic right or even as a commodity). We suggest that the social right to water include not only water for domestic uses but also water for food production, as both are necessary for survival.[2] The right to water underpins all other social rights. At the same time, this right exists within a larger context of the reality of water infrastructure and management, behind which lie powerful economic and political interests (Levy 1992, 144). Thus understanding water as a "foundational" social right, and suggesting water policies based on such a right, often results in serious challenges to the economic and political status quo (Bennett 1995b; Kahrl 1982; Reisner 1987).

Over the last twenty years, the concept of citizens' rights across the world has dramatically expanded. One hundred and seventy-one nations signed the declaration emanating from the 1993 World Conference on Human Rights in Vienna that emphasizes the universality, indivisibility, and interdependence of civil, cultural, economic, political, and social rights. Citizenship is now seen as encompassing not only civil and political rights but also economic, social, and cultural rights (codified in the U.N. International Covenant on Economic, Social, and Cultural Rights of 1966 and signed by all Latin American states; CEPAL 2002; Bustelo 2001, 4–5; Gros Espiell 2001, 134). In the reality of Latin America, however, civil and political rights have been separated from the others and are increasingly implemented, while economic, social, and cultural rights remain vague and unapplied in any systematic way. It is argued that implementing economic, social, and cultural rights is costly, and the conditions of poverty and scarcity that prevail in Latin America mean that resources do not exist to make these rights a reality (Bustelo 2001, 19; Gros Espiell 2001, 136–39). The result is that while lip service is paid to indivisible human rights, social, cultural, and economic policies that could reach all citizens are not developed and implemented and are instead addressed in a piecemeal fashion. Yet, implementing civil and political rights takes resources as well, and their current implementation means that they have priority over social, cultural, and economic rights. Thus advances in legal and political equality coexist with persistent social and economic inequality (Barrig 2001, 30), and human rights are treated as divisible.[3]

Across the world, people enjoy or are deprived of rights based on cultural frameworks built from multiple interlocking variables such as age, income, social rank, race, ethnicity, religion, and gender. For example, higher income groups always have better water supply, and often better water quality, than lower income groups. The right to use a particular resource is frequently linked to rights to other resources (Netherlands Development Assistance 1997, 4–6). In rural areas, the right to water may be linked to a prior right to own, rent, or use land, while in urban areas it may derive from the right to land titling (as opposed to invaded land that cannot be titled).[4] In some countries and cultures, both men and women have the right to inherit family land; in others, only men or widowed women have that right. When the right to irrigate is linked to land rights that women do not have or when families squat on urban land that they cannot title, which means they have no rights to municipal water, women and poor families find themselves with responsibilities for water management without the attendant rights.

Gender and Household Water

In many regions of the world, including Latin America, women's work tends to be culturally associated with and defined as belonging to the private spaces of everyday life, and men's work is seen as belonging to the public spaces. The work of managing water in the household falls primarily on women because historically they have been, and especially among the poor continue to be, the managers of the sphere of reproduction, while men's role in relation to water tends to occur within the sphere of production.[5] Under conditions of abundant and clean water delivered to household taps, people pay little attention to their water supply. However, when potable water service is erratic, unreliable, or insufficient, and when water quality is unreliable and unhealthy, as is the case in poor urban Latin American neighborhoods and low-income rural areas, then household water management becomes a labor-intensive, physically demanding, and even stressful part of everyday life.

Within the Latin American household, women are generally responsible for all tasks involving water: cooking, cleaning, laundry, bathing children, and caring for sick family members. Water scarcity and poor water quality complicates these tasks. Residents in poor urban neighborhoods often get their water either from community faucets that function a few hours each day and service as many as one to two hundred families each or from trucks that deliver water once or twice a week (Bennett 1995b). In rural areas, poor households get their water from community wells, nearby rivers, or irrigation ditches.

The lack of home water connections and the lack of round-the-clock water service create hardships. Someone must be available to collect water whenever it appears at the community faucet or whenever the water truck shows up. Someone must carry home daily multiple heavy pails of water from the community faucet or the village well and store it in large barrels or tubs. Someone must do all the water-related household tasks by transferring water from the large barrels and tubs to smaller receptacles. Someone must ration the household's water to hedge against the community faucet or village well having a dry day (or days) or the water truck failing to show up. Someone must heat water—often on open fires or propane stovetops—for laundry, for bathing, and for cooking. That someone is almost always a woman or a child.

The use of community faucets, water truck deliveries, village wells, or irrigation ditches as sources of household water results in multiple transfers of water before consumption. Water is usually stored in containers scrounged but not made for that purpose; these containers do not have fitted lids, and family members who are not educated about hygiene dip dirty hands into the water and do not keep the makeshift lids on tightly. Therefore, water must be boiled before it is consumed and this is an extra daily household task involving heavy lifting, and time, time, time. This work falls, again, to women.

Thus, water development policies and projects, always presented as gender neutral, in practice, almost always have gender-differentiated outcomes (World Bank 2001, 14). Based on their different roles and responsibilities, women have different criteria for evaluating proposals on water services (Zwarteveen 1994). Improving water supply and quality for poor urban neighborhoods benefits women most directly. Such projects free women and children's time and energy so that they can more actively and successfully engage in school and/or work (Jarman 1997, 188; World Bank 2001, 23–24). Family income can rise as a result. Better household water supply often results in improved family health, and good health is the primary asset of the poor (Chamber 1989, cited in Jarman 1997, 188). In contrast, water rationing has an immediate detrimental effect on women and children because it affects their household labor as described above, while men remain comparatively unaffected (Bennett 1995a).

Though planners and policy makers signal the enormous costs of improving water supply for all, a gendered analysis shows that water resource projects are vitally flawed when the role of women is left invisible. Acknowledging women's expertise and needs regarding water resources leads to more comprehensive planning, more effective projects, and significant gains for women, as well as for their families and communities.

Gender and Irrigation

In rural areas, investments for improved irrigation systems are usually also gender biased and benefit men, leaving out women irrigators. The purpose of any irrigation system is to transfer water from a source (a lake, river, or groundwater) to the field and apply it to crops to allow agricultural production. Irrigation systems are complex, combining infrastructure and technology to make water available (through pumps or dams in rivers for instance) and to transport it (most often through canal networks). Next to these *technical* elements, irrigation systems also comprise *normative* elements (the rules, rights, and obligations related to the distribution of water, the organization of operation and maintenance, conflict resolution, etc.), *organizational* elements (related to the human organization necessary to govern, operate, and sustain the system), and *agroproductive* elements (soils, crops, technology, capital, labor, and the capacities and knowledge of the art of irrigation; Mollinga 1998; Uphoff 1986).

Agriculture in Latin America, like elsewhere, is by far the major user of fresh water—about 80 percent in 1990 (WMO/IDB 1996). A gender division of labor that defines agriculture as a male occupation and women primarily as housewives irrespective of their contribution to family agriculture characterizes many Latin American countries (Deere and Léon 1987). General abstractions about irrigation and gender in Latin America are difficult, if not impossible. First, irrigation systems vary tremendously in terms of technology and infrastructure but also in terms of management. The mountain irrigation systems in the Andes, built and managed by farmer communities (Boelens and Hoogendam 2002), have little in common with the large-scale pump irrigation systems in the coastal plains of Peru (Vos 2002) or the large surface irrigation systems in México (Kloezen 2002). Direct user participation in the Andes has rather different accountability mechanisms than the representational participatory management of many Mexican large-scale irrigation systems.

The degree of public involvement in funding and operation and maintenance also differs widely. The roles of governments, markets, and civil society in irrigation water allocation and management is intensely debated in much of Latin America. International lending agencies strongly in favor of reducing government budgets and public involvement in managing irrigation, promote strategies that combine decentralization and privatization with market-based allocation of water (Ringler et al. 2000). Such proposals often meet with much resistance.

Important differences also exist in gender relations and in the intrahousehold and intracommunity organization of production between countries, regions, and even within irrigation systems. The three-hectare farm of Inés, a female farmer in Ecuador whose husband has a paid job in town (Arroyo and Boelens 1998), is difficult to compare with the large agribusiness farms of more than one thousand hectares in the Bajío in Mexico (Kloezen 2002). Inés conducts all farm activities herself, sometimes with help from her children, and also plays a prominent role in the water-users' association. Ever increasing male migration from rural areas to cities has forced Inés, like many other *indígena* peasant women in the Andes, to assume more responsibilities than are considered normal or desirable in prevailing culturally gendered ideologies (Boelens and Zwarteveen 2002b). Because of male migration, women may either take over the farm—inducing a process of feminization of agriculture—or decide to rent out their land. In the whole of Latin America, it is estimated that women head 26 percent of rural families (Vargas 1998).

In contrast, the largest irrigated commercial farmers in México provide a near perfect embodiment of rural masculinity. For those landowners, agriculture has become an enterprise and does not just encompass the physical task of working the land (which is in any case often done by hired wage laborers, some of whom are female) but also engaging in the politics of farming: talking with other men about government policies, socializing with government officials, making business deals with salesmen of agricultural inputs, and so on. Women are part of the farm enterprise and may accompany their husbands to town to purchase agricultural inputs, make water payments, rent machinery, or conduct bank transactions (Monsalvo-Vélazquez 1997), but they are mostly not identified (nor do they identify themselves) as farmers.

Food and Agricultural Organization (FAO) estimates show that women make up 22 percent of the rural labor force in Nicaragua and Honduras and roughly 30 percent in Costa Rica, El Salvador, and Paraguay. The Andean countries have by far the highest percentages of women working in agriculture, with more than 50 percent in Bolivia and Colombia and as much as 70 percent in Peru (FAO 1998). Most of these women work as unpaid family labor on family farms. If a pattern can be discerned from the various ways in which farming in Latin America is organized, it is that women's involvement increases in degree and importance with a decrease in farm scale and level of commercialization. Active female involvement with farming and irrigation is much more common in poorer households with smaller farm holdings and is often driven by poverty rather than greater gender equality or emancipation.

Women's water needs are only partially shaped by their gender as gender interacts with class, wealth, ethnicity, and so forth to structure an individual's possibilities for controlling water. Yet, and in spite of the enormous diversity that makes generalizations difficult, two facts stand out when reviewing the evidence about gender relations in irrigated agriculture in Latin America. Both formal rights to water and decision making about irrigation water distribution and other irrigation matters are largely concentrated in the hands of men (Boelens and Zwarteveen 2002b; Buechler and Zapata Martelo 2000; Deere and de Léon 1997; Monsalvo-Velázquez, Zapata, and Manzanares 2000). Because formal control over water lies with men, the feminist project in irrigation largely consists of challenging and questioning this gender disparity.

Control over water is important because water for irrigation is a resource associated with great power and is therefore highly contested. All over Latin America, social groups can be found struggling not just over the physical control of water and irrigation systems but also over the right to define and organize these systems. To give just two of many examples, when an irrigation project in Lake Totora in Bolivia extended the available supply of water, its distribution became a topic of fierce conflict between two villages, Tiraque and Punata. Tiraque contested the project's initial plan to divert all extra water to Punata (Gerbrandy and Hoogendam 2002). In Ceceles, Ecuador, indigenous people had gradually acquired formal and informal rights to irrigation water that more than a hundred years ago belonged to the hacienda owner. Despite these rights, irrigation water deliveries were insecure and irrigators constantly had to defend their rights from claims by other parties. The question of who has the authority to decide about water allocation is central in these struggles as the following quote of a Ceceles farmer illustrates: "It doesn't matter if they say the government gives water rights—we have water rights" (Boelens and Doorenbos 2002, 228). Ceceles farmers built their own nine kilometers of secondary canal to secure their water supply and also threatened to blow up a dam if they were not included in plans for improving water availability: "you dynamize the system, or we dynamite it!" (228). Struggles over irrigation water also occur between peasant communities and state agencies (such as in Ecuador where the *indígena* movement has created its own water law as a protest against the law the state aims to adopt) (Boelens 2001), among different communities (such as when several communities claim water from a river), and among different members within a community (e.g., when irrigators take water out of turn or steal water).

All these struggles are to some extent gendered as men and women are differentially involved and positioned in them, and gendered metaphors are used to defend and claim rights. However, most of these water struggles do not directly occur along gender lines in the form of direct disputes over water between male and female members of communities and households. Few, if any, records of female irrigators and farmers organizing to demand more control over water *as women* exist. This is partly because rights to water are often directly linked to rights to land, and gender-based disputes over water are frequently subsumed in struggles over land (Deere and León 1997). The prevailing ideal model of organizing intrahousehold affairs and relations in much of Latin America is one of harmony and collaboration, of mutual support and help. Men are (seen as) the heads of households and often also the ones who deal with all extrahousehold matters, but they do so on behalf of the rest of the family. Even though intrahousehold realities can only be partly understood when this ideal is used as the main explanatory framework, it does provide an important normative reference and thus shapes the ways in which women and men articulate their wishes or needs, including those about water.[6]

Most women do not identify individualized, independent control and rights over resources as an important need. Irrigation itself, as is explained in greater detail below, is often clearly seen and identified as a typically male domain and activity. For women, claiming irrigation rights would imply explicitly challenging these norms and thus also challenging the power and ability of their husbands to properly carry out their manly roles—and doing so comes at high social costs. The need to struggle for formalized and individualized water rights may also not always be very high because formalized rights and institutionalized powers only partly determine actual access to water. In the absence of formal rights, female farmers (and others) may therefore still be able to access water. In many irrigation systems in Latin America,[7] the "real" user, the one actually cultivating the plot, is not the person who is registered in the *padron de usuarios* (registry of rightholders). Often family members farm and attend meetings. Land and water titles may also be sold or rented (see Ahlers 2000c), or the land maybe divided among heirs. Formal registration often matters less than social awareness and knowledge among the group of irrigators of who is in charge of irrigating a plot. In most communities of irrigators, everybody knows each other, and usually a high degree of social control prevails. Actual irrigation water distribution to fields often differs significantly from official schedules and allocation patterns planned before the season, which results from both the difficulty of physically controlling water as well as from the challenge of effectively monitoring and controlling the behavior of all irrigators. Physically accessing water without having formal authorization to do so is quite easy and a common practice.

Actual water distribution often occurs through less formal (but often regular and sometimes normalized) arrangements among field neighbors or between gate operators and irrigators. Often gender differences in strategies and available networks for making such arrangements are found because struggles over water are part and parcel of wider social relations, identities, and networks. Brunt (1992), for instance, illustrates how male farmers in an irrigation system in Mexico invite canal operators and irrigation agency personnel to bars and brothels and offer them drinks and food and even women to make them more disposed to act favorably toward their needs. These actions are not accessible to women farmers who have other options such as making canal operators the godfather of one of their children (Brunt 1992), or offering them money for a couple of beers or soft drinks (Ahlers 2000c; Monsalvo-Velázquez et al. 2000). Even without formal rights, women (as well as men, for that matter) can physically access water as the following quotation from a fifty-year-old Mexican woman illustrates: "in the payment slips, my name does not appear, they are still in the name of my father . . . it doesn't matter if it is in my name or not, what matters is that I get water when I need it and that's it" (118).

Hence, gender-based irrigation water conflicts and discussions are more likely to be about the terms and conditions of access and about the control over benefits of use than about control and rights per se. For instance, studies show that women are often more interested than men in using irrigation facilities for purposes other than just irrigating the main crops. Such uses include watering gardens or feeding animals and place specific demands on the quantity, quality, and timing of water deliveries.[8] Women and men may also have different preferences for the operation and scheduling of irrigation water deliveries. Because of their domestic workloads, women often have less flexibility and less time to spend long hours in the field for irrigating (Jácome and Krol 1994). Workloads are also the reason why, in some communities, women prefer the flexibility of a continuous water flow though it might increase the total time spent on irrigation. In contrast, men may prefer nonpermanent rotational turns of water that enable them to irrigate with a larger flow in less time (Hendriks 2002). Many studies also report women's reluctance to irrigate at night.[9] Women fear gender-based violence, and going out at night may also reflect negatively on their social status *as women* and arouse a husband's jealousy and anger. Dark nights are typically also the times when most water stealing occurs. Men share this reluctance to irrigate at night, and studies note that as night irrigation cannot always be avoided, women (just as men) do irrigate at night when they must.

Almost everywhere in Latin America, men dominate irrigators' associations both in numbers and in influence.[10] Because membership in organizations is typically linked to having titles to land and water, women are generally underrepresented in the public political spheres of life. And because mostly men hold such titles, women are denied membership; even when they are active in farming and irrigation, women's absence limits their opportunities to control, or even have input in, important decisions about water distribution and the allocation of resources for operation and maintenance.

In rural areas, irrigators' organizations are among the most visible and strong community organizations and provide an important channel for information and resources to and from the community. Leadership positions in water-user associations are often important political positions, offering opportunities for expanding political relations and social standing at regional and state levels (Rap, Wester, and Prado 1999). Control over water thus both depends on and accompanies control over other resources and information. Participation of women in water-users' organizations for irrigation not only improves women's access to and control over irrigation but also may contribute to wider goals of women's empowerment. Exclusion of women from water users' organizations can be interpreted as denying them economic rights and complete citizenship (Bhalla and Lapeyre 1997).

Women's lack of more or less formally recognized powers, claims, and rights to irrigation water is not only unjust, undemocratic, and inequitable, it may also lead to inefficiencies. For irrigation systems to run smoothly and effectively, there must be a balance between *rights* (to water, to infrastructure, and to participation in decision making) and *responsibilities*. The reasoning behind this insight (which has become common wisdom in irrigation policymaking circles) is that those who most need access to a resource, or those who use it most, should also be granted the rights of access and control.[11] Without secure rights to a resource, users will be less motivated to make the investments necessary to maintain and improve it. Without secure rights, the ability to invest in the resource may also diminish because of lesser control and less access to support services such as information and credit that are often directly linked to ownership. A balance between responsibilities and rights is also important because those who most use a resource know it best.

Another inefficiency that the artificial division of male and female spheres regarding water creates is that planners almost never recognize that irrigation systems can be designed to also provide water for domestic use. If irrigation projects were designed with data regarding their potential for providing household water as well as irrigation water, both productive and reproductive work could benefit.

Irrigation as Masculine Identity and Culture

Improving women's control over irrigation is not something that can be achieved solely through changes in policies and laws. Female water users themselves have to raise their voices and demand accountability from irrigation water providers and women themselves have to be willing to struggle for more control. Increasing women's control is a struggle not just over water as a resource and over the power to phrase water policies and laws but is also a struggle to change "water cultures."[12] Articulating women's water needs requires challenging deeply rooted and culturally embedded associations between irrigation and masculinity. Most irrigation professionals are men, and professional involvement with irrigation is very much identified and perceived as a male activity. The attributes and skills seen as characteristics of good irrigation professionals—such as technical dexterity, physical strength, spatial orientation, and mathematical skills—are normally perceived as male. In this sense, masculinity and the professional irrigation identity can be seen to mutually constitute and define each other. As Lynch (1993) suggested, the characteristics and culture of the "bureaucratic tradition" to which irrigation institutions and policies are tied is one that strongly associates decision making and power with masculinity. The almost hegemonizing power of this tradition has long been maintained, and continues to be maintained, through the socialization of generations of male engineers and bureaucrats and is sustained and legitimized through the powers and financial resources of irrigation bureaucracies or *hydrocracies* (Rap et al. 1999). The ideal engineer is thus also a near-to-perfect embodiment of cultural masculinity. The strong normative link between irrigation professionalism and masculinity not only makes it difficult for female irrigation professionals to be taken seriously, it also creates strong barriers for (male or female) irrigation professionals with nonengineering backgrounds. An example is the resistance the first economist to become director of the Comisión Nacional de Agua in Mexico faced (Dávila-Poblete 2002). To argue that women's needs should be addressed, that their knowledge should affect decision making, and that their contributions should be valued is to challenge the bureaucratic tradition at its roots. It is to challenge the ways in which the bureaucracy of the water sector constructs knowledge and defines its job, it is to challenge the maleness of the profession and thus its seriousness and importance, it is to question its legitimacy.

The various and numerous irrigation activities women do are not only unseen but also tend to be defined as "nonirrigation"—irrelevant to the irrigation profession—and even as "nonprofessional." When women are cleaning canals or irrigating, they are seen and said to do so on behalf of their husbands, who are considered the "real" irrigators and farmers. Though a slight exaggeration, it is almost as if irrespective of *what* women do in irri-

gated farming, the very fact that a woman is doing the job is enough to qual-
ify the work as "nonirrigation." An example of an irrigation project NGO in
Ecuador illustrates the persistence of the belief that irrigators are men. Staff
of this NGO planned all meetings with water users on weekends because
most men in the communities where the NGO worked left home during
the week to work elsewhere. Women were left in charge of irrigating and
farming. Despite the women's responsibilities, the staff continued to identify
the men as "the real farmers" and the ones with whom to have meetings
(Boelens 2001).

The supposed physical strength or technical dexterity required often jus-
tifies defining irrigation as a masculine activity.[13] In some countries in the
Andes, the maleness of irrigation is further confirmed and expressed in cultural rules that stipulate that women are not to come close to irrigation in-
takes or to walk on canal bunds.[14] This would "pollute" the irrigation water
or lead to droughts.

Gender ideologies also have it that men are more qualified to represent
the household in community and other public matters, including participation in irrigators' meetings (Ahlers 2000c; Boelens and Zwarteveen 2002b).
In Latin America, as in many other countries of the world, the exercise of
political authority is socially and culturally associated with men. Gender
identity partly determines the right to speak and to have a voice and the
ways in which one's voice are heard and interpreted. Even if women participate in meetings, social practices and norms that define what sorts of interaction are permissible and what the modes of conduct should be constrain
their freedom to publicly interact with men. To be outspoken and have
strong opinions are positive characteristics when found in men, a way of
defining and reconforming masculinity and male superiority. In contrast,
when these characteristics are found in women, they reflect negatively
on their status as women (Ahlers 2000c; Boelens and Zwarteveen 2002b;
Monsalvo-Velázquez et al. 2000). In a small-scale irrigation project in
Ecuador, almost as many women as men participated in the users' organization. Nevertheless, observations during meetings showed that while on the
average regular male members spoke about twenty-eight minutes, female
members only spoke three and a half minutes. The women said that they
were reluctant to voice their concerns at meetings because they were afraid
to make mistakes and to be ridiculed (Krol 1994). Women in irrigation districts in Mexico explained in similar terms why they chose to remain silent
at meetings, even though they recognized that many men made irrelevant

and thoughtless comments. The few women who participated in meetings usually sat in the back of the meeting room and tried, as much as possible, to go unnoticed to avoid being asked a direct question (Buechler and Zapata 2000). The one role in organizations that often still is deemed compatible with a female identity is that of treasurer: women are assumed to be more honest.[15]

The underrepresentation of women and their indirect participation not only destroys the democratic character of decision making but also may negatively affect the responsiveness of organizations to the needs of women. It is more than just a symptom of gender inequality—it is one of the factors that perpetuate it. Ahlers (2000c, 166) concludes that the lack of accepted public space may force female irrigators to resort to alternative strategies for accessing water. Some women invest a lot of time and energy in creating and maintaining good relations with influential men in ways that do not compromise their social status or make them liable to accusations of immoral behavior. Many women also rely on their sons for the day-to-day politics of irrigation.

Decreasing the gender gap in irrigation challenges the strong ideological and cultural associations between irrigation and masculinity. Improving women's control over water implies redefining and reshaping the water world in ways that allow women to become legitimate and respected inhabitants of that world.

The Connection between Gender and Water

Important gender divisions that allocate many water responsibilities to women but vest most powers and rights in men characterize most water worlds. The precise nature and form of these divisions is markedly different between the domestic water sector and irrigation. Wherever domestic water cannot be obtained by simply opening a tap, women's responsibilities involve much time, energy, and money. Women's primary role is seldom accompanied by a parallel high presence in water-related decision making, to the detriment of both efficiency and equity.

Gendered ideologies often denominate irrigation as a male domain. Though irrigation water demands are often not neatly gender specific, women seldom actively participate in water-users' organizations. Female farmers often succeed in physically accessing water when they need it, for instance by making use of the rights of their male family members. Their weaker formal rights to water, however, lead to greater reliance on less formal and therefore less protected forms of access. The fact that women, just as men, have clear ideas, wishes, and demands about infrastructural and operational irrigation matters underscores the importance of gender analysis for irrigation planning.

Water worlds are not just gendered at the level of users. Even where most water policies no longer assume gender neutrality of users, water users typically continue to be conceptualized as atomic individuals. Though such methodological individualism allows seeing men and women as distinct social categories, it does not allow the much-needed understanding of gender as social relations. Such understanding involves approaching women not only as individuals and as a social category whose problems appear to be somehow connected to characteristics of this category but also as parties to sets of social relations (involving resources, rights, responsibilities, and meanings) with men and other women through which what it is to be a woman, in that time and social place, is defined and experienced (Jackson 2002).

The very distinction between water for household use and water for irrigation builds upon and further strengthens the categorical thinking typical of methodological individualism, with the discursive construction of women's water needs as confined to the "private, domestic" sphere, and those of men occuring in the "public, productive" sphere. The tendency to clearly delineate separate women's and men's water domains obstructs rather than helps a good understanding of the many connections between men and women and between the varied uses and users of water. The framing of water policy needs to be changed and an enabling environment created and sustained purposefully to allow better recognition of the importance of a gender perspective for the water sector. Considering water as an inherent social right of all human beings and understanding water within larger political and economic contexts of production and consumption behind which lie powerful economic and political interests are two important steps in the right direction.

The biased ways in which women are represented in water policies tie in with the ways in which gender roles are molded and perceived in professional water cultures. Both the domestic and the irrigation water professions share a strong, technical engineering heritage, and both have typically attracted higher numbers of men than women among their professional ranks. The health and basic needs approach of the domestic water world tends to cherish a professional culture of "help." Those who need help, those deprived of water, depend upon the goodwill and technical expertise of the benevolent water professional to improve their position. It is not difficult to see how a picture of poor victimized women who need help provides the perfect mirror to strong protectionist men providing this help. In a highly diluted form, as in a watermark on expensive writing paper, the picture of the benevolent male helper can indeed be seen to color today's water policy deliberations and practices. It works as an almost invisible barrier against approaching and recognizing women as active and knowledgeable actors capable of articulating their own water wishes and demands. The professional culture in the irrigation world can likewise be seen to appeal to very gender specific ideals of expertise in which women figure as "the other," lending professionals their virile distinction.[16]

Making the water world more habitable for women requires changes at many different levels and in many different arenas. It requires changing divisions of labor that allocate water responsibilities to women without granting them the associated rights, and it requires changing existing routines of public decision making to allow women to participate. It requires changes in laws, infrastructure, and organizations. It also requires changing the terms of water policy discussions, because reducing the gender gap in control over water is not just a direct struggle over the resource water but is also and importantly a struggle over the ways in which water needs are defined. In both the domestic water and irrigation water sectors, albeit in very different ways, creating legitimate discursive, legal, and organizational spaces for women to articulate and defend their water interests means that deeply embedded cultural and normative associations between water and masculinity need to be challenged. This is necessarily a long and often a difficult process, and it may be one that is painful and risky. However, not making the attempt may well come at an even higher price: that of human misery, deprivation, and poverty as a result of ineffective, inefficient, and inequitable water management.

3 Global Water and Gender Policies: Latin American Challenges

G ender equity and its relation to water policy is generally not central and, in many cases, is completely absent from the discourse of the government and international institutions that determine public policies in Latin America. Given that only a decade has passed since governments in the region have explicitly addressed gender as an issue and that only very recently has the connection between water and gender been made, to expect that substantial initiatives have begun is unrealistic. Nonetheless, examining the intersections between water and gender policies to date and exploring where these intersections might lead is worthwhile. To understand these issues, a brief description of the process of globalization and the prevailing neoliberal economic model in Latin America is key because this is the context under which gender equity and water policies have developed.

Neoliberalism and Globalization in Latin America

After the Second World War, almost all Latin American nations developed mixed economies with highly centralized government control and economic regulation. Nationalization, most commonly of petroleum, mining, communications, and banking industries, shifted these sectors to state control and ownership. Governments adopted an import-substitution-industrialization (ISI) development model, which lasted until the 1980s in most countries. Latin American governments adopted what is known as the "neoliberal model" in the late 1980s in response to the severe economic crises that swept the region after failures with ISI and the excessive growth of foreign debt.

Unregulated markets and the reduction of state involvement in the economy via the shift to mixed private-public ownership of state enterprises or their outright privatization characterize the neoliberal model. Neoliberalism is "where the fundamental nucleus of economic performance is the market," and the market is the regulator of social relations of power (Solís de Alba 2002, 48). Reducing the size of the state overall is a pillar of the neoliberal model, accomplished through decentralizing, reducing the state apparatus by decreasing its personnel, and legal reforms designed to favor private entrepreneurs and foreign investment.

Across the globe, nations have experienced varied and unequal effects from the application of the neoliberal economic model and the process of increased articulation with international markets known as globalization. An overarching outcome has been an increasing gap between rich and poor, both within countries as well as between developed and developing countries. As the rich get richer and the poor get poorer, broad sectors of the population are pushed into living conditions of great vulnerability and exclusion. Women, children, and elderly persons have been the hardest hit.

The high mobility of capital and human resources that characterizes globalization has reduced or eliminated ties to a permanent working place in a locality, community, or even nation and has diminished the sense of belonging to a particular social group, such as factory workers or agricultural laborers. Spatial mobility has turned into a powerful stratification factor as new social, political, and economic hierarchies are built and rebuilt daily on a world scope. With these changes, a new asymmetry emerges between the extraterritorial nature of power relations and the overall territoriality of people's lives as a whole (Bauman 2001).

Because the political and academic worlds and leaders and activists in social movements use the concept of "globalization" in different ways (Bauman 2001; Chomsky and Dieterich 1996), a comprehensive definition is needed. We have chosen the one used by the Economic Commission for Latin America and the Caribbean (ECLAC), which defines globalization as the "growing influence exerted at the local, national and regional levels by financial, economic, environmental, political, social and cultural processes that are global in scope" (2002, 17). This definition highlights its multidimensional nature and acknowledges its worldwide effects.[1] It recognizes that globalization is not only an economic phenomenon. "Indeed, although the economic facet of globalization is the most commonly referred to, it acts concomitantly with non-economic processes, which have their own momentum and therefore are not determined by the economic sphere" (17).

Among the noneconomic effects of globalization has been the growth of national and transnational social movements. These include women's movements, which have brought gender issues to the global agenda, contributed to a redefinition of citizenship, highlighted the changing boundaries between the public and private spheres, and led to a heightened emphasis on human rights (Guzmán 2002).[2] These women's movement efforts have significantly influenced gender equity policy implementation in Latin America, leading to the creation of governmental gender-related institutions. To date, however, the influence of women's movements on the development of policies at the intersection of water and gender issues is only nascent.

Neoliberalism and Water

By the 1990s, the state apparatus had been reduced in most Latin American countries and large numbers of state-owned firms privatized. Privatized sectors include electricity, communication, transportation, banks, and others (García de la Cruz and Sánchez Díez 2002; Solís de Alba 2002). As part of the spread of the neoliberal model, national governments applied the principles of neoliberal policy to the natural resources sector. Specifically in the water sector, for the state to reduce its role in infrastructure construction and maintenance and in water resources management in general, this policy has translated into increased participation by both the private sector and different water-user groups.

Thus, in the last decade, water has gone from being a social good to being an economic good. Furthermore, since the Second World Water Forum in The Hague in 2000, it has also become a strategic resource, a scarce good that the government has to regulate closely and that international organizations that deal with natural resources must monitor. These significant changes have occurred without adequate preparation in most Latin American nations, where the legal instruments regulating water sectors have not been modified for decades. Water legislation has not been updated since 1927 in Honduras, since 1942 in Costa Rica, and since the 1960s or 1970s in Panama, Bolivia, Peru, and other countries. Some countries have no specific legislation on water use at all, and water resources are subject to laws on land use or are under "goods and services" (e.g., Belize, Guatemala, El Salvador, Nicaragua, and others). Current globalizing trends are forcing Latin American governments to modify their outdated national water laws and to look for ways to open water markets.[3]

As governments have proactively sought to reduce the role of the state in the water sector, the need for a participatory approach to integrated water management has become more apparent and thus there has been increased participation of the private sector in infrastructure construction and maintenance, drinking water supply and sanitation management, and conservation activities. Also the participation of water-user groups in irrigation water management and financial participation of water users via higher tariffs has increased. Meanwhile, the state has retained control of the regulatory process, setting the conditions that encourage and protect private sector participation.

The rapidly expanding global interdependence of nations and economies has heightened concerns among governments about the local impacts of the neoliberal model. This interest has led Latin American governments to put renewed emphasis on alliances established between neighboring countries, for example, with the North American Free Trade Agreement (NAFTA), the Southern Common Market Agreement (better known as Mercosur— Mercado de Cooperación del Sur), the Asia-Pacific Economic Cooperation (APEC), and other bilateral agreements.

As a further impact of the increasing global interdependence of nations, starting in the 1990s, the United Nations convened a series of summit meetings and international conferences—which government representatives, NGOs, and individual citizens attended—that examined some of the major problems of our time, debated proposals to address them, and reached political consensus, setting a course toward a new era in world affairs: children (New York 1990), the environment (Rio de Janeiro 1992), human rights (Vienna 1993), population (Cairo 1994), women (Beijing 1995), social development (Copenhagen 1995), human settlements (Istanbul 1996), food (Rome 1996), racial groups and indigenous people (Durban 2001), and the elderly (Madrid 2002). At all these meetings, the issues of water and of gender have been present to some degree.[4]

The growing presence of water as an issue addressed in such a diversity of fora is because water, of all the natural resources, is without a doubt the most crucial. Not only does life depend on water, but all productive and most reproductive activities require it on a daily basis. At the same time, among the groups targeted to achieve a participatory process, women are the most important because they are part of all social strata, all age groups, and all cultures; belong to both the spheres of production and reproduction; and contribute actively to the development of their countries. Given women's central role in the social structure and water's importance for sustaining life, integrated water resource management policies at the local, national, regional, and international levels should give both priority.

Examining the evolution of the summit meetings and international conferences that have shaped global policy statements on water demonstrates if and how the different bodies charged with developing water policies did so in ways that promoted women's participation in water resource management. In a parallel vein, an assessment of how institutions in charge of developing gender policies have addressed water management is needed as well. We find that even though gender and water are interconnected, water management agencies and water supply operators, as well as the offices and ministries in charge of gender equity issues, continue to have separate or parallel agendas.

Linking Water to Gender

Our point of departure in analyzing the evolution of water resource management policies is the principle of sustainable development, which the Brundtland Commission defines as "development that meets the needs of the present without compromising the ability of future generations to meet their own needs (Comisión Brundtland 1998, 460).[5] The concept acquired legitimacy at two key gatherings dealing with environmental issues, the 1992 Rio "Earth" Summit and the 1992 Dublin Conference. The 1992 United Nations Conference on Environment and Development, known as the Earth Summit, brought together the largest number of heads of state to ever attend a UN conference.[6] It was without a doubt a watershed for sustainable development policies because countless international meetings, events, studies, reports, and publications followed, all aimed at developing projects and programs for the conservation of natural resources. To implement these programs, the UN Commission for Environment and Development authorized $600 billion (mostly in the form of multilateral loans and grants) to 150 developing countries (United Nations 1992c).[7] As well, sustainable development secretariats or government ministries were created in most countries.

After the Dublin International Conference for Water and Environment, all national and international gatherings included water on their agendas and endorsed what are today known as the Dublin-Rio principles (United Nations 1992a).[8] These principles were later reformulated during other international gatherings where the issue of water, which initially had been viewed as being on equal terms with other resources, gained importance and primacy. This was especially true after the International Conference on Water and Sustainable Development held in Paris in 1998 (World Water Council 2000a, 3). The Dublin-Rio principles became the basis for the design or modification of water management policies by various United Nations agencies, multilateral banks, and governments in both the developed and developing countries. International bodies such as the World Water Council (WWC) and the Global Water Partnership (GWP) were established on the basis of those principles, with the WWC in charge of developing a vision for sustainable water management and the GWP in charge of creating frameworks for action that could be implemented on a regional level.

In Latin America, the issue of water had been under discussion since 1967 with the Charter of Punta del Este of the Organization of the American States. In 1977, Mar del Plata, Argentina, was the site of the first and only United Nations intergovernmental conference on water (the United Nations Conference on Water). This gathering set the basis for declaring the 1980s as the International Water Supply and Sanitation Decade (World Water Council 2000a, 3). Despite the decade's supposed focus on water, for the most part, water resources management in Latin American countries—just as in other countries of the world—was only one of many elements of development policies. Water took on a more predominant role in policy making during the 1990s.

Water's status as distinct from that of other natural resources (such as forests, land, and air) was affirmed in 1997 with the convening of the First World Water Forum, in Marrakesh, Morocco, which recognized that "in recent years it is clear that there is a chronic and harmful crisis surrounding water resources" (World Water Council 2000b, xii). In the late 1990s, both the World Water Council (WWC) and the Global Water Partnership (GWP) expanded their work. The WWC prepared the "World Water Vision for Life and Environment" (World Water Council 2000) while the GWP developed the "Framework for Action towards Water Security" (Global Water Partnership 2000) both used in the design of government plans and programs at the national, regional, and international levels. These documents in turn were the basis for GWP's document, "A Way Forward: From Vision to Action" (Global Water Partnership 2000).

In March 2000, the Second World Water Forum was held in The Hague, Holland, with representatives from all countries, private enterprises, NGOs, professionals, donor agencies, academics, and intellectuals. The WWC issued the following mission statement: "To promote awareness of critical water issues at all levels, including the highest decision-making level, to facilitate planning, management and use of water in all its dimensions on an environmentally sustainable basis for the benefit of all life on the earth" (World Water Council 2000a, 4). The objectives of the WWC are:

1. To identify critical water issues of local, regional and global importance on the basis of ongoing assessments on the state of world water.

2. To raise awareness of critical water issues at all levels of decision making, from the highest authorities to the local level.

3. To provide the forum for a common strategic vision on integrated water resource management on a sustainable basis, and to promote the implementation of effective policies and strategies worldwide.

4. To provide advice and relevant information to institutions and decision-makers on the development and implementation of comprehensive policies and strategies for sustainable water resources management, with due respect for the environment, and social and *gender equity* (emphasis added).

5. To contribute to the resolution of issues related to transboundary waters (World Water Council 2000, 4).

The fourth objective's limited reference to gender issues could be interpreted as a sign that the WWC believes that policy makers should only take environmental, social, and gender equity into consideration, rather than implementing concrete measures to address them. Alternately, the issue of gender may only be mentioned because given the political climate encouraging inclusion of women, it is deemed necessary to mention it. But a simple mention is not enough. Incorporating the goal of gender equity is a complex process that requires the design of management policies or action strategies aimed at fostering the inclusion of women in decision-making bodies at all levels.

While the WWC developed the vision, the GWP crafted a proposal to implement Integrated Water Resources Management (IWRM). Besides broadening the Dublin-Rio principles, it was to make recommendations for putting them in practice. The third principle of the resulting document focuses on the role of women and notes the need to pay attention to (1) [the] involvement of women in decision making, (2) women as water users, and (3) [the fact that] IWRM requires gender awareness (Global Water Partnership 2000, 17–18). This is one of the few documents that recognizes that when one speaks of "gender balance," the concept is not simply about counting the number of males and females, but rather it has to do with attention to the needs of both genders.

At the same time that the above document was being written, GWP was developing the Framework for Action to achieve water security, which "constitutes a key component of strategies to meet International Development Targets for 2015 related to reducing poverty, improving health, eliminating malnutrition and maintaining a healthy environment" (Global Water Partnership 2000, 2). This framework follows the lines of Agenda 21, approved in Rio de Janeiro in 1992, where the first section, "Social and Economic Dimensions" notes that "[a]n effective strategy for tackling the problems of poverty, development, and environment simultaneously should begin by focusing on resources, production and people and should cover demographic issues, enhanced health care and education, *the rights of women*, the role of youth and of indigenous people and local communities and a democratic participation process in association with improved governance" (United Nations 2002, sect. I, chap. 3, emphasis added).

The background to this is that Agenda 21 holds that marginalization leads to greater poverty and at the same time poverty leads to greater environmental degradation because those who are marginalized must overexploit nature to achieve a subsistence living. This assumption led Agenda 21's strategic actions to be oriented toward alleviating poverty and combating economic marginalization. Thus it notes that "[p]overty is a complex multidimensional problem with origins in both the national and international domains. No solution can be applied globally. Rather, each country must design its own programs to tackle poverty in ways that are appropriate to the local contexts. The eradication of poverty and hunger, greater equity in income distribution, and human resource development remain major challenges everywhere. The struggle against poverty is the shared and collaborative responsibility of all countries" (United Nations 2002, sect. I, chap. 3).

On this basis, the governments of the different countries of Latin America developed action plans in which they presented general guidelines for implementing poverty alleviation programs within national frameworks of "sustainable development," taking as their main goals caring for the health of the population and stimulating the participation of civil society.

Thus, the institutions in charge of implementing the poverty alleviation programs promoted the participation of civil society with shared responsibility for the planning, implementation, evaluation, and supervision of environmental and natural resource policies and for the fight against poverty. They also recognized that involving women was fundamental to achieve these objectives. All this has remained, however, at the level of formal pronouncements that have not been translated into concrete actions. The series of legal or constitutional measures and reforms that were decreed—which in the case of water resources promote the participation of civil society and its involvement in decision making aimed at water preservation, conservation, and distribution—did not include ways to actually foster the participation of women, who are at a disadvantage compared with men because of the historically embedded cultural norms of social participation.

Though it is true that most governments relied on Agenda 21 and that the latter mentions women throughout its forty sections,[9] Agenda 21 lacks mechanisms for overcoming the discrimination that affects the female population. Specifically, such proposals should include:

• Implementation of measures to strengthen and foster institutions, nongovernmental organizations, and women's groups that can train women in the use and management of natural resources.

• Fostering a reduction in women's enormous workload through the establishment of daycare centers, an equal division of domestic tasks between men and women, and the use of environmentally healthy technologies.

Another limitation on incorporating the recommendations and commitments developed as international tools for public policies is their emphasis on the situation of poor women without taking into account the legal, cultural, economic, and political obstacles faced by the female population as a whole. The documents discussed above (Agenda 21, GWP's Framework for Action, etc.) that consider the situation of women also fail to address the inequalities that exist between women and men or the power relations established between them; that is, they do not incorporate a gender focus. In addition, these documents have tended to assign women the role of "environmental guardians" or "administrators of the environmental crisis in daily life," without taking into account that this is the responsibility of society as a whole. Finally, these policy documents consider women to be a "vulnerable group" rather than citizens with rights (Rico 1998a).

The next major world conference was the World Summit on Sustainable Development in Johannesburg, South Africa, held in 2002, ten years after the Rio Summit. At the regional level, Latin America held its Preparatory Conference of Latin America and the Caribbean for the 2002 Johannesburg World Summit in Rio de Janeiro, Brazil, in October 2001. In the document, "Rio de Janeiro Platform for Action on the Road to Johannesburg 2002," the governments of Latin America "Recognize[d] that gender equity has been fundamental in advancing efforts to achieve sustainable development and that the full participation of women in policy formulation and implementation should be strengthened at the local, national, regional and global levels" (CEPAL, PNUD, PNUMA 2002, 55). Regarding water management, this document proposed changes in the cultural and social perception of water, putting an end to the culture of waste and building a culture of scarcity on the basis of the interaction between problems of water quantity and water quality.

At the Summit, the water sector set up the "Waterdome,"[10] where all the panels on water were held (e.g., on topics such as water and environmental sustainability, water and food, and others). The panel on water and sanitation "underscored the need for a multisectoral, people-centered, integrated water resource management approach. Speakers highlighted the importance of regional management of water resources, access to clean water, the linkage between sanitation and poverty reduction, capacity-building and awareness programs, and appropriate pricing based on end-users' financial resources" (International Institute For Sustainable Development, 14–15).

As a result of the discussions held at the Waterdome, one of the final agreements reached at the Johannesburg Summit was the objective of "[P]roviding access to at least one billion people who lack clean drinking water and two billion people who lack proper sanitation" (Johannesburg Summit 2002). Such agreements, however, run the risk of being no more than political declarations—and even as action plans they are impossible to fulfill—if they are not accompanied by the development of common agendas between the water and gender sectors and the elaboration of concrete implementation commitments with adequate funding. As an illustration, the Johannesburg document makes general statements such as: "We are committed to ensure that women's empowerment and emancipation, and gender equality are integrated in all activities encompassed within Agenda 21, the Millennium Development Goals, and the Johannesburg Plan of Implementation" (www.earthsummit2002.org). This commitment, however, is not backed up in the section titled, "Making it Happen!" or in any other part of the document. This leads to the question of whether gender equity is a serious objective within water resource management policies.

In March 2003, the Third World Water Forum took place in Japan. Its two main objectives were to monitor the progress of major water-related actions undertaken at international/regional/national levels from March 2000 to March 2003 and to follow up on commitments made during the Second

World Water Forum in The Hague (2000) toward the achievement of global water security.

At both the Johannesburg and Japan summits, specific actions to foster the participation of women in the water sector were led by the Gender and Water Alliance (GWA), which was formed during the Second World Water Forum and one year later became an associated program of the Global Water Partnership (see www.gwa.org). These actions have included electronic conferences—held simultaneously in English, French, Spanish, and Portuguese—carried out in 2002 in different world regions on the implications of incorporating a gender analysis in water projects. In addition, the GWA led the Water and Gender Panel at the Third World Water Forum in Japan.

The GWA maintains that "optimizing development implies recognizing that women and men have different requirements and often unequal opportunities for domestic and productive uses of water and the use of catchment areas," and that "women and poor people generally have fewer opportunities to share in and benefit from development and management." It calls for "more effective mobilization of human resources and institutional capacities . . . to achieve a more logical and equitable sharing of burdens, benefits and responsibilities between women and men" (World Water Council 2002b, 16).

Despite the advances detailed in this section the reality is that, to date, programs in the water sector have paid little attention to issues of gender equity and even less to the creation of an enabling environment to facilitate women's participation in water management and water policy formulation.

Linking Gender to Water

How gender policies include or affect water management is essential for understanding how gender and water management play out at the grassroots level.

During the last decade of the twentieth century, the strengthening of democratic institutions across Latin America, the peace processes in Central America, as well as the efforts of the women's movement to raise greater public awareness about the situation of women have all contributed to the increasing inclusion of a gender perspective in the region's economic and social development.

The Fourth World Conference on Women held in Beijing in 1995 stimulated deeper institutionalization of the gender perspective in many countries through strengthening national mechanisms for the advancement of women and for gender equity. In Latin America, the Regional Programmes of Action on Women of Latin America and the Caribbean 1995–2001 (ECLAC 1994), the Santiago Consensus (ECLAC 1998), and the Lima Consensus (ECLAC 2000b) have led to gender equity policies becoming part of governmental objectives at the ministerial level or other high levels through the creation of National Offices for Women in all countries. Among the principal accomplishments are changes in national legislation aimed at assuring equality before the law for men and women, and the signing and ratification of international legal instruments such as the Convention on the Elimination of All Forms of Discrimination against Women (CEDAW) to assure the protection of human rights for women in all spheres (UN 1979).

Efforts to strengthen the autonomy of women and the exercise of their citizenship, problems that specifically affect women, such as family violence, poverty in women-headed households, maternal mortality, and the exercise of sexual and reproductive rights, have become a part of public debate and of governmental agendas. The effects of these advances for women, however, vary considerably both across the region and according to the particular issue involved.

The National Offices for Women have faced significant obstacles on at least four levels (Bravo and Rico 2001, 19). The first has to do with their technical consolidation and management capacity. The second concerns their actual power and capacity to negotiate and reach agreements within the state apparatus, above all at the level of decisions that are made in what are considered the "hard" sectors, such as economic policy, and sectors whose policies are supposed to equitably benefit the whole population. The third level is the weak reception that gender equity issues continue to have within civil society, especially among private sector management and labor unions and even with nongovernmental organizations with which the National Offices for Women have had an uneven relationship. Last, a lack of reliable data seriously constrains decision making and stems from the meager amount of statistical information disaggregated by sex because most state sectors do not generate gender-specific data.

The prevailing gender system also shaped and constrained the institutional agendas of National Offices for Women.[11] Therefore, macroeconomic issues, sectoral reforms—such as health care, education, and public services such as water, telephone, and electricity—and state processes—such as modernization and decentralization—have only been partially addressed, if at all, by these institutions. And, in turn, various commissions, secretariats, ministries, and other state bodies in charge of the above macroeconomic and development issues do not consider the National Offices for Women essential partners in negotiation or policy-making processes.[12] This view results from strong ideological resistance to prioritizing gender equity among government officials, technical specialists, and decision makers, whether they are men or women. Few understand the situation of women and the inequality they face, nor do they comprehend the benefits that a gender focus can provide to projects, institutions, and communities. Internal strategies and methodologies are absent, and these combine with bureaucratic inertia to prevent incorporating a gender approach into sectoral policy planning.

This situation points to the difficulty of making public policies when the existing gender system overlaps with other social institutions. Modifying any one social institution, whether it is the family, the economic system, the political system, or the culture itself, has a feedback effect on the gender system. Simultaneously, changes in the gender system that are produced by conjunctural dynamics (economic crises, migration, natural disasters, etc.) or by global trends (technological development, internationalization of economies, globalization of human rights, etc.) are key to the way institutions are structured and modified at the macro- and microsocial levels.

That gender policies and government policies for other sectors have developed independently, each with their own terminology, objectives, and priorities exacerbates these problems. The scant attention paid to water issues in gender equity policies and in the nearly nonexistent attention, beyond rhetoric, to gender equity in programs and legislation dealing with water vividly illustrates this. Thus the gender approach in International Water Resources Management is unfinished business.

Women's advocates during the 1990s focused on building institutional spaces for gender issues; the challenge for the present decade is to infuse gender issues across the public agenda, along with attempts to broaden governmental gender agendas.[13] What is needed is to move from the "must be" embodied in international agreements and policy statements to the "must do" of formulating and implementing public policies that can have a synergistic influence on sectoral efficiency and on gender equity, through poverty reduction, a better distribution of resources, and the broadening of opportunities for all.

At the international level, the first efforts to take up the issue of gender and water date back to the 1980s, when the International Research and Training Institute for the Advancement of Women (INSTRAW)[14] and the

Senior Women's Advisory Group on Sustainable Development (part of the United Nations Environment Programme, UNEP)[15] played a crucial role. These agencies fostered debate not only on women and water but also more broadly on the links among the exclusion of women, the roles women fulfill, and the problems of degradation of natural resources. These early efforts affected the International Water Supply and Sanitation Decade (1981–1990) by calling attention to the importance of promoting women's training and their participation as water suppliers for their families. They also helped shape the agenda of the 1992 International Conference for Water and Environment and led to the third Dublin principle on water and sustainable development.

Along with the strategies adopted at the 1985 Nairobi World Conference to Review and Appraise the Achievements of the United Nations Decade for Women: Equality, Development and Peace, the above efforts were the first steps in officially incorporating the environment and natural resources into the discussion on women. The Nairobi Forward-looking Strategies for the Advancement of Women, however, contain few concrete references to water because its focus was principally the "egalitarian" participation of men and women particularly in the workplace. Nonetheless, the strategies insist that: "Rural women's access to land, capital, technology, know-how and other productive resources should be secured. Women should be given full and effective rights to land ownership" (United Nations 1986, para. 182), and "women must have the same opportunity as men to participate in the wage-earning labor force in such programmes as irrigation" (UN 1986, para. 224). It is emphatic that "governments should . . . apply special remedial measures to relieve the burden placed on women by the task of fetching water." It also calls for women to "be included by governments and agencies in all policy planning, implementation and administration of water supply projects and trained to take responsibility for the management of hydraulic infrastructures and equipment and for their maintenance" (para. 188). For urban areas, it notes that "efforts to improve sanitary conditions, including drinking water supplies, in all communities should be strengthened, especially in urban slums and squatter settlements" (para. 225).

The Beijing Platform for Action ten years later did not mark any significant advances. Water is mentioned in connection to women in only three of the twelve areas of special concern where strategic measures and changes in values, attitudes, practices, and priorities at all levels are required: women and health, women and the economy, and women and the environment.[16] It is in the area of "women and the environment" that the clearest links are drawn between women and water. This section of the Platform for Action responds to concerns about the lack of recognition of women's contributions to natural resource management and protecting the environment, as well as the lack of adequate support for those contributions. It poses as a strategic objective the need to "integrate gender concerns and perspectives in policies and programmes for sustainable development" and notes that among the measures that governments need to adopt is to "promote knowledge of and sponsor research on the role of women, particularly rural and indigenous women, in food gathering and production, soil conservation, irrigation, watershed management."[17] In addition, it establishes as an unfulfilled goal to "[e]nsure that clean water is available and accessible to all by the year 2000 and that environmental protection and conservation plans are designed and implemented to restore polluted water systems and rebuild damaged watersheds" (United Nations 1995, para. 256 f, k, and l).

A balance sheet of the first five years of implementation of the Beijing Platform for Action was presented to the UN General Assembly in June 2000. It identified the lack of attention to the economic and social determinants of health, such as access to drinking water, as one of the obstacles to women's health. It recommended that governments should "[e]nsure universal and equal access for women and men throughout the life-cycle, to social services related to health care, including education, clean water and safe sanitation, nutrition, food security and health education programmes" (United Nations 2000, 24).

The few references to water resources in international agreements on gender described in the preceding pages underscore how limited the concern with gender-water connections is among governments all over the world—governments that are promoting gender equity in their programs and policies—and how underdeveloped the links are between water policy and gender policy. Little progress has been made toward the goal of bringing water management issues into gender equity discussions and toward meeting the challenge of reducing gender gaps in the access, use, management, and control of water. Thus, the theme of water has had an extremely limited presence in Equal Opportunity Plans that are the main policy instruments used to articulate gender issues with different areas of state activity. These plans, which aim to reduce the existing gaps between men and women and tend to be connected to National Development Plans, clearly point to the complexity and the systemic nature of gender inequalities. They also make clear that joint actions based on common objectives are indispensable. Up to now, however, the record shows that, in general, Offices for Women do not include within their plans the objective of reaching agreements or consulting about common action strategies with the institutions charged with water resource management at the national level.

As an exception, Costa Rica's 1996–1998 Plan for Equal Opportunities among Women and Men is one of the few that includes specific objectives related to water. The plan proposes to "foster appropriate use and management of water and hydrological resources" through well-defined goals applied to specific communities. For example, one action is to "develop a program that targets at least ten communities for training on the management and prevention of pollution in rivers and streams, in which women shall have equal participation." Another is to "foster the creation of at least three committees for watershed conservation in each of the country's administrative regions and to ensure the observance of current legislation regarding women's participation in the committees' leadership" (Centro Nacional para el Desarrollo de la Mujer y la Familia 1995, 60, 61). This plan, unlike most others, has concrete and quantifiable objectives aimed at giving women opportunities to participate in integrated water resources management.

In sum, we see an absence of gender policies that focus on integrated water resources management as distinct from other natural resources and a dearth of water policies that have incorporated a gender equity perspective. This leads to the question: What tools will women, and the population as a whole, have to face privatization policies based on the neoliberal economic model that pursues financial rather than social interests? Though over the last decade there has been a significant pattern of privatization in the water sector, as well as the rise of water markets, those in charge of women's programs fail to engage in joint planning with water institutions and vice-versa.

Despite the fact that government institutions in charge of women's policies try to infuse a gender approach across all sectors, in practice their work reflects sociocultural gender patterns that assign certain activities to men (primarily in the public sphere and in the area of production) and other activities to women (reproductive work in the domestic sphere). This means that traditional gender roles continue in the water sector as well. For example, projects addressing domestic drinking water generally prioritize only reproductive needs where women are perceived to have a major role. Such thinking fails to recognize that water is also an input for many traditional productive activities that women in Latin America carry out in their homes or on their land, both in rural and urban settings, including preparing food, baking bread, doing laundry for third parties, managing household vegetable gardens, and raising animals. These activities, rooted in women's historical roles in the household and shaped by the prevailing gender system, represent a fundamental part of family income and—until women's roles change—will continue to be essential for family nutrition, health, and subsistence. Water is an input for other productive activities also carried out by women, such as irrigation (see chapters seven and eleven).

Change is needed in the way that gender policy decision makers design and implement programs. General statements, such as those recognizing women's contribution to a country's development, are already acknowledged by all sectors. It is necessary now to go beyond exposing problems to advance jointly developed strategies for water and for women. In addition, most equal opportunity plans have not yet been sufficiently monitored or evaluated. This means that we cannot draw any conclusions as to their accomplishments based on their proposed objectives and actions. Finally, it is essential that programs be adequately funded and staffed. Permanent line items must be created in ministry budgets to fund the mainstreaming of gender equity across the public agenda.

In any discussion of water and gender policies in Latin America, it is crucial to take into account activities carried out by civil society, specifically by women's organizations, because of the importance of the women's movement and feminism in the formulation of gender equity goals, and because their efforts to promote sustainable and equitable development predated governmental efforts. Meetings in preparation for the Earth Summit in 1992, such as the Global Assembly on Women and the Environment: Partners in Life (1991) and the World Congress of Women for a Healthy Planet (1991), arrived at a framework presented in "Women's Action Agenda 21" that called for participatory democracy (including the full participation by women on an equal footing with men) and universal access to information (World Congress of Women for a Healthy Planet 1991).

Women's nongovernmental organizations and feminist academics have emphasized that a gendered approach makes it possible to identify the heterogeneity of social actors important in the water sector, a heterogeneity that includes not only gender but also ethnicity and social class. This concept has encouraged many technical cooperation agencies to adopt broader perspectives that can address varied needs. Furthermore, nongovernmental organizations have tried to push for gender-oriented actions that involve women and men.

Despite all the contributions of the feminist movement and nongovernmental organizations that work on women's issues, in general, water issues are not their priority. The lack of linkages between gender and water issues at the government level is reflected in civil society as well (Red Mujer y Medio Ambiente et al. 2000).[18] No significant and systematic pressure from either civil society or the NGO sector to place the water issue on the governmental agenda of the National Offices for Women has occurred; and institutions in the water sector are even less likely to exert any such pressure. Therefore, women's organizations have not pushed for the fulfillment of the international accords on water agreed to in Dublin, Rio, and Beijing. Nor have they involved themselves in activities to monitor the implementation of these agreements.

The Gap between Talk and Action

The process of globalization in Latin America embeds water and gender policies in the neoliberal model. The neoliberal model has led to a reduced role for the state in economic development and social welfare, accomplished by increasing the roles played by the private sector and promoting the participation of civil society. In the case of the water sector, private sector investors and water users are held co-responsible for preserving and conserving water resources. Based on the belief that privatization will improve water allocation, there has been a push to modify water legislation to create incentives for private sector participation in both service provision and the creation of water markets. Water services management, however, needs to improve so it can meet the steady growth of multiple users competing for water, increasing demand by users, and growing contamination. Thanks to the multiplicity of international and regional conferences, there is a greater awareness of the need to reach sustainable development goals, which require reconciling economic, social, and environmental objectives (CEPAL 1998, 7). At the same time, incorporating a gender perspective into water policy and planning has rarely moved beyond mere words.

Regarding gender policies, though some countries have established foundations for gender equity, in many cases, this is isolated from mainstream policy making and in others is not widely understood or recognized. Gender policies rarely take an environmental approach; they tend to view water resources as just another issue. Thus the possibility for linking gender and water policies remains rhetorical.

In general terms, ten years after the Rio Summit, a period with multiple meetings at the governmental level as well as among nongovernmental organizations, neither international agreements nor Latin America's water management systems have shown significant progress in achieving their goals.[19] In some countries, water resources management has actually deteriorated. One explanation lies with the growing role of the private sector and the corresponding reduction of the role of the state, which has created an imbalance whereby the state's capacity for providing for the population has been significantly reduced.

The institutional structures that the governments of Latin America adopted both for water resource management and to promote gender equity are vastly different because of each country's particular characteristics. In some countries, a government agency is in charge of water management at the national level within a secretariat or a ministry of development, agriculture, or housing, while in other countries water management is in the hands of agencies that are in charge of given regions, encompassing watersheds or geopolitical divisions such as states or provinces. In yet other countries, one government office is in charge of water for agricultural uses, while other water uses fall under different sectoral ministries or secretariats.[20]

In the case of gender policy, some countries have National Women's Offices responsible for promoting gender equity in national life with high enough ranking in the state hierarchy to give them a degree of autonomy and power to secure compliance with their decisions by other parts of the state apparatus. In other countries, however, the National Women's Offices remain subordinate to other state agencies; and in some cases, they are grouped or clustered with different areas of sectoral interest, such as in Bolivia, where the Vice-Ministry for Women currently remains under the Ministry of Peasant, Indian, Gender, and Generational Affairs.

Institutions in both the water and gender sectors have barely begun the task of linking interests, objectives, and goals within their own sectors. In addition to considering inter- and intrasectoral coordination, new policies must offer diverse options based on an integrated, gender-sensitive approach because real solutions require real social changes. For example, technical changes in the water sector or simply increasing the participation of women in the political sphere via quotas will not suffice either to improve water services or to improve governance.

The authorities and institutions in charge of water resources management are not yet sufficiently convinced or trained to be able to include gender equity as a basic criterion in policy formulation. Such a shift involves the political will of government officials, the transformation of norms and procedures, and the systematic application of new planning methodologies so that the unequal and self-perpetuating effects of gender gaps in sectoral public policies are analyzed before, during, and after policy implementation. Only with an extensive process of social change can gender bias be avoided in the design of policy and practice.

Despite all the talk, most policy makers still do not link the dominant gender system and the situations of inequality between men and women that prevail in the water sectors. By not analyzing how policies, projects, and programs have a differentiated effect on women and men, gender biases in formulation and planning go undetected. As a result, no corrective measures are taken, nor are preventive measures adopted that could avoid the differentiated effects. Most water sector decisions continue to be made based on the false assumption that they are gender neutral, that the population is a homogeneous whole, and that benefits reach everyone equally.

PART TWO

Neoliberal Policies and Their Social Impact

The last few decades have witnessed the spread of globalization and more recently the widespread adoption of the neoliberal model of development. These have combined to lead to deepening inequality in Latin America, as demonstrated by the growing gap between rich and poor. In general, the market orientation that characterizes neoliberal policies has been implemented with little regard for social effects. The chapters in this section explore these impacts on the water sector in Mexico, Bolivia, and Argentina, as well as the popular responses to them.

In particular, the case studies allow us to examine how the privatization of water services works in practice. They also present the oral testimonies of women who participated in the social movements that have opposed privatization. Their testimonies are powerful indicators that when the public feels distanced from decision making that affects them negatively, they are capable of carrying out protests fierce enough to overturn important agreements between national governments and multinational corporations.

4 Gender Dimensions of
Neoliberal Water Policy in Mexico and Bolivia
Empowering or Disempowering?

D ecreasing quantity and deteriorating quality of fresh water sources encourage the water sector to anticipate severe water crises as demand
from the domestic and industrial sectors steadily continue to grow.
The international lending institutions, world water committees, and mainstream environmental actors argue that these crises are a result of the failure
of state management and thus may only be deflected by introducing market
mechanisms in resource management. Though they share a consensus that
water rights must be clear, private, and individual for markets to work effectively, they simultaneously recognize that water is a basic human need
(Briscoe 1997; Cosgrove and Rijsberman 2000; Postel 1997; Serageldin 1995;
World Bank 1993). This tension appearing in World Bank, World Water
Council, Global Water Partnership and World Watch rhetoric between water as commodity and water as a basic need is not reflected in their policy
recommendations. Their recommendations reflect a dramatic shift away
from defining water as a public good to treating it as a commodity, translated into a singular policy framework, with a one-size-fits-all solution.

This switch in emphasis and policy raises important concerns from the
perspective of gender. Women and men have differential access and control
over water and its policy developments. Women's knowledge and labor investment in the productive uses of water remain largely unrecognized, and
increases in the efficiency of water allocation are likely to come at their ex-
pense.

The neoliberal features of contemporary water policy reflect a global
trend of economic liberalization with policy increasingly formulated and

regulated transnationally while the responsibility for water management is transferred to the water users. This has three effects: (a) market mechanisms and trade dominate policy frameworks, (b) global policies are implemented without regard to local differences in a "cookie cutter" fashion, and (c) the responsibility for resource management is taken from the state (the public domain) and handed to individual stakeholders (the private sector). A gender analysis grounded in empirical data demonstrates that current developments driven by the increasing individualization and commercialization of water rights, enhance trade but simultaneously encourage concentration and dispossession of water rights.

This chapter sheds light on gender and contemporary water policy using cases from Mexico and Bolivia. Both countries designed their recent water laws in consultation with the World Bank closely modeled on legislation introduced in Chile in 1980. Chile was the forerunner in adopting neoliberal restructuring in Latin America and introduced a Water Law in 1980 of which privatizing water was a significant component (Bauer 1998; Ríos and Quiroz 1995). Mexico's Water Law was adopted in 1992 in preparation for the signing of the North American Free Trade Agreement (NAFTA) with the United States and Canada. Meanwhile, Peru, Ecuador, Venezuela, and Bolivia have followed suit, implementing the Chilean model almost verbatim. Where Mexico implemented its water law with little public protest (even though the launching of NAFTA two years later provoked considerable unrest), Bolivia's rural and urban protests prevented the 1998 Water Law from coming into effect.

While Mexico and Bolivia have historically distinct political and economic trajectories, they faced similar Structural Adjustment Packages and identical water legislative advice linked to lending conditionality from the World Bank. The outcomes of their (attempt at) implementation, however, strongly diverge. International policies and local practice interact dynamically and continuously shape social, political, and economic relations accordingly. Gender relations are integral to these dynamics and thus provide a perspective that allows us to understand the shaping and effect of these policies. Therefore, the discussion focuses on whether, and if so how, commodifying water will affect gendered use of it and whether market mechanisms will affect gendered access. As the agricultural sector uses an estimated 70 percent of available fresh water, the politics of irrigation provides a starting point in understanding the intra- and intersectoral competition for water and its gender dimensions.

Neoliberalism and Water Policy

The global, political, and economic conjuncture of the last two decades saw a crescendo of neoliberal popularity economically and politically restructuring society. Instead of national economic growth, today participation in global markets defines development, with adherence to global policy frameworks instead of national priorities (McMichael 1996). Structural adjustment policies that the International Monetary Fund (IMF) and the World Bank introduced in the 1980s conditioned limited public spending and encouraged private sector involvement. Underlying these policies is the objective of promoting global free trade, facilitated by transnational agreements such as the North American Free Trade Agreement (NAFTA) and regulated by supranational constitutional bodies such as the World Trade Organization (WTO; Gill 2001). Not only does this reconfigure the state and its responsibilities, it also implies a focus on economic rationality with a renewed emphasis on efficiency, financial incentives, individuality, and competition (Benería 1999).

With the liberalization of the economy, and fueled by the persistent emphasis on failing state management, water-related policy shifted from significant public agency control to a retraction of the state to facilitate the privatization of natural resources. Water economists argue that the world is facing fresh water scarcity, as demand increases while quality is deteriorating (Briscoe 1997; Rosegrant and Binswanger 1994; Young 1986). They maintain that with most of the readily available water resources already developed, new projects accrue higher financial and environmental costs. Increasing competition for water from the municipal and industrial sectors, they argue, can only be effectively accommodated by market mechanisms efficiently reallocating water to its highest value use. Under this logic, for water markets to function, resources need to move from the public to the private sector, with water rights divorced from land and given the characteristics of private property (Briscoe 1997; Holden and Thobani 1996). After three decades of investing in water infrastructure, the World Bank formally adopted the market approach in 1993, redirecting its lending policies to legal and institutional reforms that encourage water markets to emerge (World Bank 1993, 21, 66). This "new" policy closely follows the neoliberal framework as it demands the decentralization of resource management, a greater reliance on pricing, increased participation by stakeholders, and a shift to defining water as an economic good (World Bank 1993, 13).[1]

The World Water Forum in The Hague in 2000 consolidated the 1993 World Bank principles, primarily concentrating on fine-tuning and implementing them. The comprehensive strategy for the twenty-first century, accepted at the 2002 Earth Summit in Johannesburg, confirms an apparent water consensus. Even though the 1992 Dublin conference is often cited as the first moment of global consensus in defining water as an economic good (Cosgrove and Rijsberman 2000; World Bank 1993), the Dublin principles reflect a far more socially complex analysis of water management.[2] In particular, they recognize gendered access to water and emphasized water as a basic right instead of a need (its current formulation). While the World Bank acknowledges that the fluidity and public good characteristics of water cause market externalities and a high risk of monopoly control, it persists in policies favoring a market orientation with appropriate financial incentives for water resource management (Bond 1997; World Bank 1993:27, 2000).

Privatization of water is often misunderstood to mean complete private ownership of a resource or asset, shifting both the entitlement and management of water from public to private hands. A more accurate understanding is to distinguish between privatization and commercialization because though marketing of water embodies both, they may not be equally applied. Privatization concerns the reorganization of water allocation. Entitlement is changed from public to private rights and management is no longer exclusively the domain of the public sector. These private property characteristics define access to the resource and its reallocation, while formally it is still understood to be a public good. Commercialization involves the introduction of economic institutions into the water sector to guide distribution, including the market, competition, and efficiency (Bakker 2002). In Mexico, privatization was limited to changing ownership from public to private entitlement while management was decentralized but not privatized, allowing the public sector to maintain a certain level of control. Commercialization, however, was implemented to its full extent. The proposed Bolivian Water Law attempted both full-fledged privatization and commercialization.

Exchanging or trading water rights has always been part and parcel of water management practices. Different today, however, is the combination of rights taking on private and alienable characteristics in a context that promotes global free trade. The local and state institutions are encouraged to withdraw and actors such as lawyers and notary publics take the place of water judges and historic decision-making procedures. As a result, both the community and the public sector relinquish control.

Does this neoliberal framework translate into improved water management as demand from the industrial and municipal sector grows? Mainstream concerns generally revolve around the quantity and quality of water, while this chapter focuses more on concerns related to social equity. Why should social equity be a concern when water resources are shifted from the public to the private sphere? First, by center staging only an economic concept of efficiency, economic maximization standards become the measure to define successful management, overshadowing other values such as equity or environmental sustainability (Spiertz and Wiber 1996). Second, economic efficiency tends to disregard sectors outside the formal economy, thereby undervaluing uses of water and labor not recognized as economically productive, for example, homestead production and local ecosystem regeneration. A solely economic rationale neglects social relations that are not competitive or goals that are socially instead of economically important (Benería 1999). Third, commodifying water and introducing individual rights in combination with quantifying nature exclusively in terms of monetary value, transforms collective water users into individual market players and creates a negotiating arena unhindered by notions of community or social equity (Lipschutz 1998; McAfee 1999).

Gender and Neoliberal Water Policies

Improving gender equity in water management means addressing the institutional and social barriers women face to formal and informal access to water. These barriers concern the decision-making process determining the allocation of water, how it is used, and finally the control over the actual volume of water delivered. Access to water and land rights is structurally gendered (Ahlers 2000; Arizpe and Botey 1987; Deere and León 2001; Zwarteveen 1997c). Groundbreaking work for Africa by Dey (1981) and Carney (1988), for Asia by Zwarteveen and Neupane (1996) and Illo (1988), and Latin America by Bennett (1995b) and Lynch (1991) among others show how women have struggled for access to both domestic and productive use water in contexts that do not recognize them as fully entitled.

I argue that unequal gendered access to resources is perpetuated and legitimized by the introduction of market mechanisms in the water sector. Underlying this analysis is the recognition that gender identities are dynamic and complex, that nature and society mutually constitute each other, and that gender relations involve cooperation as well as conflict. Similarly, natural resources cannot be understood as separate entities but as interlinked and riddled with multiple cultural, economic, and historic meanings.

To understand the gendered effects of markets, the assumptions that inform the logic of market allocation of resources as well as the epistemological tradition underlying neoliberalism must be made explicit. The allocation of resources in the neoliberal paradigm assumes that rather than public regulation, economic rationale, and efficiency are more appropriate forces to reach welfare maximization. Neoliberalism's epistemological roots lie in western science and intellectual experience that reflect a very particular representation of reality excluding observations from other sociocultural perspectives informed by gender, color, class, or ethnicity. Its fundamentals are reproduced and legitimized by specific interest groups and institutions that promote it, such as the World Bank and the International Monetary Fund (Goonatilake 1984; Harding 1991; Mohanty 1991).

Consequently, all market participants are expected to behave in a manner familiar to those who promote free markets. The "separate self model" of an unbounded individual making rational choices based on utility maximization harbors a western androcentric bias, which ignores those responsible for reproductive activities and societies geared toward collective decision making and responsibilities (Benería 1999). In practice, markets reproduce the social relations of the society they develop in, as the Mexican case shows. Women and men relate differently to the market because much of women's labor is either unpaid or underpaid. Furthermore, public space is gendered and entering into male domains has implications for the social status of women in their community. Concepts of competition and efficiency can have unintended but detrimental effects on gender, race/ethnicity, and class relations.

Efficient market reallocation requires that water rights be divorced from land rights and be granted private property characteristics through individual titling. In theory, individualization as an essential component of neoliberal policies has the potential to undermine the naïvely neutral concept of the harmonious single (male)-headed family unit. Assuring access to property rights for all members of the household, in the form of joint or individual titles, allows for a more gender egalitarian notion of household heads. Women would be less dependent on their spouses, male relatives, and leaders and formally entitled to enter the public discourse. This argument suggests that formal titles will open the doors necessary for women to fully partake in discussions over water management at all levels, and by doing so, affect decision making. Bina Agarwal (1994), for example, argues that privatization could be the vehicle of empowerment for women in relation to the other members of the household because formal titles allow women: to *participate* in the market, to have *independent* access to economic resources, to improve their *bargaining* position, to have *collateral* in order to obtain credits, and to facilitate greater *equality of rights* over productive resources. Deere and León (2001) continue this line of reasoning, pointing out that male migration has made women throughout Latin America the primary farmers in small-scale agriculture. Property rights in their name would ensure farm productivity, improve their access to credit and services, in addition to enhancing women's bargaining position within the household and the community.

However persuasive the above arguments may be, they neglect women's historic struggles to access productive resources *outside* formal structures of entitlement, as well as the intrinsic gender biases of the neoliberal context (Ahlers 2002a; Cleaver and Elson 1995; Jackson 1998). They also disregard the collective as a crucial vector in sustainable management. Finally, they fail to recognize that the alienability of individual water rights carries the danger of dispossession.

Gender relations are not solely antagonistic but involve common interests as well as conflicting ones, emotional dependencies alongside economic support. Women and men precariously balance personal and collective needs and interests in their communities, simultaneously legitimizing and contesting inequality. Collective ownership or community support should neither be assumed, romanticized, nor perceived as inherent to indigenous or peasant communities. Rather, internal gender and class inequalities need to be analyzed as articulating with socioeconomic change, contested from within and without. Nonetheless, collective decision making over resource allocation and use is effectively dismantled when rights become exclusively individual and alienable.

Formal individual rights may alleviate this dependency on social networks, simultaneously they might exclude those forms of access that have not been officially recognized but may be vital for women to realize their productive and household activities (Zwarteveen 1997c). An emphasis on individual and formal rights for women disregards the complexities of local definitions and practices of rights not reflected in state law or recognized by state institutions, with serious consequences for those social groups dependent on the primary titleholder (Ahlers 2000a; Ahlers 2000b; Simbolon 1997; Zwarteveen and Neupane 1996).

Property rights are dynamic and negotiated: social relations define the extent of entitlement, use, control, and exclusion. Water rights are typically related to other rights such as land rights, citizenship rights, and rights of original settlers, as well as affected by the type of social group, state law, indigenous, customary, folk and religious law, known as legal pluralism. Given its fluidity, establishing clear and formal property rights to water is a highly ambitious project as such rights are often unclear, undefined, and ineffective. The social and cultural constellations of power legitimize claims to water as much, if not more, than formal or legal institutions (Pradhan and Pradhan 2000; Zwarteveen 1997c). Water as a common pool resource demands some level of collective management; as such it has a long tradition of collective decision-making processes shaped by historically and culturally specific frameworks on the one hand and bureaucratic, state-induced processes on the other. Furthermore, as a common pool resource, water defies easy commodification. Not only does its collective use and fluidity cause third party effects, its multiple uses and values are resistant to a commensurable exchange value. Together these complexities form historical spatial-ecological transformations, best understood as sociolandscapes, or perhaps more appropriately *waterscapes* (Swyngedouw 1999).

How particular communities or ethnicities relate to water, how men and women relate differently because of gendered access, and how historic social relations and struggles shape the different priorities users have in time and space intersect to produce an intricate complex of multiple and often incommensurable values. As multiple values of water are attributed simultaneously, reducing water to a mere economic, monetary value is alienating. Water users move in a constellation of multiple and intersecting inequalities that both limit their scope of choice or force them into making certain choices. Their choices are not solely informed by cost benefit analyses but also by empathy, solidarity, and collective action (Benería 1999; Kabeer 2000). Commodified water is an abstract removed from its spatial and social-historic context. Capturing the value of water solely in economic terms results in a destructive fragmentation of the social and natural landscape (Ahlers 2002a; Escobar 1995; FEDECOR 1998).

Neoliberal Water Policy in Mexico

The De La Madrid presidency (1982–1988) set in motion the transformation of the Mexican State from a paternalistic social-authoritarian institution to a neoliberal one, emphasizing fiscal austerity, privatization, and liberalization (Ramirez 1995). The Salinas administration (1988–1994) consolidated the neoliberal framework in preparation for the launching of NAFTA in 1994. The agricultural sector experienced a complete overhaul in 1992, with the amendment of article 27 of the Constitution and the introduction of both a new Water Law and a reform of the Agrarian Law. A reduction of state subsidies, rigorous sanitation of debts, and the removal of guaranteed prices left farmers facing the full burden of agricultural production and competing within international markets. The safety net for marginalized farm households has been removed, while new credit and subsidy programs are geared towards joint public-private investment favoring capital intensive agribusiness (Foley 1995; Ibarra Mendivil 1996).

The 1992 Mexican Water Law rigorously changed the Mexican *waterscape.* It decentralized irrigation management, divorced land rights from water rights, and allotted them private property characteristics (Gorriz, Subramanian, and Simas 1995; Herrera Toledo 1997). The centralized power of the Mexican presidency, the close relationship of Salinas with the Mexican water bureaucracy, and their ties with the water policy sector of the World Bank, which had increased its influence on Mexico because of the 1982 peso crisis, enabled these legislative changes to happen simultaneously (Bennett 1995b; Ramirez 1995; Rap, Wester, and Prado 2002).

The 1992 Water Law[3] had, by its conception, a strong commitment to encourage water markets.[4] The National Water Commission's (CNA) mandate states that its focus is on the introduction of market mechanisms, pricing and other economic incentives to encourage more efficient use of water (Herrera Toledo 1997, 39).

Even though water formally remains the property of the state, institutional regulations are in place to treat it as a private resource (Rosegrant and Gazmuri 1996). Thus, the Mexican state partially privatized but fully commercialized the water sector.

Markets and Property Rights in Mexico

The 1992 modifications to the Constitution and the Agrarian Law thoroughly redefined land and water rights. Usufructuary land rights had been distributed among the landless during the first Agrarian Reform resulting from the Mexican Revolution, creating the so-called ejido or social sector, characterized by collective farming enterprises. The large land holdings that existed before the Revolution, curiously called the *pequeña propiedad* or private sector, were reduced to holdings of approximately 100 hectares and held private rights. Rights to water were exclusively linked to rights to land, which were initially granted to males over eighteen or to single women and widows supporting a family. Only in 1971 was this right to land changed to include all males and females over the age of sixteen (Arizpe and Botey 1987). Women accessed land largely through inheritance while men acquired land through the agrarian reforms, the redistribution of communal land, and the purchasing of rights. According to Deere and León (2001), by 1984, only 15 percent of beneficiaries of the Mexican land reforms were women.

Over time, Mexican women have established social networks to gain access to resources and to defend them when necessary. Certain male leaders are invited to be the godfathers of their children or given public political support. Patron-client relationships with the private sector are sought and nurtured, influential family members are feted whenever necessary. Among themselves, women forge informal cooperatives for making and selling *gorditas*, raising chickens, or sharing door-to-door catalogue sales. These activities not only raise money to supplement farm income but also provide each "member" entrance into the social networks of the others (Ahlers 2002b; Brunt 1992; Villarreal 1994).

As a result of the proprivatization reform, women are no longer guaranteed inheritance of land and water titles through their spouses, cutting off an important avenue of access to both resources. The contemporary alienability of rights in combination with the current precariousness of agricultural production has increased the probability that the spouse will have sold his titles. The new legislation also reversed an earlier decree that assigned collective property rights to groups of women, the so-called UAIMs (Unidad Agrícola Industrial de la Mujer Campesina or Female Farmers Agricultural Industrial Unit).

The case discussed here concerns an emerging water market in a Mexican irrigation district and is based on a research project conducted from 1996 to 1999. Irrigation district 017 lies in the semiarid[5] Comarca Lagunera, which straddles part of the states of Coahuila and Durango in the central north of Mexico. It covers an area of roughly 220,000 ha with a command area of 93000 ha, divided into 20 hydraulic subunits, organized as Water Users Associations, representing a total of 38,000 users of which roughly one third are female (Comisión Nacional de Agua 1994). The cropping pattern of the district is changing from a long history of cotton and subsistence crops to forage crops for the dairy industry. The collapse in cotton prices in 1991 and the lack of subsidies and credit facilities caused the private sector to shift to dairy farming and horticulture, while the ejido sector changed to forage and food crops or sold their land and water rights.

The current drought cycle, beginning in 1995, left the catchment reservoirs supplying the district filled to only 20 percent of their capacity. This situation has led to an increase in groundwater use, reflected by the overexploitation of the eight aquifers underlying the district (Cruz and Levine 1998). Simultaneously, the quality of water is deteriorating because of accelerating and uncontrolled growth of the textile industry since 1991. Industrial and municipal sewage is discharged into the river and irrigation canals, while the excessive mining of groundwater has resulted in the release of high concentrations of arsenic (Fortis and Ahlers 1999).

The Comarca Lagunera shows a marked difference in tenancy between the private and social sector. Concerning irrigated land, an *ejidatario/a* (the social sector) officially has access to an average of 2 ha, and a *pequeño* (the private sector) 8.3 ha in comparison with the national averages of 3.9 ha and of 8.3 ha, respectively (FIRA 1997). The high costs of electricity to pump groundwater and the increasing pumping depth, in addition to the 1994 CNA decision to cancel all concessions if not used for two consecutive years, forced marginalized farmers to give up irrigated agriculture with groundwater, and on the other hand made surface water a more interesting investment for potential water buyers. The high costs of producing traditional crops, the elimination of guaranteed prices, competition from the world market with a fall in the price of cotton, and restricted access to credit, make irrigated agriculture in the Comarca Lagunera a very capital intensive and risky activity.

After the Water Law's passage in 1992, four forces shaped the local water market. First, Mexican maize and cotton were competing on the world market with heavily subsidized producers in the United States and China who brought the price down. This meant that a large group of water titleholders, primarily from the social sector but also small holders in the private sector, were unable to make their water and land rights viably productive and hence put them on the market. By 1998, 20,000 of the 38,000 rights were traded within the irrigation district. Second, the favorable political and economic climate for agribusiness, dairy production in this case, created a demand for water rights to primarily irrigate fodder crops. Third, though drought is a regular phenomenon in the area, the Salinas administration has dismantled previously available safety nets for marginalized farmers to avoid market distortions. The current drought cycle sharply reduced surface water availability in the district while at the same time groundwater became more expensive. The drought enabled the agribusiness to employ brokers who bought water rights wholesale from entire communities of economically depressed farmers. Fourth, the irrigation agency still politically responsible for the smooth running of the irrigation district but formally sidelined in water resource management, strongly recommended a water price that buyers and sellers were hesitant to deviate from.

At the same time, the Water Law itself remained extremely unclear to all water users. Nobody felt comfortable openly discussing buying and selling water. Especially lower-income groups, and women in particular, had little access to information on pricing, availability, and legality of trading water rights. Both male and female farmers traded their rights in times of distress to large capital intensive landholdings.[6] Contrary to the general belief, women were far less prone to sell their rights permanently than men were. Instead, in the Comarca Lagunera, the majority of male sellers (73 percent) sold their rights permanently in comparison with 57 percent of the female sellers. More than half of the female sellers sold land and water titles separately while only 27 percent of the male sellers did. Both men and women confess to hardly negotiating with the buyers. Certainly under distress sales, negotiating power is limited. The interviewed women explained that they, unlike the men, always involved the local community leader to organize the sale and thus often did not directly negotiate with the buyer. This might be why women received up to 19 percent less for their water titles in comparison with their male colleagues. Often women preferred to be paid in kind to supplement household needs or to market locally. None of the women in this research had ever bought water or land titles, though the men had bought both.

The market in water rights shifted water from the social sector to the private sector. In those *ejidos* where usufructuary rights had been translated into individual rights, the communities lost control over the management of their water resources. In two of these villages, surveyed in 1997, more than 80 percent of the titleholders had sold their water rights, 33 percent of them women. Of the buyers participating in the study, 72 percent were from the private sector, and all of the buyers were male. In 1998, at least 8,000 of the 20,000 rights traded were bought by only nine users, all of them from the private sector holding large held capital intensive farms (Ahlers 1999; Fortis and Ahlers 1999). In contrast, in the *ejido* communities that organize agricultural production collectively, very little trading has been undertaken. In two of these communities, surveyed in 1997, only 7 percent of the total available water rights were traded, of which 27 percent by female titleholders. This pattern is consistent with experiences elsewhere in Latin America, where privatization of natural resources has resulted in a social and productive decapitalization of small-scale farmers, leading to displacement and dispossession. Alienable titles seem to make the small holder more liable to withdraw to a "poverty refuge" through the sale of land and water titles (Thorpe 1997).

In the Comarca Lagunera, not only were water rights massively sold by the social sector and bought by the private sector, privatization and commercialization did not lead to conservation or wiser use of water. Traded rights now irrigate high water demanding crops such as alfalfa, where before a range of crops with diverse levels of water consumption were cultivated. The concentration of water both in terms of space and ownership to pockets of high value and water intensive crops has left vast areas and villages without access to surface water and increasingly dependent on groundwater of varying quality.[7] Furthermore, water previously siphoned off for animal husbandry, homestead grain, vegetable, and flower production is no longer available. The soils left dry all year turn villages into dust bowls.

Privatization also has affected community cohesion. With dispossession, the community loses its grip on natural resource management, and subsequently, women lose the possible support of the community in representing their interests and securing their water (Ahlers 1999). Where before the collective served as a buffer, now the individual has to solve her or his problems without community support. Women in marginalized households who do have titles need to sell their land and/or water for a pittance to sustain their families. Those women without titles are cut off from the informal avenues of access to land and water all together. Formalizing water rights, therefore, could very well discriminate against women's access to property rights, rendering obsolete their investments in labor, knowledge, and networking. Furthermore, the buyers in this water market are all male, which raises the concern that not only do market mechanisms reproduce gender inequities, they exacerbate them.

Neoliberal Water Policy in Bolivia

Bolivia began its Structural Adjustment Program (SAP) in 1985, introducing tax reform, releasing price and interest rate controls, and liberalizing trade and the exchange rate. The Sánchez-Lozada administration (1993–1997) deepened the neoliberal project with the introduction of the Plan de Todos, characterized by privatization, decentralization, and popular participation geared toward creating an environment more conducive to private investment (Kohl 1999). The subsequent administration, headed by Banzer, secured the continued privatization of natural resources. Kohl (2002) argues that the combination of privatization and participatory mechanisms in the decentralization program guarantee the necessary conditions for transnational firms to gain access to low cost natural resources and Bolivian labor while creating a level of social stability for these firms to prosper.

In a pluriethnic and hydrologically diverse context as Bolivia, an endless array of property relations in water exists. These translate into complex arrangements related to water that vary according to region, ethnicity, and method of cultivation, and may be private or usufructuary, individual, or collective. Different forms of property regimes can exist within households, communities, or irrigation systems. Property regimes resulting from historic and sociopolitical regional dynamics, and not under private sector control, are conveniently and vaguely called *usos y costumbres* (customary practices) and differ across ethnicity, space, and crops (Boelens and Zwarteveen 2002b; Bustamante 2000; PRONAR 2000; Gerbrandy and Hoogendam 1998).

Existing water legislation dates from 1906 and allows for both public and private rights over water (Bustamante 2000; Fundación Solón 2000). The Water Law the Banzer's administration proposed in 1998 reflects the principles of neoliberalism and the structural adjustment conditionalities of the World Bank. It reinforced exclusive concessions, emphasizing private property rights and water markets (Assies 2001a). Peasant organizations and engineering associations immediately and massively contested the proposed law for its narrow mercantilist vision. In response, the Banzer administration abandoned the proposed legislation but reintroduced it in another law (2029) that focused on potable water and sanitation. This law allowed for full privatization of municipal water systems and the commercialization of water allocation.

The first project under Law 2029 took place in the municipality of Cochabamba whose water system supplies the entire Cochabamba valley, the largest irrigated area in Bolivia. The World Bank advised on the institutional and legal reform, and the Inter American Development Bank (IDB) financed a desperately needed loan to Cochabamba conditioned on fully privatizing the water system[8] (Assies 2001a; Florez and Solon 2001; World Bank 1999a, 1999b, 1999c).

The uprising over water privatization in 2000, fully discussed in chapter five by Bustamante, Peredo, and Udeata, and known as the "Water War," forced the Banzer government to retract the contract with the international consortium. A new law (2066), drafted in consultation with the coalition representing rural and urban water users of Cochabamba discarded the concept of water concessions, replacing them with a registrar that recognizes water cooperatives and local *usos y costumbres* (CGIAB 2001). Currently, a new Water Law is being designed with the participation of the government, indigenous groups, farmers, NGOs, and professionals.

The Bolivian case proves that not only can the public contest and successfully overturn an antisocial legislation, the public is quite capable of developing alternative policy. Unfortunately, this is not without cost: the government has been sued for $25 million by Bechtel, the largest interest in the consortium, for expropriated investments calculated on the basis of anticipated profits (The Democracy Center 2002). The risk of privatization therefore lies not with the private but with the public sector, as it will be the citizens of Bolivia who will foot the bill.

The State and Property Rights

The concept of cosmovision has a strong influence on the organization of water management in Bolivia. Water is not perceived as a mere substance, either public or private, but as a living entity. It is believed to be the origin of life and respected and treasured, accordingly (Gerbrandy and Hoogendam 1998). From this perspective, water is not only essential for material life but also for spiritual sustenance: natural and human resources are regarded as an integral whole. Indigenous communities throughout Latin America have strongly contested the fragmentation of water resources into individual segments captured in property rights. They fear that this will undermine shared responsibility and tear apart the collective decision making necessary for effective resource management (Boelens and Hoogendam 2002; Boelens and Dávila 1998; Escobar 1995).

In Bolivia, water rights are often mediated through formal concessions to the male head of household or through community membership. Similar to

Mexico, Bolivian agrarian reforms of 1953 distributed only 17 percent of land titles to women (Deere and León 2001). However, members of FEDECOR (Federación Departamental de Cochabamba de Organizaciones de Riego) estimated that female farmers in the Cochabamba valley hold between 5 and 40 percent of the water titles and are gradually holding more public positions in decision-making bodies (fieldnotes 2001). In addition, they are increasingly responsible for supplemental income to farming households and for managing transregional and transnational households.

Though the Water Law passed almost without comment in Mexico, indigenous and irrigation organizations in Bolivia were highly aware of the pitfalls of water privatization and commercialization. Their primary opposition to the new Water Law lay with the commercialization of water rights, the creation of individual water titles, the lack of representation of stakeholders from poor and indigenous backgrounds, and finally their lack of confidence in the state to resolve water conflicts in favor of poor farmers and the indigenous community (Bustamante 1998). The conflict over water privatization signaled the failure of the Bolivian state and its policies to reflect a multiethnic and pluricultural constituency that harbors very diverse regimes of natural resource management (PRONAR 2000; Rada Velez 2001).

As the debate over water privatization continued, male and female farmers began to withdraw from dealing with the state, insisting on the protection of their local *usos y costumbres*. To an outsider, the *usos y costumbres* seem ambiguous, as they differ tremendously between communities, are not well defined or documented, and are prone to be flexible. To insiders, however, they mean a level of autonomy from state control. Given the antagonism with the state, debating gender inequities reproduced by these *usos y costumbres* has proven difficult. Cosmovision strongly promotes gender complementarity without challenging gender inequality or the changing context of gender roles.[9] The increasing alienation from the state is taking water users to a traditionalist refuge, one that could well conceal and reproduce gender inequities.

The Bolivian case highlights the importance of relinking urban with rural water uses and users. It forces us to be more open to public participation in policy design and reconsider the importance of diversity and complexity in property regimes, with sensitivity to ethnic history and politics, as well as alternative world visions.

The cases of Mexico and Bolivia show that the underlying principles applied to new water legislation are embedded in a series of neoliberal reforms emphasizing economic efficiency over social equity or sustainability concerns. The economic restructuring of society is clearly reflected in the hydraulic policies both countries drew up: both Mexico and Bolivia reorganized water allocation shifting from public to private entitlement and moving management from the public to the private sector. Furthermore, these principles particularly emphasized the creation of water markets as an effective reallocation mechanism. Mexico privatized water rights under the umbrella of water users' organizations to fulfill full commercialization of water and create its effective marketing with the global agricultural sector in mind. Bolivia attempted full-fledged privatization and commercialization with the global water industry in mind.

The primary concerns presented in this chapter address the impacts of the increasing individualization and commercialization of water rights, which enhance trade but simultaneously encourage concentration and dispossession, negatively affecting both the social and physical environment. Given historic and structural gender inequities, these processes may play out particularly negatively for women. Introducing property rights might theoretically present opportunities to rebalance gender equity, providing women with the possibility of having individual and direct access to productive resources, and allowing them to translate usufruct rights into capital. These rights, however, are embedded in historic structural gender inequality and reproduced by the current neoliberal context. Women's access to land and titles, as well as their bargaining position in negotiating price, is highly dependent on how gender ideology has shaped property regimes in the past. This, in combination with the neoliberal paradigm, will determine their participation in the market.

Water markets, and the policy changes that enable these markets to emerge, disregard the intricate negotiating processes that shape social relations and fail to recognize—much less take into account—the incommensurable values of water. Meanwhile, those with the means to play the market and secure property rights translate a privatized public good, such as water, into an economic and political asset. The economic and politically affluent embrace market solutions because, by monetarily valuing nature, purchasing power will decide its reallocation (McAfee 1999).

The Mexican case shows that the water market not only is shaped by, and has a tendency to cater to, those with the necessary financial means but is also molded by inequities in the global and the local market. At the global level, world market prices for agricultural products in conjunction with trade agreements such as NAFTA and with World Bank conditioned neoliberal water policies leave local marginalized and subsistence farmers vulnerable and unprotected. At the local level, gender and class inequities prohibited water right sellers from being fully informed regarding pricing and legality of the trade, allowing wealthy buyers to secure water rights for extremely low prices.

When water rights entered the market in the Comarca Lagunera case, rights were sold by those marginalized in the social sector and primarily bought by the affluent in the private sector. Both men and women sold rights but only men bought them and the mechanisms of sale were highly gendered in remuneration. Individual alienable rights did not provide any empowerment for women or affect greater gender equity; rather they have disempowered untitled women by formally dismissing their indirect access to water, and encouraged marginalized female titleholders, as well as their male counterparts, to trade their rights in a market riddled with class and gender inequities. While marginalized male titleholders tend to withdraw to a "poverty refuge" by selling both land and water permanently, women in the Comarca Lagunera sell their water title separately from land and then only per season. The effects of water trading have contributed to rural poverty and community disintegration, as well as to environmental degradation resulting in islands of concentrated high-intensive farming in an otherwise barren desert landscape.

In Bolivia male and female marginalized farmers trust the state as little as they trust the markets. There, women confide that they would rather fall back on historic *usos y costumbres* and fight their battles within their communities to effect change because their communities, unlike the state, respect incommensurable values of water. The collective organization around resources has political dimensions in an ethnically divided nation. Not only did rural and urban users fight a common cause, they then actively engaged in redrafting more socially just legislation. The Cochabamba experience is particularly instructive in highlighting that privatization of water as not an urban phenomena or limited to just the municipal water and sanitation sector.

The question posed earlier whether neoliberal water policy induces improved water management as competition for water increases must be answered negatively. Lessons learned from the Mexican and Bolivian experiences are that the one-size-fits-all water policy of the neoliberal model undermines access to water outside the formally recognized structures of entitlement; it has a high tendency to result in dispossession and concentration of water rights simultaneously solidifying gender inequities; it disregards both multiple values of water as well as diversity in modes of expressions and meanings reflected in its institutions of distribution and allocation.

Instead of perceiving the intricacy of water rights over time and space as a priori problematic, it may be more useful to understand them as the historical products of social political—and thus gendered—contestation over productive resources. Though diversity in property regimes often seems either incompatible or irresolvable within a coherent national policy framework, the richness in variety provides a matrix which, when critically analyzed, may deliver new structures of entitlement more amenable for social justice along gender, class, and ethnic lines, and in so doing create more environmentally sustainable water resource management objectives.

Several themes for policy consideration should be taken into account. The first is a renewed appreciation for collective property regimes in water management. The second is a search for entitlement that does not reproduce historic inequalities. In this sense, both the Bolivian and Mexican experiences provide arguments against the formalization of historically unequal access to water and its alienability. Whether rights should have an individual dimension within the collective, either at community, system, or state level, remains open for discussion. The essential issue to remember is that water is a common pool resource and that alienability of water rights has a greater tendency to lead to dispossession instead of conservation. Finally, this chapter calls for a move away from a one-size-fits-all policy framework. The objective of integrating water quality and quantity concerns with social equity implies a pluriform water policy that recognizes that multiple uses and values exist within a dynamic hierarchy. The question remains how to maintain pluriformity within national legislation while simultaneously providing legislation supporting equity for all.

5 Women in the "Water War" in the Cochabamba Valleys

Telling the story of women's participation in the "Water War" in Cochabamba, Bolivia, in April 2000, establishes the degree and form of women's involvement in the Cochabamba mobilizations and deepens the analysis of the role of women in the management and use of water in daily life. Identifying what women's participation contributed during the conflict, as well as how the active role women played affected their positions in their organizations, as water users, and as members of cooperatives is also important for understanding Bolivia's social movements.

What has come to be known as the Cochabamba Water War was a transformative event for the significance of water as well as for water policy. Suddenly topics such as access to water and water rights, privatization, structural adjustment, poverty, and citizen participation and conflict were on the public agenda. Almost the entire population of the region participated, no matter what their social class. Different issues combined as in a kaleidoscope: poverty and marginality, discontent over the lack of access to drinking water and demands for access to water and other services, the existence of community water management practices, and an Andean vision of natural resources rooted in the agrarian world that has recently spread to the urban milieu.

The articulation of these issues had several dimensions and facets: ethnicity, gender, and class were expressed in a varied dynamic of social protest, associations, alliances, recognition, and negotiation. Women were one of the most important currents in the movement as they are mainly responsible for the everyday work of managing water and irrigating fields. In the urban sphere, women are the ones who manage water consumption, distribution, and storage, a crucial role because in many parts of the city, households are not connected to the water distribution network, or water simply does not get there. This close relationship between water and women's everyday lives shaped their participation and their connection to the larger discourse of the protests, which through the slogan, Water Is Life, asserted an inalienable right to water.

Women, Water Rights, and Resource Management in the Cochabamba Valleys

Cochabamba is a department[1] marked by the lack of water. Even though residents and visitors speak of its temperate climate, its beautiful small towns, and its varied *criollo* food, its lack of water is always mentioned. Only 55 percent of the urban population and 46 percent of the rural population have access to drinking water and sewerage systems (Bolivia Public Expenditure Review, World Bank 1999b). Because of this scarcity, inhabitants have a heightened awareness of water management issues. The constant concern with water goes a long way to explaining the degree of involvement in the conflict, which drew on longstanding demands for water services and access as well as on the recognition of the need to defend their own water systems and the municipal water distribution system. These all came into play in the face of a privatization process that threatened to take away the population's right to water.

The region's diverse inhabitants, however, do not all have the same relationship to water rights and management, and this varies depending on their social, geographic, and cultural location. This means that a consideration of each particular social group in the conflict must take into account the differences in access and control and in norms, procedures, discursive arguments, and demands. Thus for women, the different forms of access to water, the degree of participation in its management, and place of residence all influenced their position in the conflict (see table 5.1).

Urban Area: Women as "Users" of Water

A large part of Cochabamba's urban area has access to drinking water through the Municipal Drinking Water and Sanitation Service (Servicio Municipal de Agua Potable y Saneamiento, SEMAPA), a water supply operator with mixed public-private financing. SEMAPA is subject to the provisions of Law 2066,[2] which regulates the supply of drinking water and sewerage services and also establishes users' rights and obligations.

Users generally acquire the right to service when they buy a residence or

Table 5.1 Forms of Access to Water and Participation in Water Management in the Cochabamba Valleys

Type of user	Forms of access to water	Participation in water management	Place of residence
Consumer	Through the company that provides the service	None (only in SEMAPA* through neighborhood committees)	Urban zone
Associated	Through water board, neighborhood committee, or cooperative	Direct if holder of water rights	Urban periphery
Communal	Through communal systems	Direct if holder of water rights Indirect, through husband or son	Rural zone

Note: SEMAPA is the Servicio Municipal de Agua Potable y Saneamiento (Municipal Drinking Water and Sanitation Service).

building by paying a connection and installation fee. There is no data on the number of women who directly hold this right to service in the city of Cochabamba, but in practice women have a far more direct relationship with water as part of their role in social reproduction than men, both for everyday chores and because they usually pay for the service, resolve billing problems, and register complaints.

The rights acquired by users by paying for the service connection are to:

• Receive a continuous supply of drinking water of acceptable quality and in adequate amounts, according to prevailing norms,

• Request the measurement and verification of their water consumption,

• Request that the service provider check for leaks inside their building that may not be visible,

• File complaints for overbilling, bad service, or negligence on the part of the service provider, and if necessary to appeal to the Superintendent of Basic Sanitation, and to demand that the service is functioning adequately (Mattos Crespo 1999).

In formal terms, there is only a service provider–client relationship, and users have no participation in water management. As a result of the conflict analyzed in this chapter, however, the public has gained a greater degree of participation through using the Neighborhood Committees to democratically elect representatives to the water company's Board of Directors.[3] Thus there is now a somewhat greater degree of community control over water administration, planning, and management.

In terms of the participation of women, although they have more to do

with daily household water use and its "quality control," nothing particularly favors their inclusion over that of men in either the Neighborhood
Committees or the SEMAPA Board of Directors. Some authors such as
Salazar (2000), Dibbits et al. (1995), Peredo (2001), and others have suggested that one of the effects of the regulations resulting from the 1993 Law
on Popular Participation (see note 3) has been to displace women's participation to the benefit of men because meeting times and meeting dynamics, the
ways leaders are elected, the mechanisms used to administer resources, all
tend to limit women's participation. Until the 1993 law, their participation
had been greater through housewives' committees, "soup kitchens" *(come-
dores populares),* production groups, groups organized for supervision of the
neighborhoods ("barrios"), and others.

Water Committees or Cooperatives in the Urban Periphery

Because SEMAPA is unable to provide service to the entire city, the population of the urban periphery gets water through its own systems, generally
from groundwater sources managed by cooperatives, committees, or associations. By investing either cash or labor to build the systems, water users
have greater direct participation in peripheral water systems than they do in
the municipal water systems that have no social participation Although, as
happens so very frequently, women become invisible under the general category of "families served," the possibilities for participating in meetings
where decisions are made and in the organizational structure are greater
than when a municipal water company provides the service. Thus, decisions
such as the fees to join the system, tariffs, investments needed to expand the
pipelines, and so forth are all issues that are usually managed in a more
transparent way with greater social control, including the participation of
women. The tendency of these organizations and the very conceptualization
of the drinking water and sanitation projects in Bolivia is to consider men as
the heads of households. In practice, however, it is women who are more involved with specific water management issues because these are a daily concern due to their roles in the task of reproduction.

Individual or Family Rights in Rural Areas

In Bolivia, because of the weak and precarious presence of the state in rural areas, peasant or indigenous organizations are in charge of most irrigation and drinking water systems, involving both women and men in the
technical and operational tasks of water access, administration, and distribu-

tion. Currently women play a central role in water distribution and consumption, basically because during recent years family structures in rural areas have suffered the effects of increasing migration. Today, the temporary migration of *campesinos*[4] to the cities no longer respects the seasons or the agricultural calendar but rather is determined by alarming rural impoverishment. As a result, women take on a greater role in tasks culturally assigned to men and for ever longer periods of time, and women and children have become responsible for almost all agricultural chores.

Thus agricultural and water management tasks are largely feminized, and women collect water for family consumption, take their animals to communal troughs, and monitor when they can irrigate, all from the same source of water. Despite this reality, in the Andes, the majority of water rights still are registered in men's names, whether for irrigation or drinking water systems. This formal registry, however, does not translate into a limitation on access to water, because in practice it is a family right available to all members. Nevertheless, certain rights, such as participation in decision-making bodies, are linked specifically to the holder.

In general terms, the number of women and their degree of participation in leadership positions diminishes in inverse proportion to the size of the system. While at the family or neighborhood level a more direct degree of participation is likely, in larger organizations, this participation is more restricted. The reasons for women's absence in leadership roles has to do with level of education, abilities in speaking Spanish, limitations of time and availability, and so on (Boelens and Zwarteveen 2002a). But underlying this is the commonly held cultural belief that the qualities required to actively participate in public meetings or in leadership positions are male, this reality tends to limit spaces for female leaders.

Research in the Andes (Boelens and Zwarteveen 2002a; Gutiérrez and Cardona 1998) has shown that just because women do not speak in the community's general assemblies does not mean that they do not influence important decisions related to the management of water systems through less public channels. For example, it is common knowledge that men must first consult with their spouses before most decisions are made. This makes it very difficult to make decisions at a single community meeting as nonlocal organizations working on rural development sometimes want to do. Consequently, analyzing in greater depth decision making in Andean communities beyond the public or formal spaces where these processes take place is very important. The existence of nonpublic spaces for decision making related to water management does not negate the desirability or necessity for women to participate more explicitly in public spaces as well.

This raises debates between "we must respect traditional forms of participation" and "we must promote more direct and explicit forms of participation in which the value of women's work and contributions to the organizations is made more evident" (Peredo 2001). Though women participate, have influence, and many times decide, their participation is not necessarily reflected in structures of representation and decision making, perhaps least of all when negotiating and reaching agreements with public or state bodies.

Prelude to a War Foretold

The city of Cochabamba and the urbanized areas toward Sacaba (to the east) and Quillacollo (to the west) have a population of approximately 730,000 inhabitants. The Municipal Water and Sanitation Service covers about 55 percent of the demand for drinking water (Gandarillas 1997). According to Ledo (1997, 28), "close to half of the water produced for domestic consumption (4 million cubic meters) . . . was devoted to the consumption of the residents of the old urban core and the northeastern part of the city, where about 27 percent of the total population lives. The remaining 73 percent of the population have access to only 50 percent of the volume produced." The zones that have less access to water are also the poorest areas in the city (see the highlighted cells in table 5.2).

Water scarcity has made the valleys of Cochabamba the site of conflicts and tensions for a long time. Some of the first legal cases recorded during the colonial period had to do with disputes over water. The origins of the contemporary conflict, however, have to do with an urban-rural confronta-

Table 5.2 Forms of Access to Water in Cochabamba

Zone	Public cistern	Own well	Water truck	Run-off	Neighbor
Northeast	14.9%	0.0%	0.6%	0.6%	1.2%
South central	4.5%	0.6%	**24.5%**	1.2%	1.3%
Northwest	5.1%	2.1%	13.5%	1.9%	3.7%
South	0.0%	0.6%	**45.1%**	0.0%	0.0%

Source: Ledo 1997
  Note: Boldfaced figures show the correlation between lack of water access and impoverished areas.

tion that goes back to the 1960s when SEMAPA first attempted to drill wells in the Central Valley to improve the supply of drinking water for the city. Because the Misicuni Multiple Project[5] that would supply water from the high mountains to Cochabamba by tunnel has constantly been postponed, a major part of the company's response to growing demand was based on utilizing underground water.

Conflicts and tensions around water reached a breaking point in September 1999, when the government of former dictator Hugo Banzer, fulfilling a commitment made to the World Bank to privatize, gave the concession for the SEMAPA water company to the "Aguas del Tunari" consortium (a Bolivian subsidiary of an international consortium headed by the multinational engineering firm Bechtel). The concession contract established company control of the exploitation of water sources and service provision in almost the entire province of Cercado where the city of Cochabamba is located and in the future along the Central Valley-Sacaba conurbation axis. Several irrigators' organizations and small neighborhood, communal, or municipal drinking water systems were within the concession area, so these legal measures affected their rights. As well, the contract guaranteed the company a 15 percent rate of return and pegged the tariffs charged by the company to the U.S. consumer price index.

Law 2029, which regulates the provision of drinking water and sanitary sewage services, was also passed shortly after the privatization of SEMAPA. Among its provisions were that concessions (both large and medium sized companies) would have exclusive rights in the provision of sanitation services and in the use of water sources for forty years. All others (water committees, cooperatives, communal systems, etc.) would have a nonexclusive, and therefore, temporary license for five years. A further provision of the law gave sanitation sector authorities the power to assign rights to water sources, without establishing any criteria, limits, rights, and obligations and also permitted the expropriation of water sources as needed.

In response to government actions that affected the lives and the rights of multiple social sectors in Cochabamba, peasant organizations and water-user organizations in areas of the urban periphery carried out the first roadblocks on November 4, 1999. The broad base and determination demonstrated by the roadblocks forced the government authorities to negotiate, resulting in an agreement between the Superintendent of Basic Sanitation and the *campesino* organizations of Cochabamba's Central Valley that required the Aguas del Tunari consortium to respect *campesino* water sources.

The negotiations, however, left unresolved the provision of drinking water and sanitary sewage services under Law 2066, which benefited Aguas del Tunari to the detriment of cooperatives and of community water centers and systems.

Because this remained unresolved, the *campesino* sector restated its demands, now joined by various city organizations angry about water tariffs that were to be increased between 40 percent and 200 percent[6] with the rise in rates to cover the cost of future improvements and outraged about irregularities that were discovered regarding the signing of the contract.[7] The resulting social movement organized itself around the Committee in Defense of Water and Family Budgets, which along with other organizations would subsequently make up the Coordinadora Departamental en Defensa del Agua y de la Vida (Coordinating Committee in Defense of Water and Life).[8] The Coordinadora's considerable initial achievement was to link the urban and rural populations in opposition to the concession to Aguas del Tunari and to Law 2029.

The Water War

Nobody would believe how Cochabamba, a "garden city," suddenly became a real battleground . . . these are days when a majority of the people of Cochabamba and its environs stood up in the face of an irrational hike . . . in water tariffs by the recently created "Aguas del Tunari" company and against the imposition of the latest Law 2029 on drinking water and sewer services. Two days of intense struggles, not seen in Cochabamba in the last 50 years. The mobilizations grew spontaneously with the support of the Coordinadora . . . people came out into the streets in massive numbers: thousands and thousands of people, youths, even children, women in fancy clothes and women in polleras,[9] peasants, older men with no weapons other than their indignation and their voices lifted in protest, faces daubed with bicarbonate and many with handkerchiefs over their mouths and bottles of vinegar in their hands to counteract the effects of the tear gas. And while the hours and the anguish increased, the bonfires multiplied, the noise of empty pots and sticks banging on tins and anything the demonstrators found around them also increased. A true war scene, the noise of shots, shouts, people running, broken bottles in the streets, nuns from various churches aiding the wounded, women who threw paper and water from their windows to reinforce the roadblocks. (*Bolivia Press*, Special Edition No. 1, 2000)

The mobilizations began in January 2000 with roadblocks on the highways of the country's main axis (which connects Bolivia's principal cities of La Paz and Santa Cruz via Cochabamba), which led to the first confrontations with the police and military. Negotiations between government ministers, civic leaders, and leaders of the Coordinadora finally ended with the signing of the "Regional agreement for provision of water, defense of people's budgets, peaceful coexistence, and respect for human rights." This agreement established a commitment to create working commissions, made up of both the government and civil society, on the fee structure, on the revision of the contract signed with the Aguas del Tunari consortium, and on the revision of Law 2029. After several weeks, negotiations broke down in the working commissions dealing with the concession contract and the fee structure but moved forward in the commission drafting modifications to Law 2029.

The breakdown in negotiations between the government, civic leaders,[10] and the Coordinadora led to the organization of another protest action, "peacefully taking over the city of Cochabamba," on February 4, 2000. This mobilization was violently repressed, leading to a major conflict that culminated in several wounded, a number of arrests, and the signing of a new agreement called the "Cochabamba Settlement," in which the government promised to freeze water tariffs at 1998 levels until an agreement was worked out.

As a way to pressure for its demands, the Coordinadora carried out a "Popular Poll"[11] in which the population was asked whether they agreed with the fee increases, the concession contract, and the privatization of water. Nearly 50,000 people participated, and the results led the Coordinadora to demand that the contract with Aguas del Tunari be annulled and that Law 2029 be immediately modified. As negotiations continued at an impasse, the Coordinadora called for a total work stoppage and the "takeover of the city of Cochabamba" on April 4. Thus began the final battle in the Water War, the two most dramatic weeks in recent Bolivian history.

People from neighborhoods in the urban periphery and peasant communities from the rural areas marched toward the city to support the blockades and marches. Life on the streets became intense, with news breaking every minute. Unprecedented solidarity and cooperation emerged, either because of news regarding the government's response, or because of news about the company, or because of initiatives taken by the Coordinadora, or because of the aggression and offensives by the military forces, or simply as a defense from the police forces and from the tear gas, and the bullets of the military forces. People from different social classes who in everyday life had little to do with each other became part of a single group in the streets, even putting their lives at risk. "Water Warriors," street brigades of men and women from the ranks of the unemployed, the poor, youths, and vagbonds, formed, and these demonstrated incredible discipline, in the process often giving new meaning to their lives.

Faced with a rebellion that appeared unstoppable, the Banzer government began to negotiate (April 6, 2000), and the highest departmental authorities announced the cancellation of the contract with the consortium (April 9, 2000). Then, when the conflict appeared resolved, the police violently broke up a negotiating meeting between the Coordinadora and the government, the central government denied that the contract had been cancelled, and several Coordinadora leaders were arrested. These events infuriated the population even further, resulting in constant clashes between the forces of law and order and the "Water Warriors" in the city's street and plazas. In an attempt to regain control of the situation, the government declared a state of siege in the whole country.

On April 10, the Superintendent of Basic Sanitation sent a note to the Aguas del Tunari consortium canceling the contract for "reasons of force majeure."[12] That same day an agreement was signed in which the government committed itself to: (1) Return the management of the drinking water and sewerage company to SEMAPA under a transitional board of directors with both governmental and nongovernmental representation, including legally recognized entities such as nongovernmental organizations (NGOs) and labor organizations. This board had responsibility for orchestrating a long-term solution to the water issue and to amend Law 2029 on the basis of the popular poll carried out in Cochabamba on March 26, 2000. Despite these promises, the population remained mobilized until finally, at dawn on April 15, after two long weeks of conflict, the parliament approved the amended version of Law 2029 (now Law 2066), meeting the movement's principal demands.

Women as Actors and Symbols of the Rebellion

One of the stories that passed from mouth to mouth in the streets of Cochabamba during the conflict was about "La Coordinadora." When the leaders of the Coordinadora sought refuge in a convent, the nuns agreed and asked, "But where is La Coordinadora (Ms. Coordinator)? She must be a very brave woman, right?"[13] Making the Coordinadora a *woman* went from being an anecdote to being a story of identity for the women who participated in the Water War.

To tell the truth, at first even I was curious as to who "La Coordinadora" was, that friendly lady, that brave woman. But later I have become aware that really men, children, and especially women participated in the struggle for water. This has marked a chapter in the history of Cochabambans; we know very well that women from the provinces or from the countryside are the ones who most fought in the Cochabamba Valley.[14] (Amanda)

"We Women Have Known How to React When Extreme Things Happen. . ."

Women played a fundamental role in the mobilizations not only through their active participation but also in the issues the movement emphasized, the way demands were raised and their interpretation, and thoughts about the movement. According to the women protagonists themselves, the roles and activities that they took on during the Water War were chiefly:

• Keeping watch at key places as well as at the blockade points;
• Responding to police repression with sticks and stones. In some cases, making sorties to try and prevent arrests;
• Providing protection against tear gas: vinegar, wet cloths, lemons, Vaseline, etc.;
• Serving as roadblock delegates or chiefs, and carrying rocks, wire, etc., to enforce the blockade;
• Closing the *chicherías* to avoid the tendency to go drinking;[15]
• Cooking in communal kitchens with food supplied by all the communities.

Women irrigators recall that when they first entered Cochabamba not all inhabitants of the city welcomed them. Social discrimination and prejudice against the campesinos is very strong among many city residents who would tell them, "Just leave; what are you doing here?"

The city people, those in the old downtown, threw rotten tomatoes at us: "these kacachakis, laris,[16] Indians, look how they are filling the streets, how they dirty everything." They even threw urine at us. Then we said, we are fighting for everyone. . . .

Unfortunately it hurt me that the city people did not help us much, they closed their doors, when there was teargas we didn't know where to go, where to hide, we asked for a little water, some gave us some and others didn't. That has hurt me, because we are all human and between all of us we should help one another. . . .

This initial rejection gradually changed as the confrontations spread and negotiations became tenser, making it clear that the rural sectors were also defending urban demands against the fee hikes.

They trembled when they got their bills; they had this problem, and who helped them? . . . would the people in the old downtown alone been able to defend themselves? All of us irrigators, all of us have united and in this last mobilization they opened their doors, they offered us a glass of water because it really is for everybody and we were fighting for everybody. . . .

It was precisely the women who forged the first links of solidarity in the streets:

The women would tell me, "we have many people from the communities who have come to do roadblocks on the avenue and many of them are hungry, we need something!" I told them, "'Mamacitas' We are the women, we will go ask!" So, we went house to house to ask for whatever they could spare, and then we made that communal kitchen so that the people from the surrounding communities could sustain themselves.

"Going to ask," showing their own strength and vulnerability is a feature of the female discourse towards Cochabamba society during the Water War. This is a very feminine approach: to articulate being a mother, suffering, tenderness, love, courage, and protest as a way to challenge injustice. This strategy made it possible for the rebellion to become generalized and expanded the participation of women from the countryside, from the neighborhoods in the urban periphery, and from the city center itself:

And we women thought, so what are we going to do? Are we going to just stay and watch, with our arms crossed while they are gassed, run over, killed, beaten, and that's it? Can't you see? We are women, and we are not going to be able to do anything. Then they said, since the women and elderly can't go, well, let's do something; let's block the road!

They combined their sensitivity as women in the face of abuse, violence, and injustice with their need to become social actors when confronted with stereotypes of what women, and elderly women, should be. This led them to be protagonists in the protests.

At the meetings, many women were appointed as blockade leaders along with men, to make sure that there was no drinking and that communities showed up for their scheduled shifts.

My zone also carried out pickets and passed out cards to those who were there: "and whoever doesn't show up to help with the blockade won't get water, if we ever get it." So everyone showed up, like soldiers. I was in charge, I had an aide and I posted block leaders.

During the conflict, women used several identities and signifiers that shifted along a continuum from strength to vulnerability. Their choice of identity varied according to the needs at any given time within their own organizations, as well as in confrontations with the military forces and during interactions with different social groups and classes:

The police hesitated when they were going to beat us because we would say, "Cowards! Don't you have mothers and sisters? Don't you drink water? Yes, we're fighting for you too!" Besides, it is women who provide the courage. We are more determined. . . . It is easier for them to grab the men, the youngest men, and they take them away; with the women it is a bit more difficult, we always stop them.

The conflict deepened and became increasingly radical, as a local report shows: "The voices of protest are on the rise. The statements made by many women and men from different parts of the city on open mikes made available by radio and television stations indicate that the people have gained consciousness and are increasingly angry. . . . They report that airplanes from La Paz are arriving to unload large numbers of soldiers. The city seems to be at war, there is broken glass in the streets, burned tires, piles of garbage, pieces of wood and stones in the middle of coca[17] leaves. The people seem fearless, they have risen to their feet, and all they want is to be heard" (*Bolivia Press 2000*, Special Issue, April 7, 2000).

Women actively participated in caring for people during the mobilizations:

The women helped people who were choking from the teargas, because they had water, salt, bicarbonate, menthol, white flour, vinegar, we had everything we could; there we were with all that stuff. And for those who were choking we had cigarettes to roll, paper and matches to light them and make smoke to counteract the effects of the teargas; that was what women did.

Women were also appointed to monitor and prevent excesses by the protestors, prevent excesses of violence, and prevent alcohol consumption:

Because some "compañeros" would go to have a drink, the government would say over the radio that the blockaders were a bunch of drunks, but this wasn't true, because we were all aware that we had to make sure our traditions and customs were respected (FEDECOR workshop, December 2001).

All these activities were carried out in addition to fulfilling the traditional role of women in the home. For peasant women, this implied enormous sacrifices because during the most intense periods to go out and mobilize, they had to abandon their homes, their crops, and their animals:

Truthfully, it meant suffering for us, it was not nice, we left our little animals and all our chores, we women had to come running, with slings, with ash. . . .

We could not even get back to our houses to cook, and all of us left our houses, only the babies stayed behind. We got up at 4 a.m. and would leave food cooking.

Women, Leadership, and Decision Making

Although women were active participants, carrying out countless duties, and played a key role in negotiations at the micro level, in the confrontations, on the barricades, in weaving together the solidarity networks between urban and peasant sectors, and in disseminating information in the mass media, their participation dropped dramatically at the level where decisions were made, where face-to-face negotiations with the government took place. "Even though it was obvious that there was women's participation," said one woman, "we were not taken into account. Those who would lead, who would make up the commission that would be part of the Coordinadora, and who would come to represent the Coordinadora, were all men, and we women had to do other things, anything but be the leaders."

Many women not only led the actions in the streets and headed groups at points of confrontation, but in their own organizations they were also managers of water. These roles, however, were not always recognized or legitimized. The following comment in which a woman even decries her gender identity reflects this situation:

I am sorry I am a woman, how I would have liked to be a man. That way I could be general secretary, that way people could say that I managed and was part of the leadership. But I'll never get to be general secretary because of that flaw, that I am a woman. Because I am a woman I won't be made a leader. In the countryside especially, machismo predominates, and they say, "How can we be under the command of a woman?"

What the Water War Accomplished

An evaluation of what the Water War accomplished reveals the following gains:

• The SEMAPA water company recovered its public status, now with a greater degree of public participation and control on its board of directors.

• There were amendments to thirty-six articles of the Law on Water and Sewerage Services, guaranteeing, among other things: respect for small water systems, recognition of *campesino* rights to their sources of water and water systems, community control over contracts and readjustment of tariffs.

• International financial institutions became more open to dialogue and public consultation before formulating legislations and norms related to water.

However, many challenges lay ahead, because:

• The problem of water in Cochabamba remains unresolved and more than 50 percent of the population still has no access to services. No new short-run sources of water are easily available: remaining underground sources require major investments and are very difficult to tap.

• The Bolivian government forced SEMAPA to sign a forty-year concession contract, which established that the agency must pay a yearly fee to the Municipal Sanitation Department equal to 1–3 percent of its yearly income (from customer payments) and excludes it from receiving public subsidies earmarked for the water sector. In addition, because SEMAPA has partial public financing, it is subject to an additional tax of 1–3 percent of its yearly income.

• Another battle in this war will be fought before the International Centre for Settlement of Investment Disputes operated by the World Bank, where the consortium has filed a claim seeking both losses and punitive damages for having their contract in Bolivia canceled.

• Finally, despite all the mobilizations to defend current water sources, these rights are not secure because the implementing legislation for Law 2066 which makes these rights legal has not yet been approved.

What Changed for Women?

Experience shows that explicit processes of reflection and education that highlight and emphasize women's contributions and their value to the community are required to combat self-perceptions that diminish and camouflage women's important responsibilities by subsuming them within the traditional daily female tasks. In the case of the Cochabamba women irrigators, however, a process of self-valorization, in which they recognized the importance of their roles with respect to water, took place by leaps and bounds precisely because the April actions placed them in the eye of the storm. As one of them pointed out, "we have begun to have value, to value ourselves." Some women underwent even more profound processes, asking questions about their role as leaders and as activists. Their experiences in the "Water War" generated greater commitment to their own organizations and increased expectations regarding their roles within those organizations:

I don't want to stay at home anymore, I want to participate because I also have an equal right. So that is why we have to start organizing ourselves, we women must educate ourselves. . . . We have the strength to participate and learn. We are strong; at least in our communities we are no longer afraid. We bundle up our toasted corn, our cheeses, our dried meat, and just go off to the struggle.

Another movement protagonist explained why she is continuing to participate and presented a critical perspective, contrasting the level of women's participation with the lack of recognition from their organizations and from society as a whole:

We are not struggling for something meaningless; we are struggling for the truth. . . . We left our homes, we left our chores, but we are not struggling for no reason, we are struggling for water and the day will come when we will be recognized. . . .

Women's demands and mobilizations had concrete results. For example, the neighborhoods of the southern zone such as Alto Cochabamba gained the support of SEMAPA to build their own drinking water system with community labor, although of course this did not solve the problem in the whole city.

Water got to marginal zones and neighborhoods where before people had none. . . . This is what is important about this struggle, because it shows that we can get drinking water and sewerage services to marginal zones and neighborhoods, and that the struggle of the women of Alto Cochabamba has not been in vain.

Finally, participation in the April mobilizations enabled the spread of solidarity networks among women from different social classes and places of residence around a common struggle:

I've witnessed women's solidarity in the streets, I've seen women from all social classes offer each other mutual support, giving each other refreshments, nuns bringing things, ladies who were watching from their balconies who said, "we should help, we will give newspapers." There was solidarity, and this has made us discover that we can indeed build solidarity aside from the political differences that may separate us. That has helped us recognize ourselves as women, it has helped us to say, yes, we can change the state of things that affect us. . . .

The social conflict that took place in Cochabamba is paradigmatic of the tensions that exist around the issue of water today on a world scale: the scarcity of drinking water, the precariousness of access for people in the urban periphery and rural areas of low-income countries, the marginality of large groups in terms of water rights, the fragility of distribution systems, the privatization of services versus community or state management, questions of efficiency and sustainability, daily uses and customs regarding water, the role of women, and finally the social conflict that can be unleashed around water. Behind all this, there are contrasting visions of water: the pressure for privatization policies connected to profitability versus visions of communal use of water based on solidarity, rooted (as in this case) in longstanding sociocultural fabrics.

Though the conflict between Cochabamba society and the Aguas del Tunari consortium was a local one, which took place in one of the poorest countries of Latin America, it established an important precedent for the social currents that champion a vision of water as a common good for humanity. Reacting on the basis of their most vital daily needs, men, women, children, the elderly, youths, members of community and neighborhood organizations in the city and countryside, that is, the society as a whole, mobilized in a defense of water that in the process acquired a major collective significance: the struggle for life.

Bolivia and Cochabamba have not been the same since. "I drink water, therefore I am, therefore I vote," is a graffiti painted on one of the walls of the city, indicating that water is an issue for everyone, that it is a basic right, and that this has become part of collective consciousness. The empowerment experienced as a result of participation in collective social actions and negotiations gave an impetus to irrigators' and users' organizations, to the cooperatives, the neighborhood organizations, and women's organizations.

Therefore, we can speak of a before and an after in terms of the Water War: of changed relationships with the authorities and institutions; of the increased capacity to negotiate and reach agreements with government bodies; of the growing involvement of the population in decisions having to do with natural resources, as well as of the dynamic within popular, civic, and social organizations; and of women's organizational dynamics and power relationships.

In Bolivia the state is weak. Although it set out to implement a water management system for the whole country, the state-run or municipal-run companies left many urban areas without coverage—especially in the urban periphery. These areas therefore developed their own rules, distribution systems, and criteria for assigning water rights and tariffs. In rural areas, water management—understood as the organization of activities and resources to take water from its source to its end user—is in the hands of community organizations that operate on the basis of their own *usos y costumbres* (customary practices).[18] These more traditional forms of water management are governed by a vision of water as central to the common good, are based on a deep respect for nature and on an assumption that water and land are not only essential for life itself but are themselves living entities.

The Water War served precisely to give new value to the traditional perception of water, which under current socioeconomic models runs the risk of subordination to the unilateral logic of development and commodification. Different visions of water were apparent during the Water War, ranging from that of urban water consumers to rural irrigators and farmers. At the beginning, the rural groups and irrigator organizations were harassed and discriminated against because they had "invaded" urban space. Largely thanks to the role of women in the conflict, this tension gradually diminished, and bonds of solidarity developed between groups from the urban periphery and the rural groups, as well as between women from irrigators' organizations and women from urban water users' groups and cooperatives. This process meant that demands related to the customary practices increasingly made more sense to the urban population and became central to the demands of the Coordinadora in its negotiations with the government.

Women participated in the Water War based on their specific societal roles, but these roles took on a double and complementary significance: strength and vulnerability. This confirms Chaney and García Castro's (1993) argument that women's political participation is more socially legitimate if it is based on their traditional roles. However, women's leadership in the decision making and negotiation process was not an accurate reflection of their level of participation in the actions and the importance of their role in water issues in everyday life.

Women's positions as block organizers or heads of street committees were due to several factors: their role in daily community water management gave them a fuller understanding of water's value as a resource; they recognized that their water sources must not be negatively affected by privatization, and they linked water with the survival of their own culture in ways rooted in their indigenous cultural identity.

For many women, the decision to participate and leave their homes, their animals, and their crops behind was a major sacrifice that was motivated simply by anger at knowing that their rights were in danger. Thinking about the importance of their daily work related to water began after the conflict as they began to assign water greater value, and this will surely become a process of empowerment and collective reflection.

The dynamic of interactions between women from different social groups is interesting. Though the need to differentiate is very pronounced in Bolivia's class and almost caste structure, it was notable how peasant women found themselves side by side with middle class "ladies" and how they worked together to figure out how to confront military intervention.

The achievements of the Water War gave the inhabitants of Cochabamba an important sense of empowerment that lasted for quite some time. The transfer of water management back to the municipal company SEMAPA presents a new challenge, that of strengthening the Coordinadora. In the face of marginality, a lack of public policies that defend the rights of the population, the Water War was an episode that combined citizenship, participation, and dreams of a better life. The public in general, and women in particular, is always excluded from social policy decisions, from the distribution of wealth, from the distribution of power. The conflict was a moment when this norm of everyday life was ruptured and power resided in the streets.

The challenge that remains is how to link different levels and processes of empowerment with demands for the expansion of rights in societies built on class, gender, and ethnic hierarchies and discrimination. On one hand, how can demands based on collective visions of solidarity and communal water uses find a legitimate space where they can be applied; how can decisions on water policy, services, and the sustainability of water use truly match visions rooted in community practices, respect for nature, and respect for the right to water? And on the other hand, how can the demands and the dynamic that the actors themselves bring to these processes be incorporated as a fundamental component of future action? In other words, how can women participate and exercise their rights as citizens in the streets and at the same time overcome the barriers of discrimination and gender inequality within their own organizations or communities, especially because the latter are also directly related to the role they are supposed to play in water issues? The water protests gave women a new role, and a "struggle within the struggle," something of which the women Water Warriors of the April days in Cochabamba are well aware.

6 To Make Waves
Water and Privatization in Tucumán, Argentina

I n 1998, in Tucumán, Argentina's smallest province, a singular event occurred, one celebrated by a local population who had not yet grasped the extent of what they had achieved. "The French Want Out" read the headline in the province's most important newspaper, which went on to explain that "[t]he Compagnie Générale des Eaux, which currently operates Tucumán's water and sewerage services through [its subsidiary] Agua del Aconquija, announced that it will initiate a national and international process to leave the province" (*La Gaceta* 1998). What happened in Tucumán to convince a powerful European corporation to abandon operations after just five years? How had this occurred in a country where the privatization of state-owned service enterprises had become an excellent business for French, Spanish, and Italian capital?

In 1994, the French firm Compagnie Générale des Eaux, which operates water and sanitation services in fifty-six countries, and Dycasa, a Spanish dredging and construction firm, formed a consortium called Agua del Aconquija S.A. Just before the bidding began on the privatization of the province's water system, the provincial government raised water tariffs and instituted service conditions less favorable to users to make the public company more attractive to bidders. The consortium immediately faced sustained protest from water users throughout the province. Many citizens felt that their rights had been violated and opted for a strategy of civil disobedience, refusing to pay their water and sewerage bills.

Women played an important role during the four years of protests. Many of these women had previous experience in social struggles, but others were participating in public protest for the first time in their lives. The role of women in this social protest, though local in scope, had global consequences because one of the largest international corporations in the water sector was involved.[1]

The protest was both urban and local and took place during a decade characterized by the rapid expansion of social conflict throughout Argentina in opposition to the neoliberal economic model. The macroinstitutional transformations initiated in 1991 as part of the neoliberal package had resulted in increased unemployment and cut backs on social rights that had been won during the twentieth century. Setbacks were greatest with respect to labor and social security legislation, in particular regarding working conditions for labor and retirement policies. For example, laws providing for "flexibilization" of the labor market not only contributed to a substantial increase in unemployment (the unemployment rate was greater than 20% in the 1990s) but also to increased precariousness of working conditions for those who continued to be employed. Furthermore, unregistered and informal employment increased substantially. Social protest grew steadily during the 1990s, from the capital city of Buenos Aires to the interior of the country, including the northwest province of Tucumán (Giarraca 2001).

These protests incorporated social actors not represented by the traditional political groups, such as unions or political parties, and involved new forms of public participation, such as roadblocks, "piquetes," civil disobedience, "escraches," protest tents, and "cacerolazos."[2] According to Della Porta and Diani (1999), effective public protest is characterized by its ability to mobilize public opinion through the mass media that serves as an intervening actor to exert pressure on key decision makers. While collective action erupts into public space as a result of concrete demands, success requires an accompanying discourse that makes the actions visible—the mass media often provides such a discourse.

Several factors made the protest over water services in Tucumán unique. First, it was directed at a large foreign corporation at a time when new potential investors were demanding that Argentina guarantee them juridical security. Second, it was an urban movement that began in the small cities and towns in the interior of Tucumán province rather than in the provincial capital. Third, the participation of women was decisive in maintaining the momentum of the struggle throughout the entire four years.

The protests successfully used civil disobedience, a type of public protest that as one author contends, even theoreticians of liberalism do not consider criminal when it is aimed at defending acquired rights (Colombo 2001, 1).[3] When this is taken into account, they accept an extrainstitutional basis for breaking norms and agree that civil disobedience can strengthen rather than weaken the rule of law. This type of action, however, is not easy to achieve for reasons that range from emotional factors (such as fear of repercussions) to personal principles regarding what a "good citizen" should be (in the case of Tucumán, not wanting to be categorized as a debtor).

The Tucumán residents who organized the protests not only had to begin an offensive against a corporation that undermined user rights, they also had to establish alliances with municipalities, adopt a stance vis-à-vis the water authority's workers' union, and propose alternatives for water and sewerage service management. At this last step, the organization's limitations became evident because in the end it gave in to the solution the state proposed. Though organized citizens accomplished a remarkable feat in forcing a multinational corporation to leave the country, their actions did not lead to a conclusive success because the corporation had to be replaced. Nevertheless, the process itself is an invaluable learning experience especially when the state reinitiates the privatization process.

A few words are needed about the authorship of this article. It was written by a social scientist whose work focuses on the social worlds of Tucumán (Norma Giarracca), together with one of the women who initiated the protest over water services in Tucumán and led it to a safe harbor (Norma Del Pozo), a collaboration uncommon in the social sciences. Norma Del Pozo's oral testimony, as well as that of other participants, appears in the text in quotations identified by initials within parentheses. However, Del Pozo's participation is not limited to explanatory narratives because the compilation and organization of the material, the interviews of other participants, and the analysis and interpretation of the facts is the product of this partnership.

The Setting

Tucumán is the smallest province in Argentina; it covers 22,524 square kilometers, a mere 0.8 percent of the country's total territory, yet it has the highest population density, 50.7 persons per square kilometer. It urbanized early so that by the beginning of the 1900s, 40 percent of its population lived in small cities. Unemployment is high, in recent years reaching 20 percent or more than 100,000 people. The overall social welfare of the population in Tucumán is lower than the national average; for example, the infant mortality rate is more than three points above the national average, a significantly higher rate of infant deaths.

The province's main product is sugar cane, which accounts for more than 50 percent of its gross agricultural output. In recent years, agroindustry has expanded, and exports of citrus fruits, especially lemons, have grown considerably. In the 1960s, the region began to industrialize as well as to expand its tourism and financial sectors. The capital is San Miguel de Tucumán, with a population of close to 600,000. Almost all the province's other cities are located in the southern sugar cane region, and the sugar agroindustry was critical for the region's urbanization process. As the sugar mills were built, towns grew around the mills, and over time these expanded to become small cities. These, from San Isidro de Lules (closest to the capital) to Concepción (furthest south), are strung along the province's most important highways. Though none has a population of more than 37,000, these cities serve as the seats of county government as well as of the *delegaciones comunales* of their surrounding rural townships.

During the 1960s and 1970s, Tucumán was the site of union struggles by peasants, sugar industry workers, and state employees, especially schoolteachers. This social unrest led some left wing organizations to consider it a key province for organizing and for political action. As a result, even before the coup d'état in 1976, Tucumán endured a high degree of repressive military operations.

At the start of the 1976–1983 dictatorship, General Antonio Domingo Bussi, a military officer who had previously worked in Tucumán, was appointed governor. A native of Buenos Aires, Bussi utilized extreme repression and local residents were executed, "disappeared," and imprisoned without due process of law, in an atmosphere of terror that prevailed for many years. But Bussi also implemented economic policies that expanded public employment and achieved economic growth and development. For a significant part of the population, his economic policies neutralized the effects of the terror and repression, and especially in urban areas, Bussi had considerable support. Once democracy was restored, the political party Bussi formed (*Acción Republicana*, Republican Action) won the elections and he became—albeit with half the province actively opposed—a democratically elected governor.[4] Human rights organizations denounced national policy that prevented legal actions against the dictatorship's military personnel and blamed this policy for the return of autocrats such as Bussi. As a democratically elected leader from 1995 to 1999, General Bussi and his administration faced one crisis after another, and the legislature accused him of illegal administrative acts. In 1999, *Acción Republicana*, with Bussi's son as candidate, was defeated in the gubernatorial election. With this defeat, the period when the province, towns, and even families were divided between Bussi's supporters and opponents came to an end.

Though Bussi's governorship was a reminder of the great suffering of the population under the dictatorship, it also reflected the nationalist discourse that characterized the Argentine military. This is key to understanding the role the provincial government played during the conflict with the Compagnie Générale des Eaux. While the national government, under the Partido Justicialista (Justice Party), opened the doors to transnational capital by guaranteeing stability and promising economic incentives within a strictly neoliberal discourse, the provincial government subtly reactivated the old nationalism. This found considerable resonance in a province that had historically supported General Juan Domingo Peron's highly nationalistic party (1945–1955 and 1973–1976).

While this pronationalist discourse was not the motor driving the conflict over water, nor did it provide the reason for its success, it did create a context that was propitious for the water-user organizations. In the beginning, the residents took the initiative: they organized, they petitioned, and they stopped payments on their water bills. At a later stage, the provincial government intervened. This second phase began in January 1996 when the water coming from the faucets in the capital suddenly turned a dark color due to an increase in manganese. At that point, the provincial government adopted the users' demands and unified the three branches of government in a firm stand vis-à-vis Agua del Aconquija.

All the people interviewed agreed that when the governor realized that the situation was totally out of his control, he first tried to step back and assist the national government in rescuing the Compagnie Générale des Eaux. However, it was too late: 70 percent of the population supported the "stop payment" campaign, and the corporation could not survive financially under those conditions.[5] That the democratically elected Bussi government took up the cause of the citizens of Tucumán in the conflict over water does not eclipse the actions of the residents who, after many years of fear and paralysis and *in spite* of their memories of repression and violence, once again became effective social actors.

Origins and Growth of the Conflict

During his first year in office, Argentinean President Carlos Menem approved a law to reform public administration (N 23.696), which authorized the "partial or total privatization or liquidation of companies, corporations, establishments, or productive properties totally or partially owned by the state" (Loftus and McDonald, 2001, 77). Under this law, supported by both the World Bank and the Inter-American Development Bank, public services could be privatized without any public consultation.[6] Under this program, the government of Tucumán passed a law in 1993 granting the province's water and sewerage services to a private corporation.

The water and sewerage authority in Tucumán had been managed first by the state-owned Obras Sanitarias de la Nación and then by a provincial agency, Dirección Provincial Obras Sanitorías (DIPOS). A decree by the governor established the regulating agency, the labor code, and the conditions for the new private consortium created with French and Spanish capital, all in compliance with the privatization law. The regulating agency, which played an important role during the conflict, changed its name to Ente Regulador de Servicios de Agua y Cloacas de Tucumán (ERSACT, Tucumán Water and Sewerage Services Regulatory Agency).

Some municipalities in Tucumán immediately began to worry about the future of their investments in these services as the rural townships and local residents themselves had financed most of the existing water and sewerage infrastructure slated for transfer to Agua del Aconquija. The idea of commercializing water (which until 1993 had been considered a common good) and privatizing its service led the water users to demand that the private company pay back their investments. In 1995, in a letter also signed by local residents, the municipal government of Monteros was the first to pressure the provincial government to act on the reimbursement of their infrastructure expenditures.

In June 1995, shortly before the consortium took over, new water tariffs were made public reflecting a 104 percent increase over the tariffs of the provincially owned water authority. Worse yet, this increase came at a time when salaries, pensions, and retirement benefits were frozen and when the province's main agroindustrial activity was in crisis. Monteros was the site of the first of a series of public actions—a mobilization organized by the residents, especially women, with the participation of laid-off workers from the old provincial water company and of provincial legislators who had voted against the privatization law.

From June to October 1995, mobilizations took place throughout the province, first locally because residents were unaware that others were organizing in neighboring towns and cities. Eventually, seven cities in the southern part of Tucumán province—San Isidro de Lules, Bella Vista, Aguilares, Alberdi, Concepción, Simoca, and Monteros—established contact and began to coordinate their actions.

Actually, we in Monteros were the ones who got moving and began coordinating with people in other municipalities. On October 4, 1995, we organized an event and decided to create a commission and invite more people to join us. We got together on October 6 in Bella Vista and formed the Comisión Coordinadora de Usuarios del Interior (Coordinating Committee for Consumers from the Interior). While the women did much of the work and in fact constituted the majority, only three of us were delegates to the committee. We didn't want to be visible. (NDP)

In October 1995, the new provincial government assumed office, and in November ADEUCOT (Asociación en Defensa de los Usuarios y Consumidores de Tucumán, the Association in Defense of Users and Consumers of Tucumán) was formed, with representatives from both the province's small cities and the capital. During the next few months, two important events occurred. At the official level, the provincial legislature created a committee to oversee the tariff schedule and the overall privatization process. And, through ADEUCOT, water users met to discuss a dramatic strategy: stopping payment of their water bills. While water users from the small cities and from the capital were represented in ADEUCOT, those from the interior were more active. In December 1995, they organized a consciousness-raising event in the capital, where the residents had not yet clearly signaled whether they would stop paying their bills. The most remarkable characteristics of the movement that grew in response to the privatization of water were that a high proportion of women and residents in small cities participated and that the stop payment campaign, which caused financial harm to the company, did not generate physical violence.

Dark Water Flows from the Faucets

In January 1996, when the water from faucets changed from clear to dark, in San Miguel de Tucumán many residents felt this was the last straw and reacted by joining the "stop payment" campaign. The problem with the water, which the company explained was due to an inexplicable increase of manganese at the source, lasted for about a month. The provincial government responded by fining the company and forcing it to deduct that month's charges from its billings. But more important, for the first time, the provincial government began to discuss rescinding its contract with Agua del Aconquija because of the cumulative effect of high water tariffs, poor quality service, and indications of corruption of provincial officials during the privatization process.

The executive and legislative branches of the provincial government agreed that privatization had been poorly carried out and was inadequate. The regulating agency, ERSACT, brought consumer complaints to the government because the company was unwilling to negotiate. The provincial legislature responded by asking for a substantial change in the company's attitude. The office of the provincial public prosecutor prepared a report that advised persuading the company's officers to restructure the water rates. For the water users, this new government support created a highly favorable situation.

Officials from Agua del Aconquija made it clear that they would not accept a unilateral rescission by the government of the existing contract. Some legislators, conscious of the fact that this situation could lead to repercussions from the national governing party, tried to mediate a compromise. When the company convinced the French ambassador to issue a very harsh public statement supporting its position, the Argentine national government intervened.

These alternating cycles of conflict and negotiation between the provincial and national governments and the private water company, supported by the French government, lasted until September 1996, when the government of Tucumán finally decided to cancel the contract. The contract stipulated that if either party unilaterally cancelled, Agua del Aconquija would have to continue operating the water services during an eighteen-month transition period while a new operator was found. During this transition, the government had to decide how and to whom the service would be transferred. One possibility, especially in the cities of the interior, was to hand over the service to the municipal governments.

The seven municipalities of the interior responded with the issue of a press release with their demands:

1. "Stop Payment" until a 'municipalization of water and sewerage services' law was approved.

2. All negotiations had to include the participation of local mayors and water users.

3. The transfer of services to the municipalities based on the document proposed by the public works commission in the legislature.

4. The suspension of service cuts and threats of service reductions by Agua del Aconquija.

5. A commitment by users to pay their water bills based on the former tariff structure, but only after the first four demands were met.

Meanwhile, as the water company's income dropped, it tried to collect payment by threatening the users with legal action and cutting service or by renegotiating its contract with the provincial government. User organizations, on the other hand, began looking for a legal justification for their "Stop Payment" campaign.[7]

Throughout 1996 [our] work was concentrated in each city, with the municipal authorities forming part of the commissions that supported municipalizing the service. It was a fact that Agua del Aconquija was abandoning control of the service in seven municipalities. The studies we made and conclusions we arrived at were responsible and feasible. However, we had to overcome many maneuvers (of the provincial and national officials and legislators) that were aimed at discouraging us, disappointing us, as they painted a catastrophic future regarding not only the quality of the service that a municipal company, with user input, would be able to offer but also its financial viability. We had to strengthen our persuasive power, calling on all the resources we had at hand: first, technical resources, and if these were not enough, we asked the people in the *barrios* to apply pressure. Finally, they decided to promote municipalization. (NDP)

As we will soon see, this decision to promote municipal control was not one that the users' organization could maintain.

Proposals to Replace Agua del Aconquija

Significant differences emerged between the proposals made by the users in concert with the municipalities and those made by the company's labor unions. While the former proposed the municipalization of the service through mixed companies (municipalities with user participation), the latter sought the establishment of work cooperatives. The residents opposed the labor union's proposal based on their distrust of the union itself because just as in all other water privatization schemes across the country, the union had cut a deal with the French company that guaranteed the workers 10 percent of the stock in a joint ownership program. Essentially, water sector workers were bribed to "accompany" the privatization process from beginning to end, even though this resulted in so many lay-offs that the personnel roster was cut in half (Loftus and McDonald 2001, 78). A minority of water company workers, however, opposed privatization and looked to the water users for the solidarity they did not find in their own union.

Residents combined their demand for municipalization of water services with demands made by other social actors, thereby creating links to other sectors. Different groups, from teachers to sugar mill workers, who all had begun to feel the harsh effects of neoliberal policies, organized several marches protesting the water situation. They were all neighbors and water users, and the demand for adequate water services was common to all. In mid-1997, the legislature and the governor decided that the provincial capital and its environs, totaling 100,000 water service accounts, would remain with Agua del Aconquija, and the municipalities of the interior caught in the disagreement between workers and users debated between municipalization and operation by the water sector workers. While negotiations went on, residents continued the Stop Payment campaign; an estimated 70 percent of the users held firm and did not pay their bills. The consumer organization, ADEUCOT, was sure that the seven municipalities which had abandoned the concession would agree to take over both the service and its operation. ADEUCOT prepared technical reports for the regulating agency (ERSACT) to study and determine whether it (ADEUCOT) was able to take charge of the service.

When the company rescinded the privatization contract blaming the provincial government, the government responded by in turn rescinding the contract blaming the company's noncompliance with the contractual clauses approved by the legislature. The company then announced it would take action under the International Treaty for the Protection and Promotion of Investments between France and Argentina and seek arbitration by the International Centre for Settlement of Investment Disputes (ICSID) of the World Bank. It said it was willing to collect users' debts in a "normal and logical" fashion.[8]

Despite the fact that the contract stipulated that the Compagnie Générale des Eaux could not leave for eighteen months, the company wanted to halt operations no later than November 1997. The French company felt that it was "captive, because we are not allowed to leave Tucumán" (*La Gaceta* 1998). Negotiations between the company and the provincial government concluded with the establishment of a reasonable water tariff for the transition period. Even though the Argentine national government expressed concern that the conflict might scare off new foreign investors, once the company appealed to the ICSID, the national government sided with the provincial government. The World Bank then began participating directly, advising the province on the preparation of bid specifications.

In February 1998, the Argentine government decided that the Secretariat of Natural Resources and Sustainable Development, headed by María Julia Alsogaray, a neoliberal politician, needed to monitor the Tucumán problem.[9] The provincial government agreed to the temporary transfer of the water and sewerage services to the National Public Works and Sanitation Agency, thus voiding the possibility of implementing the proposals of either the local users or the workers union. This measure, which President Menem's administration promoted, relieved the financial stress that the foreign company experienced—as it was offering services without being able to collect payment from the users—and facilitated its leaving before the end of the eighteen-month transition period. This decision was taken after President Menem's visit to France and intense lobbying by the directors of the Vivendi Group, who represented the Compagnie Générale des Eaux (*La Gaceta*, June 6, 1998).

In effect, the nation assumed responsibility for the 7.5 million pesos that Tucumán's water and sewerage services cost during the first few months of the transition period, until users began to resume their payments on a regular basis, and the National Public Works and Sanitation Agency took over the service. At the beginning, this arrangement was to last six months. However, because of national and provincial elections, massive economic crisis, and widespread critiques of the privatization model, the anticipated reprivatization of Tucumán water and sewerage services has not taken place, and five years later (in 2003), the federal agency remains in charge, with no renovations in sight. In 1999, when the new government of Tucumán took office, it withdrew the lawsuit against Agua del Aconquija, alleging that it was going to reformulate its case, but it has yet to reactivate the legal action.

ADEUCOT and the Role of Women

The organization the users created during the protests against the privatization of water services, ADEUCOT, successfully promoted legislation that currently allows its representatives to participate in all the regulating bodies that oversee public services. In the city of Lules, where ADEUCOT's president lives, weekly meetings are held, and the number of participants, rather than decreasing, has increased over time.

Early on, the users realized that they needed a structure to manage their initial, spontaneous protests. First, they formed a coordinating committee in the Monteros social club. When the number of people and the enthusiasm grew, they sought the advice of a lawyer who suggested the legal incorporation of the organization. "We started to organize when there was talk of privatizing water, when the provincial government began 'emptying' the provincial company [DIPOS], to be able to privatize it. . . . Then we began in every city in the interior: I began in Lules, Normita in Monteros, a Mrs. M in Bella Vista . . . and, well, this drive to protest connected us to leaders in other cities" (J. Abdala, President of ADEUCOT).

Nélida Gan, an active member in Lules and in those days a municipal council member, remembers that at the beginning, middle-aged people and women were the first to embrace this struggle. She was then thirty-seven years old, an experienced neighborhood political leader, who had paid for her own political training studying history, the theory of the state, and so on. She also was a housewife who looked after her three children. When asked about what motivated her to participate she says:

I was driven by a lot of anger; really, anger, because all the improvements to the water and sewerage services had been financed by the municipal governments with contributions from the residents. So it was like handing all this over to privatized companies, who, on the other hand, charged an awful lot for the services they promised and that in the future were going to ruin us because after the fifth year, I don't remember how, the rates would continue to increase . . . This was probably the main thing that made me participate.

This leader from Lules was one of the youngest women who participated; most were housewives over forty who were defending their meager family budgets. The social world in Tucumán reflects the traditional hierarchies common in the rest of northern Argentina: the supremacy of patriarchal authority, of elders over the young, of socially prominent families over popular sectors. To a certain degree, because Tucumán had been the setting for important social struggles for many decades, its traditional social fabric has larger tears in it than other regions. This is reflected in the role women play in day-to-day life and in public spaces. Compared with other provinces, women have a much higher degree of public participation; however, in their everyday relationships, the power of paternal and conjugal authority remains very strong.

The reason why mostly women initiated the social protest over water was clearly linked to their social role in Tucumán. Most women in these towns and small cities are wives or daughters of sugar cane farmers or public employees, or they themselves are public employees, such as teachers and nurses. They live in localities that combine rural and urban social worlds where a large proportion of the residents are public employees who receive their wages in quasi monies (public bonds) that make increases in public water rates extremely difficult to handle. Women are in charge of the household expenses because they have similar or higher educational levels than their husbands or fathers. This means they were more acutely aware of the increase in water rates than men. Through Tucumán's long history of social protest women had acquired considerable training and experience in organizing. At the same time as the water protest was underway, they organized against the pollution caused by the sugar mills. This is one of reasons why women protestors knew each other so well in these localities and could easily generate a network.

This network came into play when the decision to not pay water bills was made. Some of the participants explained that the decision to "not pay" was taken in the capital city of San Miguel at a large public meeting dominated by men. Nevertheless, it was women who moved the decision from words to action. Women went door-to-door convincing their women neighbors that their actions were not illegal if they carried them out together and followed the required legal provisions.

Everybody involved recognizes that women were the core activists in this struggle and acknowledges that women were the ones who held their ground when it came to the Stop Payment campaign. Nevertheless, in meetings with legislators and public officials, men assumed the principal role. A division of labor made women the territorial activists, while both men and women worked on the technical documents, but when the need for representation came about, men took over. This reflects most public participation in Argentina: women initiate movements and are the most active and the best organizers, but when the time comes to formalize organizational structures, they do not occupy positions of authority.

The male president of ADEUCOT explains the thinking behind the role women played: "There is a degree of truth in this [that women did not hold positions of authority]; participation was very well organized and some women participated; they were very active. But when it came to decision making we worked a lot, *everything had to be thought out twice,* make compromises . . . and women are very direct" (emphasis ours). Conventional wisdom in Tucumán holds that men are the ones who think things over twice, while women react more emotionally. On the other hand, the degree of women's emotional responses at the beginning of the struggle is also seen as a positive resource. Now, everyone admits that the women were the ones who held their ground when it came to the Stop Payment campaign.[10]

"They all said we were crazy, how were we ever going to win against a huge company."

"Politicians looked at us like we were crazy, and I know they were thinking 'these women.'" "In the beginning people said we were four mad women, standing up to such a monster."

When the protests began, nothing indicated that the process that had been unleashed would achieve its goals. That events occurred as they did was, as Melucci (1992) maintains, due to the clear definition of goals and the active relational process between the actors because patterns of knowledge, dense interactions, and close emotional and affective exchanges were in play.

Women were able to transfer prior participation in community projects into active social protest. Ana, a younger protestor, explains:

> I was in the school co-op, where my children went to school. But, yes, this is something else, right? I've been involved here in the barrio, in the neighborhood center, where I was part of the women's commission. But there we didn't go out and fight, we made things for the children. . . . I didn't have the experience, and besides, I didn't know anybody. We didn't used to go out; we were involved in politics, but from there to something else, well, no. . . . At the beginning in the water business, we would pool our money to go to the meetings, because nobody had a car." (Ana)

When "the French left" (as the locals describe the situation), people began to return to their towns, unaware of the immensity of what they had achieved. One of the women interviewed says that she didn't realize what they had done until a few years later, when she went to the National Women's Conference held in southern Argentina.[11] When, without any presumption on her part, she related her experience, she saw what an uproar she had caused in the conference. The next day, several participants surrounded her and kept asking her to tell her story over and over again.

All the women acknowledge that the networks they formed, especially among women, are among the enduring results of their struggle. Today, ADEUCOT defends consumers in all areas. Ana is president in her city, Bella Vista, and not only does she run a horizontal and democratic organization, she maintains a collaborative relationship with the associations in the rest of the province and with other organizations.

The women were enthusiastic supporters of the solution that proposed a mixed company, made up by small cities and users (which we have called "municipalization"). Although it was not the form eventually chosen to operate the region's water services, it is still seen as a structure that could facilitate neighborhood participation in water management. At any rate, it remains an option for the next time the water service is up for bid, especially if there is public and sustained interest in the issue. After this experience, the women of Tucumán undoubtedly are much more predisposed and prepared to participate in influencing public policy decisions such as the provision of basic services.

At the end of 2001, protests swept Argentina, the consequence of the neoliberal model that emphasized the privatization of services and other businesses and that had propelled the country into crisis. President Fernando de la Rua, elected in 1999 on promises to address the economic crisis, was not only unable to stem the problems but actively strengthened the neoliberal model. His actions led to one of the biggest mobilizations and protests of the decade, and in December 2001, both President de la Rua and his minister of economic affairs were forced to resign, and a provisional government was installed.

In January 2002, as the provisional government tried to maintain control, the banking system collapsed, many small- and medium-sized, locally owned businesses were forced to close, unemployment spiraled upwards, and large financial groups and privately owned firms engaged in massive capital flight. Citizens took to the streets and the country witnessed day after day of massive protests, as the population repudiated the results of the prior ten years of neoliberal policies. In this context, the seemingly isolated event that had happened in the small province of Tucumán six years earlier takes on greater meaning.

While the city and province of Buenos Aires had passively accepted the privatization of their water and sewerage services—through a concession to Aguas Argentinas, whose main stockholder was another French company Suez Lyonnaise des Eaux—Tucumán was actively resisting the Compagnie Générale des Eaux.[12] The general conditions of the service and rates between the two companies were similar, which raises the question why the most important and most politicized district in the country (Buenos Aires) did not react, while a highly dispersed, low-income population in the small province of Tucumán stood its ground and said "No."

We cannot answer this question. The great dilemma in social science is why, under similar macroinstitutional circumstances, certain social actors decide to act and others don't; why some go out on the streets and others resignedly accept unfavorable conditions. We can hypothesize that during the 1990s, a greater proportion of the residents of Buenos Aires enjoyed more of the advantages of neoliberal policy than did residents elsewhere in the country, simply because as the national capital Buenos Aires has a higher concentration of the wealthy and powerful elite of Argentina. But this does not explain everything. What is true is that the first place in the entire country that opposed privatization of a public service was Tucumán. And it was done by the people from the towns, by the women, using civil disobedience.

The effectiveness of the action in Tucumán was based on several elements. Because water is central to how daily life is organized, the policies implemented by the Compagnie Générale des Eaux clearly led to impoverishment and diminished quality of life. This also led to the greater participation of women, who are the managers of daily household water use. No doubt the most important strategy was the Stop Payment campaign. Local residents were emboldened by their own collective action as the creation of a collective identity mitigated their fear and strengthened their individual will to participate.

With a new national government elected in 2003, renegotiating rates for public services in general and water rates in particular has been put on the public policy agenda. In this scenario, ADEUCOT may be favored in what happens in Tucumán, and it is demanding: *(a)* a solution to the legal problem affecting the users by reviving the legal case against the French Water Company; and *(b)* that consideration be given to the proposals presented by ADEUCOT for creating a water cooperative or mixed enterprise with the participation of users, workers, and local governments (municipalities).

This "cycle of protest" (Tarrow 1997) in Argentina is proof of what different social theories tell us, that what we usually see as social organization is a social construct. But later, there is a process of "forgetting" when we "hide" the power of collective action. According to Buechler and Cylke, "the price of forgetting the human authorship of the world is a denial of the ability to change the world, and hence a loss of potential control over one's own life. Of all forms of action studied by sociologists, social movements are the most dramatic way that human beings periodically break through the illusions of an alienated and reified world view to reclaim their authorship of the world and their power to shape that world in keeping with their aspirations" (1997, 575–76). Reclaiming their authorship of the world is what low- and middle-income women from small cities achieved in Tucumán.

PART THREE

Technology Transfer and Social Organization

A common water project consists of technology transfer to local communities. Myriad organizations are engaged in transferring appropriate domestic water and sanitation technology to urban and rural areas, as well as in bringing irrigation technology to farming communities. Time and time again, technology transfer focuses heavily on the technology and ignores crucial community dynamics. Project planners and technicians are very often blind to local needs and priorities and ignore local knowledge, skills, and understanding. The heterogeneity of communities often escapes them, as does the fact that technology use is intricately interwoven with social organization.

The two case studies in this section illustrate some of the gender issues that impact technology transfer. They show that even the very first decision of who will be involved with a water project is laden with complexity, as men and women have different needs and knowledge bases when it comes to daily water usage. Incorporating both men and women from the very beginning into technology transfer projects makes the most sense but rarely happens. And even when the decision is made to incorporate both, the cultural and logistical barriers that can prevent women's full participation must be acknowledged and then overcome. Considering gender equity during technology transfer means not only understanding the social organization of a given community but also recognizing that the project itself will impact the community's social organization.

7 Irrigation Management, the Participatory Approach, and Equity in an Andean Community

> *We are too shy and too afraid to voice our ideas about water management in community meetings; sometimes we talk to our husbands, but we don't have experience talking to outsiders.*
>
> A woman from the Llullucha community in Paucartambo-Cusco

> *We don't need any more technical training, because we can do everything on our own. We can even train people from other communities.*
>
> Men from Llullucha

> *In rural communities, gender relations are as they were in the past and as they will continue to be in the future, thanks to the harmonious relationships that stem from balanced family systems. Our agency (IMA) is involved with farm productivity, and we cannot analyze the private lives of household members.*[1]
>
> Testimony of a member of the IMA management team, Cusco

These testimonies confirm the now well known differentiated impact that external projects have on gender relations, that is, on the knowledge, abilities, and self-esteem of both men and women. They also reveal the shortsightedness of planners in incorporating the complex and contradictory manner in which external intervention shaped intrahousehold dynamics—and thus gender relations. This disregard of gender as a variable often results from generally accepted assumptions that conceive the contemporary rural household in the Andes as a dualistic, harmonious arena, where men equitably direct all benefits from irrigation projects to their families, and women fulfill their reproductive role while feeling protected by their husbands. Another underlying assumption of project planners places all water management issues within the male's domain. These assumptions were central in the soil conservation and irrigation project analyzed in this chapter that was directed only at community men, seeking their participation in training and irrigation management activities as well as in decisions related to water management and ignoring community women all together.

Why is it that project activities directed toward the access and control of key community resources systematically favor men? A simple answer is that social and gender inequity is produced and reproduced by processes that are embedded in political, economic, cultural, educational, and religious institutions (Slayter et al. 1996). Though this is true to some extent, this response is too simplistic and doesn't address how power is institutionalized in daily practices. Here I argue that it may be better to study how institutional and organizational effects—including hierarchy and power—are generated and reproduced in everyday practices (Law 1992, cited in Nuijten 1998). To fully grasp the significance of inequality in gender relations, we need to study how women and men systematically construct their gender ideology and identity and how the organizing practices of everyday life are patterned to favor men.

The issue of how to design more equitable policies to promote the sustainable management of water is of fundamental importance especially in rural areas, where water rights are closely linked to land rights. Different authors (Meinzen-Dick and Zwarteveen 1997; van Kopper 1997; von Benda-Beckmann 1996) have demonstrated how the general category of water rights can be usefully broken down into subcategories, such as the right to use and dispose of water, the right to participate in water-user organizations, the right and obligation to hold a position as a water authority, the right to formulate and change regulations pertaining to water use and management, the right to sanction and enforce rules, and the right to access knowledge and information. As this case study from highland Peru shows, all these rights may be gendered at the community level, and if this gendering of rights is not considered in project design then projects themselves may perpetuate gender inequities.

The Case Study

In 1995, the SNV Netherlands Development Organization approached several different water management institutions in Peru and proposed an analysis of the effects of their community projects not only on water production but on gender relations (Batuone et al. 1996).[2] The Instituto de Manejo de Agua y Medio Ambiente (IMA, Institute for Water Management and Environment) of the Cusco regional government, where I worked as Coordinator of Research and Training from 1995 to 1997, accepted the SNV offer and chose to study a community where it had sponsored an integrated water management project for almost five years. Projects in this community, Llullucha,[3] were judged by an IMA technical evaluation to be a model for water management, and they were applied in other communities. Despite improved agricultural production and increased farmers' incomes, however, the SNV gender analysis showed that the projects' effects were not the same for men and women.

The objective of the SNV-financed study was to improve the integration of a gender perspective into irrigation projects. The study utilized the Farming System Research and Extension (FSR/E) methodology Feldstein and Poats (1990) developed, which examines gender bias. According to these authors, gender analysis can be critical for:

• Analyzing activities because this raises questions about who does what, when, and where in farm production, household production, childbearing and childrearing, and in other productive activities, including those carried out away from the farm. The analysis identifies all tasks in terms of gender and reveals important issues regarding labor shortage within households and communities.

• Analyzing resources because this identifies who has access to or control over the resources required for production. Control in this sense means the power to decide whether and how a resource is used, and/or how it is to be allocated. Access refers to the freedom or permission to use the resource. Resources include land, capital, tools, labor, services, credit, knowledge, and other inputs.

• Analyzing benefits and incentives to determine who benefits from each enterprise.

• Allowing both technicians and farmers simultaneously to become involved in a participatory consciousness-raising process.

In addition, methodologies and instruments from Participatory Rural Appraisal (PRA) were employed, and the household was used as a unit of analysis.[4] This methodology enabled the SNV research team to compare not only the farmers' and the IMA technicians' perspectives but also the male farmers' and the female farmers' points of view.

The concepts used in this study are as follows. *Agency* assumes that social actors have the capacity to process social experiences and to devise ways of coping with life, even under the most extreme forms of coercion, within the limits of information, uncertainty, and other existing constraints (physical, normative, or politico-economic; Long and Long 1992). *Social actors* are defined as knowledgeable and capable and include not only individuals but also state agencies, political parties, churches, and other organizations. A social actor is not just a synonym for the individual but is rather a social construction shaped by the culture, norms, and predominant discourses of a given society (Long and Long 1992). *Discourse*, according to Parker (1992), is a system of statements which construct an object, a set of meanings, metaphors, representations, images, and/or narratives that advance a particular version of "the truth" about specific objects, persons, or events. Discourses tend to reproduce power relations, support institutions, and have impacts on the construction of ideology.

IMA's Experience in Llullucha

When the IMA engineers first arrived in Llullucha in 1991, water scarcity was a serious problem. Two natural springs provided limited water, farmers were constantly fighting each other for irrigation water, and the lack of water meant very little agriculture was even possible. The women had to walk considerable distances to wash their clothes and fetch water for daily household needs.

Women were responsible for herding the cows and sheep; men were in charge of other agricultural activities. The men commonly migrated temporarily to surrounding villages or cities seeking supplementary income. According the engineers' first diagnosis, the Llullucha community urgently needed soil conservation projects because of serious erosion problems due mainly to overherding and to the steep terrain that allowed torrential downpours during the rainy season to carry off the topsoil. According to standard soil use classification, only twenty-four hectares of land near the village were suitable for agriculture.

Initially when IMA promoted soil conservation practices through infiltration trenches on steep agricultural lands and terracing of farmland, the *comuneros* (officially registered owners of communal lands) were unenthusiastic and only reluctantly implemented the new methods. But IMA was under pressure to demonstrate successful results to its financing agencies, so it began providing economic incentives to *comuneros* willing to apply soil conservation practices. The incentives were successful and *comuneros* finished the soil conservation work in only three months, nine less than originally planned.

In 1992, after two years of work in Llullucha, IMA decided to carry out a participatory evaluation that only included the *comuneros*, which as in most Peruvian Andean communities, were all men. The IMA engineers were surprised by the results, which revealed that the *comuneros* were not interested in soil conservation activities, especially when they were carried out in the surrounding hills, far from their plots. Rather they were very concerned about the scarcity of water and requested assistance from the engineers in identifying methods to irrigate their lands. These results prompted IMA to implement a Rapid Rural Appraisal (RRA),[5] but once again, only men were asked to participate.

The appraisal resulted in a new proposal to optimize the water supply from nearby springs via the construction of a reservoir. To maximize its use and efficiency, a sprinkler irrigation system was designed to pipe water to the fields. To implement this project, IMA established additional incentives and urged the *comuneros* to maintain soil conservation practices when beginning the irrigation project. The *comuneros* accepted this plan; however, once construction began on the reservoir and the pipes began to be laid to bring water to the fields, the women of Llullucha protested strongly because the project was preventing water from reaching the waterholes customarily used for their animals. This conflict of interest between the project plan and women's needs for water had to be solved before the irrigation project could continue.

This encounter between the women's needs and the IMA project—what I call gender interface[6]—forced the engineers to redefine their project design. An urgent community meeting was called and several women were invited, but they did not participate in the discussion or in the decision-making process. Instead, the IMA technicians and *comuneros* discussed including a watering place for cattle and installing a drinking water system close to the homesteads.

This experience generated an institutional debate on water management policies and on integrated water resource management within IMA. The staff agreed that water had to be taken into account in rural development proposals as an essential resource that determines and mobilizes the management of other resources, such as soil, plants, and cattle. This led IMA to develop Tecnologías Productivas Apropiadas (TPAs, Appropriate Productive Technologies) in 1992[7] to promote the optimal integrated use of water, based on the following principles:

• Participatory approaches are integral to the cycle of project development.

• Water management should include soil conservation practices as well as farming and agroecological practices.

• Soil conservation practices must be linked to local farming practices.

• *Comuneros* must receive training in order to become the future promoters of community development.

The following prerequisites for participation in future projects were established: that participants have land and water use rights, adopt soil conservation practices, and attend all the training activities. They also selected a subset of farmers to take specialized courses to become local promoters.

The prerequisite that participants must have land rights excluded women. Even though according to Peruvian communal land law both men and women have the right to own land, because of land scarcity in Llullucha, the community's rule was that only men were officially landholders. Women were denied the right to own land. Even widows were denied control of inherited land, which was instead under the control of fathers-in-law or oldest sons (even if the latter were still underage). Single women had to marry in order to access land through their husbands, but they had no control over it. Women who did not marry had to migrate to other villages or to the city of Cusco to work as servants because in their own community there was no way for them to access productive resources to support themselves.

The second prerequisite was that participants had water use rights. To obtain these, the landholder had to fulfill a series of requirements, including constructing irrigation systems, paying system maintenance quotas on time, cleaning the reservoir and canals, and participating in community meetings. Women were not allowed to participate in any of these activities. The informal criteria for excluding women from communal work were the prevailing stereotypes regarding the gender division of labor, cultural norms dictating appropriate male and female behavior, as well as the traditional male domination of the public decision-making process. Social norms dictated that women confine their activities to the domestic domain (although domestic was broadly defined to include such chores as herding cattle and sheep).

The third and fourth prerequisites concerned implementing soil conservation practices and participating in training activities. In the beginning, incentives meant that all the *comuneros* readily attended every training event on soil conservation practices. But they rarely shared their newly acquired knowledge with their wives, who typically learned by silently observing while working alongside the men once the IMA irrigation project produced enough water to allow more intensive agriculture. Withholding information and not transferring new knowledge to their wives was a common strategy among men, who wanted to leave no doubt as to who was in charge. Thus clearly the IMA's incentive-based technology transfer was only available to the men of Llullucha because IMA's definition of participation worked to exclude women.

In 1995, after three years of working on the irrigation project (and five years after arriving in Llullucha), the IMA project team working in Llullucha, including the author of this chapter, began its collaboration with SNV to examine the effects of the project on gender relations. SNV sent an advisor to Llullucha to help the IMA personnel with the project methodology.

When the IMA-SNV study began, the women of Llullucha had already organized to receive aid from the Paucartambo municipality to run school breakfast programs for their children. During 1995, the first year of the IMA-SNV project, the women mobilized and submitted a request to the communal authorities for a plot of communal land so that they could access the IMA project's benefits related to water management, including the TPAs. Once the women were granted the land to farm collectively, they petitioned for water rights, which was the only way to guarantee production. The community allocated the women's organization water for their lands under the condition that part of the income generated by their crops be returned to the community. Next, the women requested and received training from IMA on implementing soil conservation practices, applying the best irrigation practices, and planning their crops. With the incentives IMA provided for soil conservation practices, they bought tools and sprinkler irrigation equipment. From 1997 onward, when IMA replaced incentives with a credit program, the women's organization was one of the first to access the credit (to improve their sprinkler irrigation equipment) and was the only organization that paid back the credit on time. This resulted in ongoing IMA work with women's organizations and greater trust in women than men when it came to managing credit. By mobilizing to acquire land, the women not only received IMA training, they were able to access the TPAs, receive

IMA incentives and credit, and participate in communal meetings for the first time. The latter was an unexpected outcome that was neither proposed nor anticipated when they requested land.

The women of Llullucha were clearly not passive victims of the prevailing rules and discourses that prevented their access to land, water, or knowledge. They actively resisted, building their agency to take advantage of even the smallest openings. Long and Long (1992) and Villarreal (1994) maintain that when a social actor seeks different means to achieve its objective and avoids passivity in the face of adversity, it resists conforming to the dominant paradigm. This is what happened in Llullucha, where the women "resisted" being left without land and water and without the benefits the IMA project offered. They proved that women can participate in an integrated water management project and that water management is not the exclusive realm of engineers or men, despite the initial gender bias of the IMA water management project.

IMA, Male Farmers, and Female Farmers

In 1995, a few months before the IMA-SNV study started, IMA concluded its first participatory evaluation with a positive assessment of the project, largely because the conditions for production had improved significantly. Thanks to the new reservoir and sprinkler irrigation system, farmers could cultivate their land twice a year, and the cultivated area increased. The new soil conservation practices also resulted in better plant growth and facilitated irrigation, which in turn diminished erosion. Llullucha's farmers had more products to sell in the local market reducing temporary migration because of the increased demand for labor on their farms.

Water users organized to improve both the control and management of water, establishing a new water use organization (WUO). By the end of the evaluation, IMA concluded that the TPAs were sound, both technically and socially because they contributed to better water management and therefore should be included in any integrated water management policy. IMA considered Llullucha a successful experience of participatory intervention and chose it as a model for others who were interested in the TPA methods. Other communities specifically requested promoters from Llullucha to train them, and most of the exchanges of experience related to water management were done in Llullucha.

This is why when the SNV showed interest in the gender study—the IMA board immediately chose Llullucha. It was an opportunity to examine how well their project was moving toward sustainable water resource management while evaluating the gender effects. It should come as no surprise that the IMA could not identify the elements needed to analyze the effects—positive or negative—of its intervention on gender relations because they had not explicitly incorporated a gender approach in the first place. The IMA technicians, however, were certain that they had contributed positively to the well-being of each family member.

In general, when the study compared the technicians' and the male farmers' opinions regarding different elements of the study, they found that for the most part the (men) farmers' positions were similar to those of the technicians, and the women held positions very different from either of them. For instance, when they analyzed participation in the design, implementation, and evaluation of the project, both the community men and the technicians claimed that, excepting the first institutional diagnosis (that resulted in the soil conservation project), these processes were fully participatory. As one technician said, "All the *comuneros* were present in these events; we could not make decisions without consulting people in the communal meeting." In the same vein, one of the *comuneros* indicated, "all the *comuneros*, together with the engineers, agreed to do everything having to do with the irrigation project." We asked the IMA technicians if women ever attended these events. Their immediate response was, "Of course not, only heads of family are present in communal meetings." When asked to assess whether or not the project had been participatory, the women responded, "Yes, it was. Our husbands were consulted in communal meetings. We did not participate because we are not communal members *(comuneros)*." Thus the women saw their exclusion from the project as normal up to a point because they understood and had internalized Llullucha's communal customs. At the same time, when asked whether they thought they should participate in communal meetings, they would pause, think, and then respond that, yes, they could because they too worked the land. But the possibility of participating in meetings was a remote one for them.

This nuanced analysis highlights the complexities of fostering the participatory approach with a gender perspective. The objective is not to force participation but to be honest in appraising the impacts of projects on an ongoing basis so as to act as inclusively and equitably as possible. The fact that the women in Llullucha mobilized to get a plot of land signified social, economic, and cultural changes in the norms that shape the community's daily life. The roles of both the men and the women of the community needed to be reappraised as the women entered the farming arena independent of the men. Since, according to the IMA guidelines, only landholders could be social actors in water management affairs, the question arises whether IMA should have included the women as formal social actors once they became collective farmers even though they still were not in fact officially registered landholders *(comuneros)*.

Women, men, and technicians all agreed that the water management project provided greater water availability and improved agricultural production. An important difference, however, was that women focused on the installation of the drinking water system and of the irrigation system to grow fresh vegetables in their gardens, while men focused on availability of water in the fields. The women considered the drinking water system important because they no longer had to walk long distances to fetch water, and this saved them a lot of time that they fully used in the increased farming activities. Women—as opposed to the men who work mainly in the fields and combine this activity with communal work and training activities—have to prepare meals and look after the children, feed domestic animals, herd cattle, and cultivate their garden and fields. The male farmers take their products to the market; they do not trust their wives to do so because they are illiterate and only talk Quechua, the local indigenous language. Before the IMA project, when there was hardly any farming, the wives used to accompany their husbands when they went to trade in other villages even though there was not much to trade. With the success of the IMA project, the community has more to sell, but only the men go to market and the women stay at home because of work overload.

Questions related to the effect of the project on gender relations resulted in different points of view. The IMA technicians said they did not interfere in this matter because from their perspective the relationship between men and women was well balanced. The IMA staff was not aware that their involvement *did* affect gender relations, even if that was not their intention. This study shows the intricate and sometimes contrasting effects of external intervention on household dynamics.

One of the more noticeable effects was that, as a consequence of the new knowledge they acquired regarding water management, the self-esteem of Llullucha's men was reinforced. Their role as promoters in sharing their successful experiences with other communities encouraged Llullucha men to state: "We don't need any more technical training, because we can do everything on our own. We can even train people from other communities." This was, in fact, an important achievement for both Llullucha farmers and IMA technicians.

For the women, however, the situation was completely different. As one of them expressed, they did not even dare talk to strangers: "We are too shy and too afraid to voice our ideas about water management in community meetings; sometimes we talk to our husbands, but we don't have experience talking to outsiders." The women of Llullucha were afraid to speak in community assemblies even when invited to do so and generally felt that their knowledge base was inferior to the men's because they had not attended any of the IMA sponsored training. Despite the fact that they generally thought of their abilities as quite limited, we found that the women indeed were accessing and acquiring knowledge while the TPA project was being implemented, simply by observing and "helping" their husbands in everyday farm tasks or organizing themselves to create land-water rights. They differed from the men only because they did not use technical words to explain the water management system, but they knew how it functioned and also how to organize themselves to achieve optimal water management. When we asked the women why they were not able to state their point of view in communal meetings or in other public meetings, they answered:

We are not allowed in the communal meetings. Only the president of our organization can participate, and this only when the authorities invite her, on special occasions. Besides, the men don't listen to us, because they think we don't have any rights. But, like the men, we *could* speak out, because we also till the soil, even more than they do.

Here it is evident that the women perceived that working the land should give them the right to participate in meetings, yet they also understand that the reality is otherwise.

The women's answers show the clash between the cultural role of women in Llullucha and their new roles and activities in the community thanks to their efforts to participate in the IMA water project. When asked the same question, the men claimed the women could not participate in communal meetings because they were not officially *comuneros* and that land is only allotted to men because they work the fields and carry out communal jobs. Women only "help" to work the fields and, besides, "Llullucha's women don't have any experience participating in public meetings, and they can't talk in public. Women lack character in making decisions, and most are shy and illiterate."

When we researched the participation of Llullucha women in the emerging water user organization, we found that it was not even considered by the *comuneros* or by the engineers. There was nothing regarding how women might be able to participate in decision making or occupy a position of authority. As a result, only men discussed and decided the requirements for accessing water, and they did so according to their prevailing, typically patriarchal, ideology. Only a landholder or *comunero* could be a WUO member, which once again, excluded women. Evidence from around the world shows that despite their involvement in the everyday management of water issues, when a social organization for managing a water system is formalized, women become invisible at the formal level of participation. Even when women are present in these organizations, their participation is not equal to that of the men (Meinzen-Dick and Zwarteveen 1997; Arroyo and Boelens 1997a; Batuone et al. 1996; Vera 1996).

What IMA Learned from This Case Study

IMA technicians learned that any kind of external intervention inevitably affects household dynamics and, as a result, gender relations. The women and men of Llullucha were not passive actors in their responses to the external IMA intervention. The men developed different tactics to access strategic resources of land, water, and knowledge that reinforced their social identity and position as social actors. The male *comuneros* gained control over the water management system, creating and establishing rules that favored them over women, and they institutionalized these rules through the water user organization and the internal communal laws. In this way, women were left almost without any possibility to claim the right to access resources or to participate in a formal level. However, the women were not passive either; they organized and developed their own social agency to overcome barriers. As they sought collective land to farm, the women participated in the project, though the project design initially excluded them.

Another lesson was that knowledge confers power to those who acquire it. In addition to their legal advantage of access to land, their unrestricted participation in public spaces, communal works, and project management and training, new knowledge gave Llullucha's men—especially the communal promoters—a feeling of self-sufficiency and power. The more information and knowledge people have, the more they are able and confident about confronting and changing their situation. Information and knowledge strengthens both individuals and institutions, enabling them to construct and participate as equals in social organizations. IMA engineers realized this, and the research study made them aware that the big differences between men and women were reinforced and became even more noticeable than at the beginning of the project.

The technicians learned to recognize other social actors. The engineers' original definition of social actor was synonymous with *comuneros,* but why were only men taken into account as social actors? First of all, legally *comuneros* were heads of household, but this status was linked to the landholder and landholders were men. The women were aware of this situation and because they could not expect to achieve individual ownership of land, they attempted to gain access to the land collectively and created a new social identity as collective farmers. The women refused to conform to the project's parameters, and they looked for an alternate route that would allow them to participate. They succeeded in entering a project that not only had been designed to exclude them, but to keep them invisible. By active resistance, the women made themselves visible.

IMA also learned that the participatory approach per se is not enough to reach and include women. The technicians were confident that their intervention policy was fully participatory. Once they embarked on the project with their flawed definition of participants as only the male *comuneros* (excluding the women of the community), they continued to consider the execution, monitoring, and evaluation of the project as participatory, as well as the training activities. At all these levels of participation, women were invisible. This happened because of the engineers' completely unnuanced mythologizing of the harmonious relationship within rural families.

IMA learned that water management is a social construct based on social and gender relations. Considering gender vis-à-vis water management has direct consequences not only for the efficiency and sustainability of the integrated management water system but also on the livelihood of the water users. These relationships are particularly relevant when planning policies especially in a context of high male migration, which is the case of communities like Llullucha.

This learning experience encouraged IMA to integrate gender not only in its water management programs but also in all its institutional activities.[8] Some of the engineers have started to achieve more participative and satisfactory results now that gender has been integrated into their activities. Gender must be one of the pillars of the participatory approach, otherwise the tendency toward bias when categorizing social actors will not disappear.

The extent to which gender can be integrated with water management policies does not depend only on the resoluteness of technicians in deconstructing their ideology regarding womanhood or manhood and their willingness to cross boundaries. It also depends on the willingness and capability of authorities and institutions to listen, integrate, and promote gender equity in all types of social action.

8 Water as a Source of Equity and Empowerment in Costa Rica

G uaranteeing community access to potable water and basic sanitation requires more than technologically and financially affordable infrastructure. This was the main lesson from the "Handpump Technology" project in rural Costa Rica, implemented during two phases, between 1986 and 1991, and which I worked on as an anthropologist.[1] The project's initial objective was to test the adequate functioning of a hand pump but was broadened to include a focus on people's relationship to water that we recognized had to change if the project was to have a real impact.

Besides supporting the construction of hand-dug and drilled wells and related sanitation safeguards, the project addressed issues such as garbage dumps, the location and condition of latrines, and the disinfection of both well and household water. However, the project did not become really sustainable until the community's hygiene habits and its water use traditions were addressed. Rather than limiting input to providing technical assistance, we sought to foster the community participation of both men and women through a training process that made the technologies their own.

The project was developed for three very low-population density rural communities in the canton of Sarapiquí, Heredia Province, Costa Rica.[2] Economic activity in this area focuses on intense forest exploitation, influenced by Caribbean climatic conditions, which means a significant rainfall most of the year. The region's communities are disperse and comprise people from all over Costa Rica and even from neighboring countries. Because of this migration, a wide range of customs and habits related to water, hygiene, and sanitation are found.

Defining the Bases for Participation

When the water supply project began its first phase in 1986, it was conceived from a mostly "technical" standpoint. It did not include participatory methodologies, nor did it recognize the importance of differentiated approaches to the various groups within the communities. In part this was because the project proposal was developed without the participation of the target population.

This methodological and conceptual shortcoming actually served as an incentive to add a series of innovative elements to the project. The openness and interdisciplinary makeup of the project team, which included specialists ranging from engineering to anthropology, facilitated reformulation of project goals and methods. The first challenge was to define participation and to establish how, when, and who would participate. This was particularly important, as a principal feature of traditional water supply projects is the assumption that participation only means community members providing free labor.

From the outset, the extent of community diversity was very clear, as was the fact that these very particular realities and needs had to be acknowledged through a strategy that made this heterogeneity visible and addressed it explicitly. The need to design materials and project spaces that were as inclusive as possible and that assisted the incorporation of the realities of youth, children, and women arose from these discussions.

This led the project team to clarify the forms that community participation in water supply and sanitation projects could take in practice:

1. *Participation as cheap labor:* Some initiatives and projects consider that the community participates because it is required to contribute unpaid labor. The project is imposed from outside, and the community is told what to do and contribute. When people are participating, their role in the definition of strategies and in decision making is nonexistent.

2. *Participation as sociocultural animation:* The use of dynamic techniques to animate the community is often mistaken for a truly participatory process. These techniques are important tools if they are oriented toward reflection and consciousness raising, but they are not an end in themselves and can never substitute for a truly participatory process.

3. *Participation as a way to share "costs-benefits":* A fundamental goal for technical personnel working on water supply and sanitation projects is to re-

cover the money invested through a contribution in cash or kind from the community.

4. *Participation as a cultural obligation:* In this modality participation is conditioned by formal requirements, often in the form of contracts that detail the roles and responsibilities of each of the project partners (e.g., the government and the community). Though the community can choose to accept or reject the terms of the contract and can negotiate changes through the community's formal power structure, most often these negotiations take place with male leaders, and the rest of the community has no real access to information or decision making.

5. *Participation with the community as decision maker:* Given the limitations of the preceding approaches to participation, this alternative prioritizes local organizational and human potential and capacity so as to ensure an effective utilization and administration of community resources. The communities themselves assume the responsibility (and the right) to make decisions from the very beginning of a project, so that they can raise concerns and adjust it to meet their needs. The goal is for people to develop their own vision of the present and the future, to increase their capacity for analyzing everyday problems, their self-esteem, and their commitment to community participation in the project and beyond.

Because of the historic subordination suffered by women, they are often not taken into account and can often feel that they have no right to an opinion or to express their needs and desires. This means it is critical to create mechanisms and to offer training that allow women to strengthen their self-esteem, increase their possibilities for participating, and ensure that their contributions and work are valued. This facilitates a process where both women and men make decisions and contribute ideas, while recognizing and appropriating their own reality.

This methodological position guided project work from early on, and the perspective of making the community the decision maker is today called empowerment. Both men and women were active subjects and not simply objects of the project, transforming community participation in the project "owned" by the technical team to a sense of ownership in which the external experts only facilitated the process.

Beyond Simply Including Women

While the theoretical reference point at the start of the first phase of the project was Women in Development (WID; Moser and Levy 1986), the project team felt that this approach had a number of limitations and was not the most appropriate. We did not think that separate spaces for women were needed because often this had meant isolating them from important discussions and decisions. Nevertheless, we were conscious that participating on an equal footing with men would be very difficult because of their subordination as women. Based more on the project team's own experiences and common sense rather than on a theoretical and methodological conception, a series of conceptual and technical tools were designed that over time have come to be known as the gender equity approach.

The main project team was made up of civil and sanitation engineers and myself, an anthropologist, with assistance at different points from specialists in the fields of medicine, sociology, and economics. As well as interdisciplinary, the group was mixed in terms of sex: the two engineers were men and the anthropologist was a woman. Because the team had never worked together before, a first step was sharing "know-how" among the team members. Respect for the different disciplines was crucial at this stage, especially not undervaluing the social work compared with the engineering work. The information sharing made it possible to present the team as a unit before the community because the anthropologist knew how to install a pump, pour a concrete slab, drive a car, and had the same duties and opportunities as her male teammates, and the engineers could provide training in an accessible language, valued participatory processes, and were involved in community activities. Despite these accomplishments, some inequities in the project team could not be overcome. For example, even with the same job and equivalent academic degrees, salaries were not the same for the women and the men who made up the technical team.

The communities where we worked had strong features of *machismo,* and thus the abilities of each member of the team to address all aspects of the project became very important. The project team set an example by modeling situations and attitudes that were more respectful of women. For instance, at first, people in the communities (especially the men) expressed fear of getting into a car driven by a woman, but over time they realized that women could drive as well as men. The anthropologist's participation in the project showed that a woman could work outside the home and still be a good mother and a wife. The more equitable power relations within the team were essential in creating favorable conditions for the project. As one woman said, "the example begins at home," and this was something that the team always projected: women and men could do any kind of work; space for dialogue and mutual respect were possible; leadership was to be fostered regardless of sex; women's work outside and inside the home was valued, and so forth.

The fact that the team was mixed also made it possible for the project to have an effect on spaces and topics that were generally off limits for men. The woman anthropologist could enter homes and speak with women about sensitive topics such as sexuality and domestic violence. This presence in private spaces, in gatherings of women, gave the project a different dimension, because women felt more at ease speaking to another woman.

Epidemiological Diagnostics and Studies

Diagnoses carried out before project implementation covered the traditional kinds of information usually gathered on the make-up and composition of families, aspects of production, the physical and sanitary conditions of the environs but also included two elements that were rather novel for the time for this type of project:

1. *The identification of the most frequent diseases and their causes:* Through the diagnoses, we learned that a majority of both women and men interviewed did not understand the connection between water-borne diseases and the water they drank. More than 75 percent of the population interviewed believed that worms were caused by eating too many sweets; hepatitis was caused by too close contact with a Nicaraguan;[3] and "malaria" was a man from the Ministry of Health who came to the community on a motorcycle.

2. *Cultural uses of water:* The cultural practices associated with the use and handling of water and wastewater, as well as with the handling and disposal of solid waste, were identified. Very few people interviewed (less than 5 percent) expressed any need to improve hygiene, to increase the distance separating latrines and the wells, or to prevent animals from having contact with the utensils used to draw water. People also declared that the water they drank was "clear and fresh" and that therefore it was not necessary to treat it before drinking it.

However, the data on water contamination (more than 2,400 fecal coli forms per 100 cc) and the high incidence of gastrointestinal and other water-borne diseases led us to design a strategy that made explicit the connection between water quality and the incidence of diseases. The project team decided to carry out a series of training and sensitivity-raising activities to establish "structuring concepts" to clarify the relationship between certain diseases and water before beginning improvements of existing sanitation. Work on the structuring concepts would be fundamental if the technological introductions were to become permanent and prevent the project from becoming one more case where pumps were installed and discarded as soon as they failed.

The first activity was to demonstrate the existence of the microscopic world and how something which "couldn't be seen" was the cause of most of the diseases. For this, the team designed what we called "the flea technique." Taking a microscope to the communities, team members asked people: "Do you want to bet that the flea has a moustache?" Of course most people responded "no" until they looked through the microscope and saw that indeed fleas have a "moustache." This was the springboard for a discussion about the many things in our environment that cannot be seen with the naked eye alone. Another variant of this technique was to observe the feet of an ant and to see that they are covered with "hair."

Once we introduced this structuring concept, team members showed community residents samples of water and human excrement so that they could see the amoebas and the worm larvae and then explained the life cycle of bacteria or protozoa and how they produced diseases in people. This training allowed for important changes to take place in people's conduct, above all among the women, who were in charge of handling water in the households and who taught their children hygiene. For example, many people moved their latrines further away from wells even though this was not part of the project, and sources of contamination such as puddles of water around the house were eliminated. As the project developed, epidemiological studies of its effects showed that the introduction of the new pumps and sanitation improvements of wells, along with changes in the handling and disposal of water, had a substantial effect on people's health.

In discussions with women, they commented that the project had indirectly brought advantages, such as the reduction in the time and money invested in caring for sick people, in the time devoted to getting water, in vaginal infections, in muscular ailments associated with hauling water, and in the number of flies and mosquitoes in their houses. Generally this type of effect is not analyzed in water supply projects, even though they are among the most important for women.

Production of Educational Materials

An important strategy was the design of educational materials in the form of manuals and didactic tools for the workshops. Care was taken both with language as well as with the use of images in the production of these materials to incorporate the following criteria:

• Nontraditional male and female roles. For example, the illustrations showed men sweeping, caring for children, and assisting children with their homework. Women were shown working on the installation of hand pumps, doing carpentry, masonry, and working in laboratories.

• An equal proportion of women and men in the training manuals illustrations and in posters. Older adults, youths, children, and different ethnic groups were also included.

• Gender-neutral language. The male image was not used as "the universal representation" and nouns such as "human beings" or "people" were used. Because nouns in Spanish have gender, references to traditional tasks included both masculine and feminine forms.

• Drawings in the illustrations avoided caricatures. Images of people depicted real physical attributes such as pretty, handsome, good looking, and so on.

• Figures of men and women appeared in domestic scenes as well as outside the home. At no time were women circumscribed exclusively to private space.

• The material was designed with illustrations so that people who could not read could follow all of it.

These features resulted from what the project team learned during the six years of project implementation and entailed very close work between the team and the graphic designers. With the latter, we analyzed the stereotypes that they used in illustrations and that they viewed as "normal" and as having "nothing wrong." To a certain extent, we were training the people responsible for the material at the same time as the illustrations were being done. As a team, it was also necessary to develop skills to really "see" the images as they appeared to other eyes.

Other important criteria also affected the training materials. The publications had to be a size that allowed women and men to fold them and carry them in the pockets of their pants, aprons, or shirts. The paper used for the publications had to withstand heavy use, such as when a pump was repaired and the manual was placed on the ground or when the women placed the manual in front of themselves while they did laundry.

Training

A fundamental axis of the project's work was training aimed at two populations: communal facilitators and the communities themselves.[4] Beginning in 1989 (the second phase), the project team designed a program to train facilitators so that the communities would be able to manage their water supply and sanitation systems once the project team left. Courses were offered on the use of ferro-cement to re-cover hand-dug wells; on the installation and repair of the hand pumps; and on organization, environmental sanitation, hygiene and health, and administration. Facilitators, half of them women and half men, were selected on the basis of their level of participation in the first phase of the project.

All the communal facilitators were given tools and techniques to help them master giving public presentations. Though the training was the same for the whole group, the team worked with the women in informal sessions to deal with their fears of speaking in public and of exercising leadership. Many were afraid to talk about "technical things" or to use "pretty words." At all times, the leaders of the training process would encourage them to participate and discuss issues during the meetings and would reinforce their importance in the process.

These types of fears were not apparent among the men at the beginning. But once the training was well under way, we realized that one of the men did not know how to read or write and that others found it difficult to make public presentations. This phenomenon, linked to their masculine identity and mainly a product of stereotypes such as "men are supposed to know everything" or "men are very macho" and "should not be afraid of anything," required specific strategies. Among the actions taken were providing assistance in arranging to take adult literacy classes and holding separate meetings with the men where they could express their fears.

The women began to change with the training. The way they spoke and expressed themselves and even their personal relationships within the household began to shift, placing them in conditions and positions of greater equity. Many other changes took place as well:

• Husbands began to show that they were proud of their wives' work as communal facilitators and how they talked about "other things" when they came home: "If I had known how interesting my wife would become, I would have supported her doing something like this a long time ago. She even stopped getting sick with nerves."

• Some husbands of the future community facilitators began to share household chores so that their wives could attend the training sessions.

• Some of the husbands faced social pressure and mockery from other men in the community: "Who knows what their wives are doing, going here and there in a car!" This had to be discussed openly and individually in each case and the spouse was invited to participate in the project's activities.

• Fifteen years after the project was implemented, we were able to corroborate that the daughters and sons of many of the women facilitators were motivated by their mothers' experience to get university educations and search out other opportunities.

The process of training communal facilitators fulfilled its main purpose, as it successfully left people in the community responsible for the "technical" implementation of the project. But the training of both male and female facilitators transcended the technical aspects, changing their relationships with their community and families, as women well as men began to be respected and admired by other community members. Today, many of them are considered community leaders.

Women facilitators were affected beyond what we could have imagined. They began to make decisions about their bodies, such as dressing differently or deciding how many children they wanted to have. One of them put it this way: "the project not only taught me how to speak in public, it taught me to speak in my home, to say what I like or don't like; the project gave me the right to speak."

With the development of gender theory, a distinction has been articulated between basic needs and strategic needs (Moser and Levy 1986), with emphasis placed on the importance of the latter. Moser and Levy's work asserts that the processes of satisfying practical and strategic needs can take place simultaneously. During this project, we learned that in conditions of extreme poverty, communities need to first take care of their most elemental needs. However, the challenge for project technicians is to respond to those most heartfelt needs at the same time as working on impacting the more strategic dimension. The need for potable water and better sanitation conditions affected issues such as leadership, rights, participation, and self-esteem.

Training in the communities reproduced in many ways what we learned in educating the communal facilitators. Nontraditional methods were used to announce meetings so as to reach the greatest number of people. For example, school homework notebooks were used to invite women to meetings, and project staff contacted women and youth where they gathered (by the river where they washed and on football fields). Childcare was provided during the workshops, and lunches or dinners prepared enabling the whole family to attend the training. "Health weeks" were planned with poetry contests, puppet and theater workshops, dances, bingo games, and even football tournaments.

The project also offered training on nontraditional topics. For example, separate teams of men and women learned how to assemble and install a hand pump. It is interesting that women followed the steps indicated in the manuals more carefully than the men as they lacked the confidence that men had (the men felt familiar with the type of work and believed that they did not need to follow the written procedures). As a result, a significant proportion of the pumps that groups of women put together were installed and worked better than those men put together. This made it possible gradually to overcome the myth that women could not work with tools and technical equipment.

Our work on the "Handpump Technology" project was based on a gender equity perspective and was something more than merely "women's activity for women." This approach meant recognizing the unequal power relationships between genders and undertaking a process that would involve women and men in building equitable and participatory relationships in the project. The strategies in very diverse communities like the ones we worked in must make this heterogeneity visible and address it explicitly. Materials and spaces must be designed in such a way that they are as inclusive as possible and allow project team members to get close to the realities of youths, children, and women.

It is fundamental for initiatives or projects that address the topic of water to have the necessary time and funds to promote equity. The benefits or the goods the project produces (such as credit, materials, training, and payments for work) must be available to both men and women and benefit them equitably. This means recognizing that some women have limitations in terms of time and mobility and that these must be considered to ensure their participation (childcare, appropriate schedules).

We learned how necessary it was to have information that is disaggregated by sex to form a mixed team that facilitated entering both male and female spaces and to use nontraditional materials to gather information (e.g., meetings where flannel boards, microscopes, and methods like the flea technique were used).

In the sphere of initiatives to provide water and sanitation, services must try to make opportunities equal by means of strategies that integrate men and women and that foster women's autonomy. In this case, equal opportunities were achieved by training a group of fifteen men and women as communal facilitators; the participation of women in the spaces of traditional power (organizations and assemblies) and of nontraditional power (administration of revolving funds); and the involvement of women as planners and agents of change, not merely as passive spectators. Providing training that was aimed beyond the acquisition of technical skills and that included the development of organizational and decision-making capacities (empowerment) was also important.

Some topics that we would today call "masculinity" were touched on in a very incipient way. But these topics were fundamental, both for achieving the fullest participation of women (because what was involved was convincing and working with their husbands and companions) and for making it possible for the men to break down some of the fears and myths associated with masculinity (e.g., having to know it all, speaking well in public, the fear of losing power).

We learned that information must be accessible and available equally both to women and men; that it was necessary to have practical didactic methods (e.g., the flea technique) adapted to the community's characteristics; and that it was necessary to maintain two-way communication channels between the "external technical experts" and the "local technical experts."

The project team learned to take advantage of the possibilities offered by water and health projects to work in areas not previously assigned as either male or female activities. This was achieved by training women and men in nontraditional topics (pump installation, handling and repair, sanitary recovering of wells, bacteriological control, and disinfection systems).

When it came to implementing the project, at no time did the project team raise the topic of power relationships as it might be analyzed today. Worth noting, however, is the process of changes in attitudes both at the community level and at the personal level was not as conflict-ridden as other experiences in Latin America. We think that this was due basically to three factors:

1. The project team worked at all times with mixed groups. There were no separate women's meetings, but rather communal meetings were then subdivided by sex. This gradually eliminated some of the fear among the men about "what was done with and told to the women." The discussion spaces with women were more informal (e.g., by the river where they washed clothes).

2. The project took place over a significant period of time, and therefore the changes occurred slowly. This made it possible to learn about and work on the problems that arose in power relations. In this regard, it was important that the male technical experts could talk with other men from the community about the importance of the women's work, especially because "the engineers" were highly respected by the men of the communities.

3. The space of water provision was a feminine space par excellence (drawing water, washing clothes, carrying water, water storage). Therefore, the men did not express or did not have fears regarding women's participation or decision making in that area. This point was fundamental because by starting with an element that was recognized as culturally feminine, there were no contradictions. As the project advanced and women gradually took on other responsibilities, the community had "accepted" seeing women in greater leadership roles.

PART FOUR

Participation and Cultural Change

Among the key principles of the gender perspective is that community participation is crucial for attaining development with equity. This holds true when the gender perspective is applied to the water sector as well. However, community participation cannot be conceived of solely on a pragmatic or instrumentalist basis. Rather, it must be seen as a fundamental right of all citizens—the right to intervene actively and exercise power in all social processes that affect their well-being.

With this in mind, this section offers three case studies that analyze the process of participation of women in the use and management of water resources at the local level, beyond the world of policies, programs, and projects. These three studies signal that across Latin America cultural changes are taking place in women's identities, roles, and their exercise of citizenship. These chapters demonstrate that cultural change occurs in a seamless, multi-directional and continuous process where traditional norms and customs in regards to water persist alongside new forms of action that redefine daily life, gender relations, and the role of women with respect to water in their communities.

9 Women, Equity, and Household Water Management in the Valley of Mexico

During everyday conversations and public meetings in the community of La Purificación Tepetitla, people commonly say that *"el agua es la vida del pueblo"* ("water is the life of the *pueblo*").[1] La Purificación Tepetitla consists of approximately 6,000 residents living in the northeastern foothills of the Valley of Mexico, just outside Mexico City. Over the last few decades, the foothills region has developed stronger ties to Mexico City, and as a result, La Purificación Tepetitla and most other formerly small, *campesino* communities have grown rapidly and become more urbanized. In this periurban context, the management of piped water supplies for household use has emerged as a prominent community issue.[2]

Although men occupied the formal positions of authority over the community's piped water system when it was first installed in the 1980s, women increasingly ensure that water is distributed equitably to all households that pay user fees and fulfill customary labor obligations. More women are being elected to the community's Drinking Water Committee (Comité de Agua Potable) and various other civil and religious posts previously held by men. Women's increasing participation in water management has been a central aspect of local efforts to counter the negative effects of Mexico's economic crises and the neoliberal reforms of water management. By drawing particular attention to women's participation, the present analysis reveals how women extend the seemingly private issue of household water consumption into the public sphere and, in the process, help create a more equitable approach to water management.

Women and Water in the Valley of Mexico

The Valley of Mexico faces an environmental health crisis due to water shortages, water pollution, and ground subsidence as aquifers become depleted (Kasperson et al. 1996; Melville and Cirelli 2000; Restrepo 1995). The metropolitan area of Mexico City dominates the valley, with nearly 20 million inhabitants (INEGI [Instituto Nacional de Estadística, Geografía e Informática] 2000). Rapid population increases combined with water scarcity have led to the development of one of the world's most elaborate and costly hydraulic infrastructures, carrying water from distant sources both inside and outside the valley (Bribiesca Casterjón 1960; Cirelli 1996; Flores 1995; Melville 1996a, 1996b). Despite these efforts, many people in poorer neighborhoods have scarce amounts of water for drinking, bathing, preparing food, and disposing of human waste (Flores 1995; García Lascuráin 1995). These amounts often fall short of the thirteen gallons of water per day that, according to Gleick (1996), is the minimum amount of water humans need. In contrast, households in Mexico City's wealthier neighborhoods often receive more than ten times that volume of water per day, with municipal governments often heavily subsidizing costs. Because the burdens associated with water scarcity fall disproportionately on poor and powerless groups, some observers argue that the current situation violates basic human rights (Restrepo 1995).

Though access to and control of water is often determined along class lines, and water is an increasingly scarce and costly resource for poor Latin Americans, recent studies in Mexico and elsewhere in Latin America affirm the importance of understanding the intersection of class-based inequality with gender differentiation in household water management as women often shoulder the greatest burden of inadequate water supplies (Bennett 1995a, 1995b; Scheper-Hughes 1992; Tortajada 2000; Whiteford 1997). In the Valley of Mexico, women of poorer urban and periurban neighborhoods constantly expend considerable time, money, and labor ensuring their households have enough water for domestic use (Flores 1995; García Lascuráin 1995). These women, however, are rarely elected public water administrators and have little access to the public institutions that oversee piped water service. This exclusion leads some women to engage in individual and collective efforts, including participating in social movements, protests, and community mobilizations to gain access to adequate household water supplies (Bennett 1995a, 1995b; Cox and Annis 1988; Elmendorf 1981; Ennis-

McMillan 2001a; Morgan 1993; Scheper-Hughes 1992; Tortajada 2000; Whiteford 1997). This reflects broader Latin American trends in the wake of the economic crises of the 1980s, where women simultaneously reinforce and transform their traditional roles as wives and mothers to gain access to basic necessities such as water (Escobar 1992; Escobar and Alvarez 1992; Jelín 1990; Safa 1990; Stephen 1992). Because women often have the primary responsibility for managing crucial household resources, their increasing role outside the household in accessing such resources indicates how social change and power struggles over household consumption spill over into social relations outside the domestic sphere.

As development specialists explore how to incorporate women into water management, it is critical to realize that installing piped water systems involves more than simply applying engineering principles and transferring new technology. Water control systems are also cultural systems that emerge from particular histories, meanings, and practices. In the communities of the northeastern foothills of the Valley of Mexico, community-based water management is formed by a culture and history of irrigation that emerges from community efforts to counter outside threats to local control of crucial water resources. Ethnographic studies in the region reveal how communities manage piped household water supplies in a centralized and communal fashion rather than using market-based principles of distribution common to urban areas (Aldana Martínez 1994; Gómez Sahagún 1992; González Rodrigo 1993; Palerm Viqueira 1993, 1995; Rodríguez Rojo 1995; Sokolovsky 1995; Viqueira Landa 1994; Wolf and Palerm 1955). Local authorities mobilize corvee labor for piped water projects, withhold a household's water supply to impose sanctions if needed, and use traditional principles of resource distribution that emphasize equitable water distribution. These cultural values can potentially overshadow traditional gender hierarchies that have limited women's past participation in water management.

This type of water management is embedded within La Purificación Tepetitla's civil-religious hierarchy of offices called *cargos*. I use hierarchy here to refer to the fact that all eligible community members rotate from lower to higher civil and religious *cargos* and through this process, gain prestige and influence in their community.[3] Civil *cargos* are usually tied to Mexico's system of *municipio* (municipal) and state government institutions, while religious *cargos* stand outside formal political institutions and entail sponsoring annual religious festivals. Civil officers serve three-year terms and oversee the direct management of the community's resources, including water. Religious officers serve one-year terms and are responsible for maintaining the church property and sponsoring the annual fiestas. Civil and religious officers typically work together to enforce local customs that link water management with *cargo* service.

Electing residents to civil and religious *cargos* involves different procedures, but residents characterize this election process as *parejo* (even or equal) as each household is required to serve. For the election of people to civil *cargos*, the community holds an assembly and votes on the slate of candidates composed of residents from households appearing next on the roster. If the assembly approves the slate, the new officers serve three-year terms in the *delegación*. Every three years, the selection process rotates among all eligible households. For the election of people to religious *cargos*, the religious officers at the end of their one-year term select the next year's group of religious officers from the households appearing next on the roster, which means that individuals cannot be elected for consecutive terms. Furthermore, individuals are rarely elected for a subsequent term until all eligible households have taken their turn at fulfilling their *cargo* obligations. Individuals cannot hold a civil and a religious post at the same time, but a person can hold a religious *cargo* one year and within a year or two be elected to a civil *cargo*. The one-year religious posts are considered less burdensome but have less authority and prestige than the three-year civil posts.

Ethnographic research both in the northeastern foothills and elsewhere in Mexico suggests that traditional gender differentiation has limited women's participation in civil and religious *cargos* until very recently, and my own research in La Purificación Tepetitla has found that women had begun to be elected to religious *cargos* but not civil *cargos* (Ennis-McMillan 2001b). Nevertheless, recent transformations in the *cargo* system have opened new opportunities for women to have a more direct influence on water management.

A Growing Foothill Community

This chapter draws from ethnographic research I conducted while living in La Purificación Tepetitla during extended stays in 1993 and 1995–1996 as well as during brief visits in 2000 and 2002. In this analysis, I draw from participant-observation data on the use of water in daily life, as well as frequent informal conversations with residents. I conducted semistructured interviews with civil and religious office holders, both male and female, and collected information during Drinking Water Committee meetings, policy discussions, community assemblies, and construction and maintenance projects. I also consulted local and national archives on water management.

La Purificación Tepetitla is part of the municipality *(municipio)* of Texcoco in the state of Mexico and lies about eighteen miles northeast of the center of Mexico City, at about 7,800 feet above sea level. Outside the community nucleus, at a lower elevation, La Purificación Tepetitla possesses an *ejido*, which is cooperative agricultural land, and a small residential area called a *colonia*. The climate is semiarid, with an average annual precipitation of twenty-five inches and an average temperature of 59 degrees Fahrenheit (Aldana Martínez 1994; INEGI 1995). The rainy season runs from June through September, with little or no precipitation during the rest of the year.

For most of the twentieth century and until the 1970s, La Purificación Tepetitla was a small *campesino* community, whose physical separation from Mexico City by Lake Texcoco contributed to the persistence of the region's rural character. The population was between 500 to 750 people, held steady by constant out-migration and little inmigration. People lived in a semidispersed agricultural setting, cultivated private and *ejido* lands, and survived on a mixture of subsistence and commercial agriculture and wage labor. Men overwhelmingly, if not exclusively, headed households.

During the 1970s, the region's population grew rapidly due to inmigration of people primarily from Mexico City and other urban areas in the Valley because of expanded wage labor opportunities in industry, transportation, services, and government for both men and women, as well as improvements in transportation and increased educational opportunities (Aldana Martínez 1994; Palerm Viqueira 1993; Pérez Lizaur 1973; Rodríguez Rojo 1995). In this new economic context, more women engaged in wage labor, increasingly establishing female-headed households. Population increases in the region accelerated after the government resettled thousands of families displaced by Mexico City's 1985 earthquake. In the late 1980s, a highway built across the dry bed of Lake Texcoco linked Texcoco and the metropolitan area of Mexico City even more closely.

La Purificación Tepetitla is no longer a small community of people who for generations have relied on agriculture to make a living but rather has grown to about 6,000 people in approximately 1,200 households located in a more compact and urbanized space. Newcomers currently represent over half the population and about 37 percent of the community's residents earn wages primarily outside the community (INEGI 2000). While a third of the households have access to private agricultural land, *ejido* land, or irrigation water, only 9 percent of the households rely significantly on agriculture (Ennis-McMillan 1998). Over time, residents have divided privately held agricultural plots and converted the land to residential use, giving some to their children and selling plots to newcomers. The main road has been paved and both public and private transportation connects urban centers. Plans are underway to pave two other main roads, and the community now has street names, house numbers, electricity, streetlights, telephone booths, and household telephone service. It also has a health clinic staffed by a medical student and a nurse, a pharmacy, a kindergarten, a primary school, a secondary school, several restaurants, and numerous small stores and other small businesses.

Developing a Piped Household Water System

Because of La Purificación Tepetitla's foothill location, it lacks both local surface water and easily obtainable groundwater sources, so for centuries, people in this and nearby foothill communities relied on surface water channeled downhill from distant mountain springs (Lane Rodríguez 1994). Most of this water was used for irrigation but a small portion was simply channeled to each household for domestic use. Before installing the piped water system, the surface water was the primary source for both irrigation and household purposes for every family and was commonly referred to as "*la vida del pueblo.*" Traditionally, men administered the surface water by serving on the Irrigation Committee, paying irrigation fees, monitoring irrigation flows, reporting problems to male authorities, and providing corvee labor for the canals and reservoirs. A separate system for managing household water supplies did not exist. Each household simply channeled a small portion of irrigation water into reservoirs that held water for drinking, bathing, doing laundry, and other basic necessities. Women rarely took on water management responsibilities outside the household and usually only then to assist male family members.

In the late 1970s, as the surface water began to dwindle and become more polluted by upstream communities, La Purificación Tepetitla sought ways to secure a reliable source of groundwater for its growing population. The community nucleus rests on a large, solid bed of volcanic rock, which has meant that numerous attempts to drill deep wells have failed. Eventually in 1980, the community secured rural development funds to drill a well in the *ejido* and install a piped system up to individual households in the foothills. Monetary contributions were collected from irrigation users, and a temporary and voluntary Pro-Drinking Water Committee (Comité de Pro-Agua Potable) formed to collect contributions from domestic users. Two men and one woman initially headed this committee, demonstrating that women have been involved since the piped water system was installed. In 1980 when the system was completed, a local civil officer oversaw the piped water accounts. At that point, 100 households out of a total of about 250 households were connected to the piped water system. A portion of the groundwater was supposed to serve as an auxiliary irrigation supply, but community assemblies later voted to reserve the groundwater for household purposes and only use surface water for irrigation. In 1982, the community established the Drinking Water Committee as a separate set of elected civil *cargos* to deal with the increasing demands of an expanding piped water network. By 2002, almost all the community's 1,200 households were connected to the piped water system and only 270 households received surface water for irrigation (the remaining 930 households did not irrigate any land). As urbanization has accelerated, the piped household water supply has increased in importance and has now replaced water for agricultural irrigation as *"la vida del pueblo."*

The piped water system pumps groundwater electrically from a well and then channels it to four stone holding tanks located at a higher elevation. From there, the water travels by gravity through smaller pipes and hoses into individual households. The community routinely rations the piped water to save on the costs of running the electric pump, and each section of the community receives at least two hours of water four days a week. Most households store water in rooftop water tanks as well as in plastic containers, metal drums, and plastic buckets. In addition, family compounds usually have a *pileta*, which is a rectangular concrete water reservoir used for doing laundry and washing dishes outdoors. Only about 20 percent of the houses have large, underground cisterns that hold 250 to 800 gallons of water. According to my estimates, an average household without a cistern typically has the capacity to store about 35 to 50 gallons of water per person per day in rooftop tanks and indoor and outdoor reservoirs. Without a public sewage system, most houses have septic tanks and also drain gray wastewater onto their properties, into irrigation canals, or into the streets.[4]

Household Water Management

Formal management of the piped water system is incorporated within the local set of thirty-four civil *cargos*, which are elected, unpaid municipal offices rotated every three years as an obligation among all households. Until 2000, however, only men were elected to civil *cargos*, and established residents with both irrigation water and *ejido* land have tended to hold the top civil *cargos* while newer residents, even those who receive irrigation water, usually hold the lesser ones. The entire group of civil officers is called the *delegación*, which is headed by three officers called *delegados* who oversee three administrative committees: the Drinking Water Committee, the Irrigation Committee, and the Citizen's Participation Committee. The three *delegados* and the three top officers of the Citizen's Participation Committee are elected locally, but they are also sworn in as *municipio* officers at the *municipio* of Texcoco. The Drinking Water Committee and the Irrigation Committee are independent of the *municipio*, which some community authorities suggest is important for maintaining local autonomy in water management. All *delegación* officers participate in developing and enforcing water policies. In addition, the *delegación* supervises a civil patrol as well as other lower-level posts and also coordinates activities with *ejido* representatives and religious officers.

Since 1994, the Drinking Water Committee has charged each household Mex$25 per month along with other administrative fees (US$1.00 = Mex$9.5). The committee's other tasks include charging for connections to the water system, repairing the system, and organizing corvee labor for water projects. In coordination with other civil officers, the committee also makes requests for funds and materials to various *municipio*, state, and federal agencies, which male officials invariably staff.

Even though a household water connection requires monthly payments, access to piped water is not simply a service for which one pays money but rather is determined by customary law embodied in local *usos y costumbres* (use rights and customs). An individual maintains water rights as long as he or she fulfills customary obligations, which include paying water fees as well as contributing unpaid labor for water projects and fulfilling civil and religious *cargo* service when called upon. To request a water connection with the civil authorities, the person must be a resident of the community and pay a connection fee. A series of community assemblies established a tiered system of charging higher connection fees for new residents because established residents became alarmed when people moved to the community and requested water connections without having made any contribution (in money or labor) to the initial installation of the water system and without fulfilling civil and religious *cargo* obligations. The policy allows established residents to be charged a lower connection fee than new residents precisely because of their other contributions. After the household connection fee is paid, local authorities draw up a document authorizing a household connection to the piped water system and requiring agreement with local *usos y costumbres*, although the specific rights and obligations are not listed. No outside government officials are involved in this process.

When the piped water system was first installed in 1980, men continued to manage the system and be the ones most likely to register a household connection in their names, just as they had with irrigation water. At that time, most households were male headed and men traditionally had taken care of water matters outside the house, such as paying water fees at the municipal offices. As a result, few water accounts were listed in a woman's name. In 1980, the first year that piped household water connections were registered, 100 households out of a total of about 250 households had piped water connections. The households without piped water continued to rely on the surface water for both irrigation and household consumption. Of the first 100 households to get the piped water connection, sixteen had their accounts listed in a woman's name, most of whom were widows, divorcees, or daughters of elderly parents. In all cases, the women were long-term residents living in an extended family whose income relied on a mixture of agriculture and wage labor.

By 1996, 865 households had piped water connections and 257 of these had the accounts listed in a woman's name. This reflects the growth in the number of female-headed households as well as a combination of other factors, including new economic opportunities for women and a traditional view of women as managers of household water. With an increasing number of women, both new and established residents, traveling to work in Texcoco and other nearby cities each day, more women have the ability to establish and maintain their own households in the community. In some cases, daughters with income from wage work have inherited family property formerly used for agriculture and built separate houses. In other cases, women moved from Texcoco and Mexico City to establish their own households in La Purificación Tepetitla. Widowed and divorced women are also listed in the Drinking Water Committee's account books as the head of the household. Still other cases involve daughters whose aging parents transferred the household's water connection to the daughter's name, and married women who inherited family property and were born in the community but their husbands were not. In these latter cases, the household usually registered the water connection in the woman's name because as an established resident, she is eligible for the lower household connection fee. Local water authorities also explain that some households register the irrigation water account in the man's name and the piped water account in the woman's name because women are more likely to be in charge of household water-related tasks.

Women's Water Interests

Regardless of the name on the household water connection, women and girls have significant water-related responsibilities: cleaning house, washing and ironing clothes, washing dishes, and cooking. Women also perform many important activities such as filling reservoirs, allocating water for domestic chores, rationing water during shortages, and making sure the household's monthly water fees are paid. Women link their private interests in household water use with the public administration of the piped water system through specific public activities. A woman who was particularly active in local water issues explained:

[W]ater probably interests us [women] more [than men] because we use it in everything, yes for everything. The man does not care. He just takes a bath and leaves and that's it. And not so with the woman, because the woman knows that everything, everything, everything in life that she does in the house is about water, is done with water. If we are going to bathe, if we are going to wash our hands, if we are going to wash a diaper, if we are going to prepare some tea, if we are going to wash a baby's bottle, everything, everything, everything is the responsibility of the woman.

In other interviews, both women and men suggested that because women take a major responsibility for managing household water, they are likely to speak out in public settings and take action on water-related issues outside the household. Women are the ones most likely to go personally to the civil offices to pay water fees and discuss water distribution problems with civil authorities, who are also often the women's kin, neighbors, or friends. Women regularly notify civil authorities of the failure of piped water to reach the house on time or in the allotted amount, leaks in the main water pipes, and improper use of water by other residents.

Women also regularly work as auxiliary civil officers to ensure fair distribution and fulfillment of monetary and labor obligations. They regularly vocalize concerns and attend community assemblies, reminding themselves and others that they have the primary responsibility of household tasks that require water. For example, at assemblies in 1995 during the economic crisis, women described the suffering they endured because of water shortages and helped form voluntary water commissions that went house to house to directly pressure residents to pay water debts.[5]

Women also increasingly join men in providing compulsory unpaid labor for water projects, called *faena*. Both men and women pointed out that an increasing number of women have the same community obligations as men because more have income and property as a result of the region's expanding wage economy. In some cases, access to wage jobs has allowed a greater number of women to gain use rights to water and other community resources. At several *faenas*, I observed women and girls hauling rocks, digging ditches, coordinating work groups, cleaning large water tanks, and laying water pipes. People explained that all households, including those headed by a widowed or divorced woman, had to fulfill these labor obligations or risk having local authorities fine them and even cut off their household's water connection.

Gender, Water, and the *Cargo* System

Local cultural values and practices regarding water management are particularly influential in how the community's traditional set of *usos y costumbres* links local water issues to *cargo* service. For most of the twentieth century, La Purificación Tepetitla's civil and religious *cargo* system followed the pattern reported for other rural areas of Mexico whereby only men held both civil and religious posts. The selection of *cargo* holders was rotated among households with irrigation water, which until the late 1970s included almost every household. In this sense, *cargo* service was a form of taxation on each household.

When the piped water system was installed in 1980, many households began relying on the piped groundwater for household use rather than the surface water from the irrigation system. In terms of the quality and quantity, the surface water was becoming an inadequate source of household water for the growing population. Because only irrigation users were obligated to fulfill *cargo* service, officials became concerned that eventually a significant number of households would benefit from community water resources without providing *cargo* service. Consequently, at a community assembly soon after the piped water system was installed in 1980, the community voted to require that all households connected to the piped water system fulfill civil and religious *cargo* obligations when it was their turn.

Residents who refuse to complete either civil or religious service when it is their turn risk having local authorities impose a variety of sanctions, the most severe of which has been to shut off a household's water supply. When I asked about the motivation behind changing the *cargo* election process by selecting candidates from the list of households with piped water connections rather than simply households with irrigation, people explained that, in accordance with local custom, it was only fair to require civil and religious *cargo* service from all households who benefited from the community's water. Again, following the same customary principle as was done with irrigation in previous decades, all residents who receive piped water must fulfill community obligations.

The change in how *cargo* officers are selected brought about by the installation of the piped water system set in motion a process whereby women eventually began to be elected to *cargos*. When changes in the election procedures were first instituted, the possibility of electing women to *cargos* did not seem to have entered into the discussion. Nevertheless, a few women were elected to lower-ranking religious *cargos* soon after the change was instituted in the 1980s, and over time, an increasing number of women have occupied both religious and civil *cargos*. The increasing participation of women in both religious and civil *cargos* seems to be an unintended consequence of emphasizing equitable procedures for selecting people for *cargo* service.

The first set of changes in the *cargo* system involved increasing the number of religious *cargo* officers elected each year from eight to forty. According to community authorities, electing more people to the religious *cargos* became necessary because the population was increasing and festival sponsorship was becoming too burdensome. Over time, with an increasing number of religious posts to fill and a greater number of women registered as heads of household, the candidates for a particular year increasingly come from female-headed households. Since the 1990s, in any given year, women have occupied a third to a half of the religious *cargos*.

When I inquired whether opposition had surfaced to electing women to religious *cargos*, some residents told me though there is always opposition to changing *cargo* customs, nobody could recall any major or sustained opposition to naming women to religious *cargos*. The notion of having a selection system that is *parejo* seems to have overshadowed concerns about traditional gendered notions of *cargo* service. Furthermore, increasing the number of religious *cargos* has meant that women could participate with men rather than replace them.

Changes in the election process for civil *cargos* came about more slowly than for religious *cargos* and women were not immediately elected. The community continued to elect only men from established families to the higher-ranking civil *cargos*, which sometimes involved skipping over individuals whose names appeared next on the roster. This election pattern seems related to traditional gender norms that tend to equate males with public leadership positions, particularly the *delegados* and other posts with direct ties to the *municipio*. In addition, electing male residents with ties to local agriculture and the use of irrigation water concentrates authority in those residents who have experience with communal water management.

Nevertheless, the entrance of women in lower religious *cargos* of the civil-religious hierarchy eventually led to women occupying higher civil *cargos* with direct responsibility over water management. By the year 2000, when it came time to elect individuals to civil posts, many candidates included women who had previously participated in the *cargo* system as religious officers. Thus, a new generation of women began entering local public office in 2000, when they were elected to nine of the thirty-four civil *cargos* in the *delegación*, with seven of these posts part of the eighteen-member Drinking Water Committee. Of the top six committee posts, women were elected to serve as deputy president, secretary, and deputy secretary, and men made president, treasurer, and deputy treasurer, but it is worth noting that two of the three women holding top posts on the Drinking Water Committee were widows and the third, an unmarried woman who lived with her widowed mother. Three women were also elected to the committee's twelve auxiliary posts.[6]

In 2002, I conducted unstructured interviews with twenty-one individuals (thirteen men and eight women) who had been or currently were holding a civil or religious *cargo*. When I asked about the recent election of women to civil *cargos*, all twenty-one individuals felt it was a good idea to have women serving in the *delegación* and that it has now become part of selecting all civil and religious *cargo* holders. While reiterating the common perspective that each property owner who benefits from piped water and other community resources should be obligated to fulfill *cargo* obligations, respondents also explained that it would not be fair to only elect males to civil *cargos* because the community was growing rapidly and the roster of eligible households includes many female-headed households. Other individuals justified the election of women to the Drinking Water Committee by noting that women had already held lower posts of the civil-religious hierarchy and were therefore familiar with customary laws and practices that linked water management and *cargo* service. Respondents noted that the election of women represented a departure from prior practices and acknowledged that the community might be reluctant to elect women to the highest posts as *delegadas.* While a few people may oppose electing women, the slate of civil officers was elected by general consensus at a community assembly that both men and women attended and apparently nobody openly expressed opposition to electing women.

Men and women responded similarly about women's service on the Drinking Water Committee. For example, a man who was serving in the *delegación* said, "Women have their ideas as well, so it is good to include their participation. Each household should participate in the *delegación.*" Of the men who were former civil *cargo* holders, one said, "Women have property and interests similar to those of men;" another said, "It is fine that women express opinions in community assemblies, but they also have to work." Likewise, a woman serving on the Drinking Water Committee remarked, "Since elections go according to a roster of all households and I am a widow, what can you do?" A woman who had previously held a religious *cargo* said, "We all have our own ideas. Each person thinks differently, so it is good to include women."

Respondents explained that to be elected to the Drinking Water Committee, eligible candidates should have an understanding of community customs, be able to read and write, and have other administrative skills related to managing the piped water system. Many women, particularly established residents, were considered knowledgeable about community customs and had experience participating in *faenas*, community assemblies, and religious *cargos*. People also said that women have more education than in prior decades and noted that the women on the Drinking Water Committee were a retired elementary school teacher, a former office worker of a government agency, and a health care worker. In this sense, as women make gains in access to education, they are seen as more qualified for public office.

Just as with religious *cargos*, women's participation on the Drinking Water Committee did not entail women replacing men but increasing the number of posts. The increase in top posts allowed more officers to share burdensome administrative responsibilities. The participation of both men and women on the committee also meant that some tasks could be assigned based on local gender expectations. For example, on particularly busy days, male officers might carry out physically demanding tasks, such as inspecting the water pipes and cutting off household connections, while women stay at the administrative offices to collect water fees. A few women said that they had no option but to carry out the civil *cargo* themselves because they could not afford to pay a man to carry out the post. Other people commented that women who are retired and widowed often had the time needed to serve in the *cargo*. None of the twenty-one respondents interviewed expressed the notion that one's gender should limit service on the Drinking Water Committee, and some suggested that gender differentiation might be beneficial since women have considerable experience managing water inside the house, which gives them insights on managing the community's piped water supply.

Despite the emphasis on including everyone, the community tends to elect established residents, both men and women, to the highest religious and civil positions and thereby ensure that customary laws are more likely enforced. In this manner, the interests of men and women from established families converge and reinforce the traditional *usos y costumbres* that emphasize communal resource distribution rather than market-based mechanisms more commonly used in urban areas.

Gendering Water Management in Mexico

While men typically control water institutions in Mexico City, one of the world's largest cities, and in other urban and periurban areas of the Valley of Mexico, this study shows women in La Purificación Tepetitla are taking on greater public roles in water management even though, in prior decades, gender differentiation had limited their participation. Women's growing participation is tied to economic and social changes that give women access to wage jobs and education that allow them to become heads of households. Although women's status is changing, both men and women often commented that women's participation in local water management makes sense because of, and not despite, traditional gender norms and expectations. Women have extended their traditional roles as managers of water in the household to community water management as illustrated by the fact that most of the women elected to civil *cargos* for the first time were *named* to the Drinking Water Committee rather than *named* as heads of the *delegación* or as members of other administrative committees.

Though it is new to see women elected as public water officials in Mexico, my analysis resonates with other accounts of women's grassroots efforts in Latin America in which women expand rather than abandon their traditional roles as wives, mothers, and daughters (Bennett 1995a, 1995b; Elmendorf 1981; Ennis-McMillan 2001a; Flores 1995; García Lascuráin 1995; Jelín 1990; Safa 1990; Tortajada 2000). Such studies show that, particularly during economic downturns, women's participation in resource distribution helps counter market-based forces that favor wealthier individuals and groups. As the Mexican state seeks to privatize water management, women participate in local efforts to maintain community-based water management systems rather than allow the *municipio* or private companies to manage limited water supplies as a commodified service.[7] Women's ideas, experiences, and leadership are valued contributions to an effective bottom-up water management approach that emphasizes participation, equity, and cooperation rather than the top-down neoliberal policies that promote competition, commodification, and exclusion.

At the same time that women in La Purificación Tepetitla reinforce and extend traditional gender expectations, their involvement in water issues signals a transformation of women's traditional gender roles. In part, this change relates to the importance placed on a system that is *parejo*, which implies that all households should participate in a community-based form of water management. Women are listed as a significant number of piped water consumers and provide crucial money, time, and labor for operating the water system. The analysis also shows that women's increasing participation in water management is supported by better access to formal education and wage work and their subsequent ability to purchase property. In contrast to the situation reported for other urban women in Mexico, women in this foothill community have access to local water institutions and, for the moment, have been able to use avenues of action other than protest to address their grievances over water issues (see Bennett 1995a, 1995b; Flores 1995; García Lascuráin 1995). The local *cargo* system has a flexible and persistent character that has helped the community adjust to the population increases, economic crises, and neoliberal reforms that have rocked the region over the last couple of decades. In contrast to market-based initiatives promoted by government institutions, autonomous community institutions emphasize equity thereby making it possible for women to participate. To date, outside officials, programs, and institutions have neither promoted nor opposed increasing women's participation in water management at the community level. Nevertheless, in La Purificación Tepetitla, a community consensus has emerged that recognizes women's contributions to the process of managing a precious community resource. This case study underscores the importance of incorporating a principle of equity—including gender equity—as a way to enhance the sustainability of community-managed water systems.

The analysis also shows how gender intersects with class and residency status because men and women from established families with ties to agriculture hold the most authority over the administration of local water supplies and obligate newcomers to participate in community customs to maintain a household water connection. This former *campesino* community has limited any attempts by newcomers and outside entities to institute a market-based water distribution system that would tend to channel water to households of higher socioeconomic strata as occurs in other areas of the Valley of Mexico and in other parts of Latin America. In La Purificación Tepetitla, women use their new positions of authority to influence the course of community development, and they help create and enforce local nonmarket policies that regulate access to and distribution of limited water supplies. Women's ability to link private interests in household water with the public water administration has allowed them to exercise and acquire a certain measure of power. As the women in La Purificación Tepetitla show us, their management of water is often at the center of the life of any pueblo.

10 Women and Water in the Northern Ecuadorean Andes

I n the past decade, research findings have led governments and local agencies to recognize the important roles women play in providing water for domestic use as well as in broader water management (Johnson and Krogman 1993; Rodda 1991; Schaefer-Davis 1996). Though the third Dublin principle highlights women's central role in water provision and management, research on the specific roles, tasks, and functions of women in irrigated agriculture, especially in Latin America, is lacking. Most information on women and irrigation comes from Africa (Carney 1988; Jones 1986; Zwarteveen 1994, 1997) and Asia (Hart 1992; Zwarteveen and Neupane 1996), which, although valuable, does not directly apply to the Latin American context.

This case study explores the factors influencing *mestizo*[1] women's involvement in the use and management of two private irrigation canals in the northern Ecuadorean Andes, providing evidence of the obstacles women face in participating in irrigation management as well as demonstrating the heterogeneity affecting the participation of women in rural water management generally. The findings are drawn from research conducted during the summers of 1996 and 1997 (Bastidas 1999) and from a broader study of the livelihood systems of diverse, limited-resource farm households in Carchi, Ecuador, from 1996 to 1998 (Bastidas 2001).

Women and Irrigation in Latin American Farming Systems

Latin American peasant agriculture was first classified by Boserup (1970) as "male farming systems" in contrast to African countries, where evidence suggests that women are more involved in crop production, especially food crops (Brydon and Chant 1989; Rodda 1991). The argument underlying this classification is that in settled farming systems with extensive use of the plow, usually men do more farm work than women. Deere and León (1982), who analyzed material from Andean regions of South America with respect to women and farm production, later challenged this assertion, concluding that the term "family farming system" is more appropriate, as they found that women, in fact, do participate in most agricultural activities.

According to Brydom and Chant (1989), who argue that beliefs shaped by religion and culture are crucial in determining male and female roles in society, the predominance and influence of Hispanic colonial values and the Catholic Church in Latin America have shaped gender roles in *mestizo* communities, limiting women to the domestic or the reproductive sphere. Despite this finding, research in Ecuador and Peru supports Deere and León's position that women's role in agricultural production and irrigation is greater than generally assumed (Villalobos et al. 1993; Lynch 1991; Jacome and Krol 1994).

A study done by Villalobos et al. (1993) in the community of Camiraya Molino in Puno, Peru, shows that in most cases women are more involved than men in managing and using water for irrigation purposes. Women participate as much as men in constructing, cleaning, and maintaining irrigation systems. This finding was attributed in part to increasing male migration to the cities, which leaves women in charge of production activities. However, although women's involvement in agriculture and irrigation activities was high, women's participation in water-user organization meetings was low.

According to Lynch (1991), female participation in constructing and maintaining irrigation systems varies widely in the Andes. She found that in Cajamarca, Peru, women worked only for short periods on small jobs, and in Puno, Peru, more than half of some work crews were women. Jacome and Krol (1994) found similar results in the *mestizo* communities of Guano, Ecuador. Because of the difficult economic situation, men migrated to nearby cities to work as drivers or construction workers to supplement the household income. Only old men and farm owners with enough land to support their families continued to engage in agriculture. In both studies, the authors found women's involvement in irrigated agriculture varied according to the migration of men and household composition.

In the case study presented in this chapter, household composition and stage in the family life cycle are used as variables to group households and examine the factors influencing women's participation in water management. The use of family life cycle as a way to group households is based on the changes that occur in people's attitudes, responsibilities, and social behavior as they grow older. According to Lansing and Kish (1957), many of these changes may be associated less with the biological process of aging than with the influence of age upon the individual's family membership. Thus, the critical dates in the life of an individual may not be his or her birthday so much as the dates when changes occur in the family status, for example marriage or the birth of the first child.

Description of the Research Area

The site selected for this study is located in the province of Carchi in the northern Ecuadorean Andes. It is part of the El Angel River water use area, which in turn is part of the Mira River hydrological system, one of the largest watersheds in Ecuador. The social and ecological diversity of this area provides a rich context for research.

The watershed of the Angel River begins in the high *paramo*[2] of the "El Angel Ecological Reserve." From this point, numerous streams form the El Angel River and eleven different irrigation canals, which provide water for agriculture (Nuñez 1997). The irrigation canals and the Angel River cross through three distinct agro-ecological and demographic zones in their trajectory toward the Mira River. In the upper zone, 2,400 meters above sea level (masl), agricultural production consists of livestock, potatoes, and basic temperate grain cereals such as wheat and barley. Most residents of the upper zone are descendants of indigenous Andean groups, who share characteristics with local mestizos but also retain many customs of their indigenous ancestors. The middle zone, located between 2,000 and 2,400 masl, is warmer and drier, and here most agricultural production depends on irrigation. Maize, wheat, and barley are the common cereals, and horticultural crops, especially beans and fruits, tend to prevail over livestock. Mestizo and white farmers predominate in the area. In the lower zone (1,700–2,000 masl), which is largely populated by Afro-Ecuadoreans, sugar cane and horticultural crops are the main agricultural products (Nuñez 1997; Vallejo 1997).

This study focuses on the livelihood system of the mestizo farmers of the middle zone in the El Angel water use area. Two private irrigation systems, the Garrapatal and El Tambo canals, were selected for detailed study during two summer field visits (June–August of 1996 and May–August of 1997) and a combination of qualitative and quantitative methods was used. When appropriate, participatory tools for gathering and analyzing information were employed. For obtaining quantitative information, more traditional statistical methods were followed. The methods and tools used to collect and analyze information included secondary information, a *sondeo* (Hildebrand 1976), and household interviews, followed by activity profiles (Feldstain and Poats 1989) and twenty-four-hour accounts (Thomas-Slayter et al. 1993).

Irrigation and Water Management in the Ecuadorean Highlands

A Brief History

Most private canals in this area, in common with other irrigation systems found in the Ecuadorean highlands, have a long history. According to Le Goulven et al. (1989), irrigation systems in the Andean areas existed long before the arrival of the Spaniards in 1530 and perhaps before the arrival of the Incas from Peru around 1470. Most existing networks, however, were built between the seventeenth and eighteenth centuries, when large land owners forced native labor to dig and maintain canals regularly destroyed by bad weather, overflows, and earthquakes.

In the nineteenth and twentieth centuries, especially in the area of Carchi, land was gradually subdivided in response to popular pressure, and this division caused changes in water use. When the largest haciendas were divided among descendants, construction of new canals settled problems created by the division of water. At the same time, the *huasipungueros*[3] claimed their water rights, which they justified by their key role in constructing and maintaining the irrigation system (Le Goulven et al. 1989).

Although land partitioning and distribution had already started in Carchi, the Agrarian Reform of 1960–1970 reinforced this process. When the National Water Resource Institute (INERHI) was created in 1966, its main purpose was to resolve conflicts among irrigation network owners and other users. Though water resources were nationalized in 1972, this did not affect all of the irrigation systems and water infrastructure; existing private water users were required to declare their water rights to have them legalized. INERHI was responsible for checking and granting water concessions and assisting farmers who had been granted legal rights to use private canals to create the Juntas de Aguas or Water User Associations (WUA; Whitaker 1990). In 1994, as a result of state modernization policies, the responsibilities of INERHI were assumed by the Regional Development Corporations, one of which is CORSINOR (Regional Corporation for the Northern Sierra), which is in charge of managing public water resources of the northern highlands (Sotomayor and Garcés 1996). CORSINOR did not assume any responsibility for the private canals (such as Garrapatal and El Tambo) whose construction, maintenance, and management remained the sole responsibilities of the users and their WUAs.

Water Allocation

In the research area's irrigation systems, water is allocated and distributed according to concessions and schedules established when the WUAs were first formed during the 1970s. During that period, concessions and turns were approved by the Water Agency of the Ministry of Agriculture and supervised by the technicians of the former INERHI. The criteria used to establish water rotations are: the time, the area irrigated, and the concession of water to each branch. In some cases, farmers receive twelve hours of water per hectare every fifteen days, while in other areas, the "water turn" is six or seven hours per hectare every seven days. In any case, water turns respond far more to local *usos y costumbres* (uses and customs) than to government authorized arrangements, a situation illustrated in detail by Sotomayor et al. (1999).

El Tambo and Garrapatal Irrigation Systems

The Garrapatal canal takes water from the upper zone of the Angel River at an altitude of 2,665 masl. In its course (11 km.), it delivers water to eight different irrigation areas, where users are organized into eleven user groups. The presidents of these user groups join to form the water user association for the main canal. Canal users live in different communities located at the margins of the canal. At the time of this research, there were 236 households using the canal, which irrigates a total of approximately 651 ha, with field size from one to five hectares. Canal users' access to a major road, city, or market ranges from ten minutes to an hour by car.

Water intake for El Tambo canal is located at an altitude of 3,200 masl. In its course (28 km.), the canal crosses the middle zone, delivering most of the water to the irrigation areas of the lower part of this zone. Most of the users live in the community of El Tambo where they are organized into a single Water User Association. At the time of this research, the community had approximately 600 people grouped in 100 families who are more isolated than those using the Garrapatal canal. Two roads provide access to the community; both are dirt, and the time to the nearest city or market is about an hour by car. The fields in this area are larger than in Garrapatal, but the area irrigated is less, about 309 ha.

The Garrapatal and El Tambo Water User Associations

The boards of the Water User Associations (WUAs) responsible for the construction, maintenance, and management of the canals are comprised of an annually elected president, a vice president, a treasurer, and a secretary. Each WUA has statutes that govern their activities and list the concessions and water turns of its members.

According to the statutes of the Garrapatal and El Tambo associations, members should meet once every two months for discussion and to collect irrigation fees and once a year to elect new board members. This is hardly ever the case. In El Tambo, farmers meet twice a year or less, and the board members have held office for as long as eight consecutive years (1989–1996). It seems that the only occasion when all members meet is when the irrigation system ceases to function and urgent action is needed. Under the 1989–1996 board, in many cases individual board members whom the majority of farmers trusted dealt with problems. In Garrapatal, because the WUA includes eleven smaller user groups, farmers are forced to meet more often, in some groups as frequently as every two months. However, the main WUA board for the Garrapatal canal[4] meets only twice a year, and not all members are present. From 1994 to 1997, the same board members held office. The organizational weaknesses of these WUAs have forced both male and female members to often find informal ways to deal with their water problems.

Women's Participation in the El Tambo and
Garrapatal Water User Associations

Overall participation of both male and female members in the Water User Association meetings for the El Tambo and Garrapatal canals is low, and when there is a crucial meeting, usually a male member attends. In only 9 percent of the households interviewed as part of the household survey (n=60) did women attend these critical meetings (see table 10.1), even though the statutes permit either the husband or the wife, or both to represent their household's interests. However, attending meetings and discussing matters are considered male activities, and the cultural barriers women face when they are with men inhibit their participation.

Common reasons given for the low participation of women in the association meetings among the whole sample are:

Table 10.1 Participation of Women in Critical Water User Association Meetings

Participation in WUA meetings	Household groups				Whole sample % (No.)
	Group 1[a] % (No.)	Group 2[b] % (No.)	Group 3[c] % (No.)	Group 4[d] % (No.)	
Always participates	0 (0)	0 (0)	67 (4)	8 (1)	9 (5)
Only when husband or male family member can't go	52 (11)	11 (2)	33 (2)	21 (3)	31 (19)
Does not participate	48 (10)	89 (17)	0 (0)	71 (10)	60 (36)

Source: Bastidas 1999
Notes: a. Households with couples with children age thirteen or younger
b. Households with couples with no children under age fourteen
c. Female-headed households
d. Households with elderly couples

- Husbands do not like their wives going out at night.
- Women lack experience (for example, in managing meetings, talking in front of people).
- Women do not have the time.
- Both husband and wife are not needed at the meeting.

As expressed by one of the women:

Meetings are on Friday nights. At that time, after cooking for my husband and the kids, I still have a lot of work around the house. . . . There is no reason for both of us to attend the meetings. Even if I go to the meetings it's only to hear what the men have to say. Men are the ones who talk and discuss. They know what to say and how to say it.

To explore the factors beyond the cultural norms that prevent women's involvement in the WUA, households were grouped into four different clusters according to composition and family life cycle.[5] The groups were: (1) households with couples who have children age thirteen or under; (2) households with couples who have no children under fourteen; (3) female-headed households; and (4) households with elderly couples. Table 10.2 summarizes the characteristics of the different household groups.

In households with children age thirteen or under, the principal reason women gave for not participating was that they just do not have the time. This group spent most of their time in reproduction activities, such as taking care of the children, cooking, cleaning, and washing clothes, leaving limited time to devote to community meetings in general. Almost half of the women in this group mentioned they did not participate in WUA meetings, and the other half participated only when the husband or other male family member could not go (see table 10.1).

In households with couples who have no children under fourteen, the researchers expected higher female participation at the WUA meetings because women were not as constrained by childcare activities. This, however, turned out not to be the case—these women participated less than any other groups (89 percent did not participate) because their sons usually attended meetings when their husband could not (see table 10.1). In 69 percent of the households in this group, women opted to devote time to other income-producing activities (unrelated to irrigated agriculture) such as knitting, managing a small store, teaching, street vending, and farm labor for hire. Women usually controlled the cash from these activities, making an increased involvement in irrigated agriculture, where they had more limited control over the income, unattractive.

Female-headed households, which made up 10 percent of the households surveyed, showed the highest rates of participation (table 10.1) with 67 percent of the women in this group attending WUA meetings, usually accompanied by a male member of the household or by a male sharecropper.[6] The 12 percent of the households where the daughter of the household head was

Table 10.2 General Characteristics of the Four Household Groups

Characteristics	Household groups				Overall sample
	Group 1[a]	Group 2[b]	Group 3[c]	Group 4[d]	
Average age for husband/wife	47/41	58/56	—/54	70/65	57/52
Average number of household members	6	4.5	2.5	2.9	3.8
Number of households	21	19	6	14	60
% of households	35	32	10	23	100

Source: Bastidas 1999
Notes: a. Households with couples with children age thirteen or under
b. Households with couples with no children under fourteen
c. Female-headed households
d. Households with elderly couples

a single mother living with her parents are not included under the female-headed household category but represent a significant social phenomenon. The high number of young single mothers living with parents is due to the urban migration of young male adults and to the difficulties young couples face in starting and supporting a family through agriculture, given the low returns and the resources needed to start farming.

In households with elderly couples, 23 percent of the households surveyed, women mentioned that the main reasons for not participating were because they were too sick or too old to attend the meetings. When necessary, a son or male relative would represent the couple's interests at the WUA meetings. Only 8 percent of the women in this group always participated in the meetings (see table 10.1).

Grouping households based on household composition and family life cycle assists in understanding the factors that influence women's participation in WUAs. The analysis shows that the 9 percent of women who participated actively were mostly female heads of households along with a few older women. Multiple household chores constrained women who still had small children at home, and they attended meetings only when the husband could not go. Women with older children, who had more time to participate, preferred to focus on increasing their own incomes, and they also had elder sons who represented the husband at the meetings, freeing them from that responsibility.

Focus groups organized with women from Garrapatal and El Tambo indicated that not all women shared the same concerns and problems when it came to water use and management. Water quality, construction of reservoirs, and water allocation are three issues that were prioritized distinctly by different women.

People living along the irrigation canals use the water from these canals for home consumption,[7] bathing, and washing clothes either because they do not have access to tap water or because the municipal water systems do not work properly. Poor water quality is one of the main problems faced by these women. A woman user explains:

This is the third time this week that I have come to the canal to get water for the house. Although we have the installations for tap water, the system never works. Some people say that it's because the tanks that collect the water are being repaired but this happens all the time . . . so we are forced to use this water for everything. I also come to wash clothes here and sometimes my children come with me to take baths in the canal.

In the El Angel water use area, waste is usually dumped into canals and rivers, even though everybody is well aware that canal water is used for irrigation and households. Most of the waste from the city of El Angel (population of 6,000) goes directly into the El Angel River, including the waste from the city hospital. According to the nurses who work in the local health dispensary, the incidence of diseases caused by parasites is extremely high. They attribute this problem to the poor water quality and sanitary conditions. This situation primarily affects small children.

Though it is the responsibility of the municipalities and the local governments to provide clean water to the rural communities and small towns, in reality, local governments take action only if a well-organized group of people exerts political pressure. Because petitions backed by an organization stand a better chance of being heard than individual complaints, the WUAs are crucial for solving these problems. One of the user groups of the Garrapatal Canal, which consisted of forty-two members, persuaded the board of the local water association to lobby for tap water from the municipal authorities. When women from the other user groups of Garrapatal sought the same benefit, they found little support from the male members.

For another group of women, all female heads of households, the main problem was the lack of reservoirs. For these women irrigating at night presents major problems, which could be largely solved with the construction of small reservoirs. One of the women explained: "If my water turn is at night and I'm working alone, I simply lose the water. It is dangerous for women to go out in the middle of the night to irrigate. God knows what might happen!" The construction of reservoirs requires the organization of several farmers because one reservoir can provide enough water to irrigate several small farms or plots. One of the female heads of household explained that because cash investment is necessary, even if the local municipal authorities provided the machinery, many of the male farmers were not willing to make the investment. Therefore, the user group took no action.

Another issue related to water turns at night is organizing the schedule. A team of outside irrigation engineers proposed a reorganization of the schedule of water turns at one of the focus group meetings that the elderly women present immediately rejected. These women, who are part of the old *huasipungueros* who remain in the area, are determined to maintain the water rights and turns they have always had. The following situation illustrates this issue.

In El Tambo, the schedule of water turns listed in the statutes is different from the schedule that farmers follow. One of the farmers explained why:

After the association was formed, the members hired a man from Pimampiro[8] who along with one of the engineers from INHERI, elaborated the water schedule for the El Tambo Canal. After the Water Agency of the Ministry of Agriculture approved the schedule, as well as the water concessions for each of the farmers and the statutes of the association, the *huasipungueros* refused to follow the water turns that had been assigned to them. A group of fourteen *huasipungueros* and their families called a meeting and asked the other members to respect their water rights and leave the water rotation schedule for them the way it had always been. All the members agreed to their petition and since then we have been using the same turns.

When the farmer said that the *huasipungueros* had asked the other members to "respect their water rights and leave the water turn schedule for them the way it had always been," he was referring to the schedule the *huasipungueros* used when they were still hacienda workers. The *huasipungueros* of El Tambo received water turns from 12:00 noon on Saturdays until 12:00 noon on Sundays, which is what the fourteen *huasipungueros* and their families wanted to keep, and did keep, even if it was (and is) not listed in any of the legal documents. Although the female heads of household have good reasons to challenge and petition the user groups for a reorganization of the water rotation schedule, they decided against conflict and respected the decision of the older women who wanted to preserve custom and culture.

These examples highlight the heterogeneity of women. While in some cases women share the same problems, in other situations women have conflicting priorities. The examples also show that it is sometimes difficult for women to voice their priorities at the user group meetings.

Participation of Women in Board Positions

A possible way to improve women being heard and addressed is to increase the number of women in board positions. Along the Garrapatal canal, the eleven user groups have between four and six board members, for a total of sixty-one board members, with the eleven presidents forming the Board of Directors for the general WUA of Garrapatal. Five of the eleven user groups of the Garrapatal canal had women on their boards, two as presidents and three as secretaries, which meant that two women were on the WUA for the Garrapatal canal. El Tambo has one WUA with eleven board members, one of which was a woman: the new treasurer. As well as a low total number of women in board positions on the WUAs—both in absolute and proportional terms—their presence on the boards doesn't necessarily mean that women's issues and concerns have a better chance of being heard at the WUA meetings. This usually depends on whether women in board positions have the power to influence decision making and on whether they are aware of the different concerns and problems their fellow female members face.

The WUA's need for literate people with administrative skills has led to the election of women board members, who all have a higher level of education than the average farmer. Of the six women board members, all had finished high school, and the secretaries and the treasurer were schoolteachers. These women are definitely not representative of the average female farmer or housewife in the area.

Irrigated Agriculture, Division of Labor, and Decision Making

Another facet of women's participation in water management is their role in irrigated agriculture, which is the most important economic activity for the small farmers in the region. There are eleven different crops in each area, although the main crop is beans, which along with maize accounts for 74 percent of the crops in Garrapatal, and in El Tambo, beans and anise cover 79 percent of the cultivated area.

Table 10.3 shows the gender division of labor in agriculture for the mestizo households in the study area.[9] Most people, 90 percent of men and 70 percent of women from the household interviews (n=60), when asked which agricultural activities men perform and which women perform, differentiated tasks on the basis of the physical strength required to carry them out. Men did most of the hard work in the field, while women were mainly in charge of activities such as planting, weeding by hand, harvesting, seed selection, threshing, and storing agricultural products.

From Cultural Norms to What Is Actually Done

Though this formal division of labor is clearly defined, what people actually do differs significantly. A focus group of twenty-one women was asked explicitly: Of the tasks that are considered mainly male activities, which tasks do you perform in the fields? The answers demonstrate that women were often more involved in field activities than what was generally acknowledged. Almost half of the women (47 percent) worked with the hoe when they worked the fields, 41 percent irrigated, and 23 percent applied pesticides. Similar information was obtained through household interviews

Table 10.3   Gender Division of Labor

	Activities	Women	Men	Both
Crop activities	Land preparation		X	
	Plowing		X	
	Planting	X		
	Weeding by hand	X		
	Weeding with hoe		X	
	Fertilizing		X	
	Hilling		X	
	Fumigating		X	
	Harvesting			X
	Irrigation		X	
	Storing			X
	Threshing			X
Rearing of small animals	Feeding	X		
	Forage gathering			X
	Watering	X		
Rearing of livestock	Milking	X		
	Watering			X
	Feeding			X
	Forage gathering			X
	Herding			X
	Fruits and vegetables			X
	Medicinal plants	X		
Reproduction activities	Preparing food	X		
	Cooking	X		
	Fetching water	X		
	Cleaning	X		
	Washing	X		
	Child care	X		

Source: Bastidas 2001.
   Notes: This table represents the formal division of labor of mestizo men and women of the study area, based on a focus group of twenty-one women and a survey of sixty households. The information was obtained from focus group meetings and household interviews.

when women were asked to describe their activities during a typical day (twenty-four-hour accounts). The main reason for the discrepancy is that most women considered themselves "helpers" in agricultural activities and did not recognize their crucial participation unless they were asked explicitly. The following response from one of the women illustrates this:

I wake up in the morning, prepare breakfast, get the kids ready for school, clean the house, and cook lunch. When lunch is ready, I have to prepare to go to the field where my husband and son are working. There we have lunch, and I help out some. When it is not harvest time, I do whatever is needed, sometimes work with the hoe and sometimes help irrigate, weed. . . . Sometimes we come back together, other times I have to get home before to do the housework and take care of the kids. If my older daughter is at home, I stay in the field from about 11:00 in the morning until around 4:00 in the afternoon.

In this case, what the woman considers "helping out" is spending half of her working day in the field farming with her husband.

The formal differentiation of tasks on the basis of physical strength is used to justify the lower wage paid to women. Although both men and women are hired to work in the fields, women were preferred at times of planting and harvesting because they did a better job and they cost less. While men were being paid US$2.50 per day of work, women were hired for only US$2.00.[10] The difference in wage rate, according to the farmers, was because the type of work that women did was not as heavy as men's work. Women accepted this disparity because of cultural norms that define gender roles in mestizo culture.

Household Decision Making Regarding Irrigated Agriculture

The study examined whether women were consulted and whether they shared in the decision on how much of the revenue from irrigated agriculture should be reinvested in crops and how much directed to household consumption. It is unfortunately impossible to compare the responses of women and men on these issues because, due to time constraints, they were not asked the same questions.[11] Women's responses about decision making fell into three groups:

• Never consulted: Fourteen percent of the women reported that their husbands never consulted them on decisions related to crop benefits.

• Sometimes consulted: Twenty-six percent of the women reported that in some cases their husbands consulted them.

• Always consulted: More than half (60 percent) of the women reported that they shared decision making with their husbands.

A pattern emerged that the husband usually managed all the aspects of crop production until the product was harvested. Then, in a majority of households, the husband and wife decided on the amount of the crop that should be left for home consumption and for seed for the next cropping season. In these households, after the sale of the product, the husband and wife negotiated how much cash should be put aside for the next cropping season and how much should be used for household consumption and other expenses. Once a decision was reached, the women stored the two amounts separately and managed the money accordingly. Though there was not much conflict on decisions regarding the amount of a crop destined for seed and home consumption, conflict was evident in deciding how much cash should be reinvested in crops and how much set aside for household expenses, with men stressing reinvestment and women household needs.

In the case of female-headed households, the women made most of the decisions regarding management of irrigated agriculture. In no case, however, did women engage in crop production ·without the help of a male sharecropper who participated in decision making. These decisions included what and how much to grow, as well as when and where to sell the product. In these sharecropping arrangements, the woman generally provided the land, cash for crop inputs, and some labor (her own and her family's), while the sharecropper provided labor and also part of the cash for inputs.

These women were faced with difficulties in controlling some aspects of agricultural production, because they insisted that certain tasks required the presence of a man. Although women could hire male labor, they said they could not trust paid workers to look after their interests in the same way a sharecropper would. One of the women explained:

Paid workers won't work at night, so I have to look for a male sharecropper if my water turn is at night. Men can irrigate at night and make sure nobody is stealing the water. . . . Also, when the canal needs to be repaired, farmers have the obligation to go and repair the damage. We [women] don't do that type of work, so we hire workers. The problem with paid workers is that if the owner is not present they don't do a good job.

In contrast to the studies cited in the literature review (Jacome and Krol 1994; Villalobos et al. 1993), women in this study area refused to do maintenance work in the canals. This was in part dictated by the mestizo culture and probably because they could still hire male sharecroppers for this job— always male relatives or farmers in the community.

The decision-making process concerning benefits from irrigated agriculture revealed that in many of the households the husband and wife shared decisions regarding the benefits from irrigated agriculture. However, negotiations in this process were not without conflict. This was probably why when women had the opportunity to engage in other economic activities, they preferred activities where they could control their own income. Even in the cases of female-headed households, female farmers shared agricultural decisions with male sharecroppers because of the difficulty of engaging in agriculture alone.

This case study shows that participation of women in user groups and WUA meetings is low (9 percent). A major reason for low participation is the cultural barriers women face when they are with men, which inhibit their participation. The study demonstrates the importance of household composition and family life cycle as factors influencing the opportunities and challenges that shape women's participation in rural water management. In this case, a gender analysis highlights not only that men and women have varying priorities regarding water, but also that different women have distinct priorities regarding water because of their different roles and responsibilities, which are not static but change over time.

One condition for ensuring that women's voices are heard and that a higher degree of female participation is achieved in the WUAs is recognizing women as resource users and managers. The study demonstrates the crucial role of women in the provision of water for domestic use as well as their important participation in irrigated agriculture. There is a clear need to make the participation of women as water resource users and managers more visible.

In terms of WUAs, the study illustrates that although the Water Agency of the Ministry of Agriculture formally recognizes the associations, they often act in an informal way. Rather than following the rules and regulations, the associations often function according to shared understandings of common objectives, roles, and expectations stemming from existing social relationships that help to preserve the harmony of the community and culture. Given this background, more research is needed to understand the internal dynamics of the WUAs and their decision-making process. Research in this area would help clarify how and why women are elected as board members and their influence in decision-making processes.

11 Women at the Helm of Irrigated Agriculture in Mexico
The Other Side of Male Migration

How do women manage groundwater for agriculture in the absence of men? All over Latin America, they take important roles as water managers during the increasingly protracted periods of migration when husbands, fathers, and/or brothers are absent. Despite this role, groundwater use by women has not received as much attention as large-scale surface water system use. This chapter addresses this deficiency and shows that contrary to the prevailing gender stereotypes that women are ignorant of how to manage water for irrigation until they are trained by "experts," they, in fact, have considerable knowledge because of their experience in agriculture since childhood.

This research, which spans from 1998 to 2002, was undertaken in an *ejido* community in the Bajío region of the state of Guanajuato, which has one of the highest Mexican migration rates to the United States and Canada, with most of these migrants male (Cebada-Contreras 1995). Despite having one of the highest percentages of its area dedicated to irrigated agriculture among Mexican states, little attention has been focused on what happens to this land when men migrate.

In the late 1980s and 1990s, the Mexican government embarked upon an ambitious decentralization of the water sector including the creation of a new federal agency, the National Water Commission (Comisión Nacional de Agua, or CNA) and a new Water Law in 1992, which transferred surface water system management from the government to users. Some research has been conducted on the canal systems and their users, including a handful of studies on female surface water users (Ahlers 2000b; Alberti et al. 2000;

Buechler 2000; Dávila-Poblete 2000; Fracchia 1999; Monsalvo Velásquez, Martelo, and Manzanares 2000; Pacheco 2000). Little research, however, has been conducted on the women who manage groundwater in these irrigation districts.

In this chapter, attention is focused on women who farm on their own and who use groundwater to irrigate their crops. Through their own words, women describe what they consider to be the hardest and the easiest tasks to perform in the fields, which often contrasts with popular conceptions of gender roles. Many of these women learned skills related to planting, weeding, and fertilizing through observation as children, when they were often present during irrigation. When women take charge of the land, they often irrigate or supervise others themselves, which runs counter to prevailing views on gender divisions of labor that irrigation is men's work and that it is physically taxing. New skills, such as driving, are required because of the absence of male household members who were likely to have been taught these skills at a younger age. Finally, the obstacles and opportunities for women to become more actively involved in decision making from the local water user level to the water basin level are evaluated.

The need to recognize women's roles in water management is key to improving the welfare of many households that depend on the work that women do in the fields. Recognizing the particular obstacles they face and making their work more visible allows governmental and nongovernmental programs and policies to gear their development efforts toward women's needs rather than to false perceptions based on popular misconceptions of gender divisions of labor. In Guanajuato state, where more than two-thirds of groundwater pumped is for irrigation, sixteen of nineteen aquifers are overexploited and static water levels are dropping an average of two meters per year. The condition of each aquifer depends on knowing who the water managers are and what their use patterns are. Failure to acknowledge women's role seriously hampers programs centered on groundwater use.

Migration in Mexico

Mexico has one of the highest rates of migration in the world and most of the flow of migrants is to the United States (Escobar, Bean, and Weintraub 1999, 8). Internal migration within Mexico has been predominantly from rural to urban areas. In 1990, however, the incidence of rural-rural migration began to increase, due mainly to the following factors: (1) severe economic crises that limited the creation of urban-based employment at the same time that the working-age population (15 to 44 years of age) increased dramatically; (2) the real value of salaries dropped; (3) informal and unprotected employment increased; (4) the concentration of wealth increased; and (5) federal funding for the states continued to be highly centralized, with the federal district (D.F.) receiving 30 percent of the federal budget even though it has only 10 percent of the population. Cities along the northern border were unable to absorb all of the migrants to the *maquilas,* as the factories strung along the northern border are known (9, 11). Those unable or unwilling to migrate to the United States in search of employment, migrate between rural areas within Mexico.

The urban labor market also was highly dispersed, became more selective, and required more training and experience. This was not the case with rural employment in fruit and vegetable production, which was more concentrated geographically and seasonally. However, this rural labor market has also become more selective, and only the best workers and those under forty years of age are chosen in many agricultural regions (Barrón and Hernandez 2000, 155–56). The real value of agricultural wages has decreased at the same time as neoliberal policies have slashed crop supports and state subsidies, causing a decline in farm income. Income is now insufficient to pay for previous levels of hired field labor at the same time that the availability of household labor has decreased (Aranda 2000, 249; field interviews, 1998–2002). This drop in income has necessitated further diversification and intensification of livelihood strategies.

The dearth of jobs in Mexico with wages that keep pace with inflation, lower farm incomes as well as the demographic increase in the economically active population, and the attraction of new migrants via existing ties between Mexicans in Mexico and those in the United States have all contributed to a rise in international migration. Guanajuato has one of the highest U.S. migration rates in Mexico (INEGI 1997, 123), with the first wave of migration having occurred during the *bracero* program of the 1940s. Most migration was and continues to be to Illinois, California, Pennsylvania, and Texas. It is estimated that in the first half of the 1990s, Guanajuato lost 7.6 per cent per year of its population due to U.S. migration (based on population figures for 1992, INEGI 1997, 123). Though much of the migration is temporary or only seasonal, migrants still send approximately U.S. $600 million per year to their communities of origin in Guanajuato state alone (Rionda 2000; Wilcox-Young 1987, 7). In Guanajuato, as in the rest of Mexico, migrant remittances are important to agricultural investments, as credit is scarce (Myhre 1998, 61; Marsh and Runsten 1998, 299). In 1994, Mexican households with between five and ten hectares of land were the most likely to have members who had migrated (21.9 percent of all migrants), with those least likely having less than two hectares of land (16.6 percent; de Janvry, Sadoulet, Davis, and Gordillo 1999, 115). According to a study of Guanajuato's rural communities by Cebada Contreras, the average age at which migrants, mostly male, first go to the United States is sixteen years old (1995, 2–4), and González found that migrants to Pennsylvania range from fifteen to forty-five years of age (1996, 5). Men in the Irapuato módulo often begin migrating because indebtedness stemming from crop failure caused by water scarcity (field interviews, 1998–2002).

Most migrants, then, are male. When they are at home, they work in agriculture either on their own fields and/or on the land of others. They usually migrate with other household members, and the duration of their absences has increased because they fear that if they return to Mexico, they will not be able to get back into the United States again. This translates into increased scarcity of male labor in rural Mexican communities that lasts for longer periods of time. Given high levels of male migration, who are the farmers and water managers in irrigated agriculture among groundwater users?

One indication of the identity of these farmers is the percentage of female-headed households in predominantly rural areas. Robles (2000) contends that reliable estimates of the percentage of female-headed households in Mexico as a whole are lacking, and she estimates they range from 17 and 29 percent, with increasing male migration likely driving the figure even higher. Undercounting female-headed households occurs also because women heading such households are accorded low status and as a result are kept hidden from researchers and sometimes even by the women themselves (31). In the Upper River Lerma district (011), where this study took place, in 1999 the percentage of female-headed households among those with less than six hectares of land and who are surface water irrigation users was estimated at 16 per cent and was especially prevalent in the *ejido* sector (Vargas, Monsalvo Velázquez, and Wester 2000). As these are the data for surface water users, and there are no reliable statistics on the percentage of female groundwater users, following Robles' argument, the figure of 16 percent is very likely to be too low.

Groundwater Irrigation in Mexico

Groundwater, usually pumped via wells, is the main source of water for domestic use, industry, and irrigation in arid and semiarid areas of Mexico (CNA/World Bank 1999 cited in Wester, Pimentel, and Scott 1999, 2). The state of Guanajuato, which occupies barely 1.6 percent of the national territory, possesses approximately 12 percent of all wells (CEAG 1998). Estimates are that 15,600 of its wells, or 75–85 percent of the water pumped from the ground, is used for agriculture (CFE 1999; Wester et al. 1999, 3). There is an alarming deficit of 1,245.8 million cubic meters per year in Guanajuato between the extraction and recharge of groundwater (CEAG, 2000). In the aquifer for the study area, that is, the valleys of Irapuato, Santiago, and Huanímaro, the water table was receding at a rate of two meters per year between 1996 and 1998 according to one hydrogeological study (Chico Goerne 2001, 47). In 1986, the water table levels in Irapuato were thirty to sixty meters in depth; however, by the year 2000, these levels had dropped to eighty to 100 meters or lower (CEAG 2000).

The National Water Commission (CNA) ostensibly controls the quantity of water pumped and the drilling of new wells; in reality, however, farmers themselves manage the water. The cost per hectare of irrigating with groundwater is greater than the cost of irrigating with canal water because of the rapid increase in the cost of electrical energy, gasoline, and diesel, which run the pumps. Privately owned wells are used by the owner who originally dug the well, or by the owner and a group of family members, or by the owner and a group of farmers. The well owner has help from the other users for the costs associated with operation and maintenance and for the deepening of the well if the well runs dry. Farmers who share wells are organized into what are termed *sociedades de pozo* or well-user groups that manage the system and share the costs. There are also wells the government originally dug *(pozos oficiales)* that are used by the group of farmers who maintain them, who are also organized into well-user groups.

In Mexico, groundwater is managed at various different levels from the basin to the user. Article 13 of the National Water Law gave the National Water Commission (CNA) the legal authority to establish Basin Advisory Boards. In January of 1993, the Basin Advisory Board for the Lerma-Chapala basin was the first established in Mexico (Scott, Wester, and Garcés 1999, 1). By the end of 2001, twenty-five Basin Advisory Boards existed in the country. In some states, auxiliary arms exist at the subbasin and microbasin level that are called Basin Commissions and Basin Committees; however, only seven Basin Commissions and three Basin Committees have been constituted thus far.

For the most overexploited aquifers, Comités Técnicos de Aguas Subterráneas (COTAS), or Technical Committees for Groundwater, were set up, made up of water users who advise the government (mainly the CNA) and act as watchdogs to prevent the misuse of water resources (Marañón 1999, 165; Buechler fieldwork August 2002). Of the forty-seven COTAS established in Mexico, fourteen are located in Guanajuato, one for each region of the state. The general assembly of the COTAS consists of groundwater users for agriculture, domestic, and industrial purposes; in Guanajuato, unlike other states in Mexico, the COTAS also include surface water users. In Guanajuato, COTAS stands for Consejos Técnicos de Aguas (Technical Advisory Councils for Water), but they have the same structure and overall purpose as the COTAS elsewhere. The governing board of the COTAS consists of twelve user representatives, three for each type of use, which means there are three for agriculture including groundwater and surface water users. Members of well user groups with land as well as private well owners with land can serve on the board and attend the general assembly. Female (or male) farmers who rent land with access to groundwater or women with informal access to groundwater are unable to join the well user groups, attend the general assembly, or be elected to the governing board. Between the level of the COTAS and the well user groups, no intermediate decision-making level exists that could allow for a greater participation by more users in decision-making regarding groundwater.

The Study Area

This study was part of a larger research project that involved 200 interviews of women, men, and adolescents in three *ejidos* near the cities of Irapuato and Pueblo Nuevo, both situated in the fertile Bajío valley in Guanajuato, Mexico, which has a long dry season that lasts from late September until the end of May. These *ejidos* are part of the Irapuato *módulo* (water-user association) in turn part of the Upper River Lerma Irrigation District 011, which has thirty-nine *ejidos* within its jurisdiction. One of the three *ejidos* studied is located at the head of the system of canals within the Irapuato *módulo*, the second is in the midreach section, and the third is in the tail end of this system of canals.

In considering female groundwater users, the midreach *ejido* was selected because it has the greatest number of wells. Women farm land with access to groundwater either on fields owned by husbands, relatives, or in-laws, or on land they rent. Sufficient quantities of surface water from the canals are usually delivered to the head and midreach *ejidos*. However, during times of drought, the dams do not fill up sufficiently with water during the rainy season, and water is not delivered from the dams to the canals. The drought conditions that existed between 1997–1999 meant that water was not provided to the Water User Association (WUA) members, who are mostly men as only those with land titles are WUA members and most women are not landowners. If their husbands or fathers who have land titles have migrated, women can pay on their behalf and receive surface water irrigation in the canals.

Water could not be delivered to some Irapuato *ejidos* in 2000 and to most *ejidos* in 2001 during the winter dry season. This forced some farmers with canal-irrigated land to rent land with access to groundwater. The midreach *ejido* has wells for irrigation utilized by individual well owners or by groups of users, but there are no female well *owners*. However, there are female groundwater *users*, who rent land with access to groundwater or who work land owned by their husband, brother-in-law, or another relative, and who enter into agreements with well owners during times of drought. These verbal agreements stipulate that farmers can receive well water for part of the land in exchange for the well owner cultivating the other part. Another way to access water is through paying a fee (about 80 pesos or 8 dollars in 2002) to the well owner per hour of pumping. Landless households generally rent land with access to wells, which women increasingly farm by themselves because during crises such as drought or water scarcity, men are far more likely to migrate.

The study area is a mid-reach *ejido* with a total of 400 hectares of land for a population of 1,605. The total number of ejidatario men and women is sixty-three and seventeen, respectively. The average landholding for the informants was 8.29 hectares. There are six government and three private wells and surface water is taken from a canal, when water is released from the dam, which depends on the water level in the dam. Grains, vegetables, and strawberries are the main crops, with principle market production rather than subsistence production and mechanized traction rather than animal traction. Agriculture represents only one of multiple livelihood strategies that households in this *ejido* engages in, which also has a vegetable packing plant where the majority of the workers are young women who work for low pay, for long hours, and without job security. Other small-scale enterprises in this periurban area located twenty-five minutes by bus from the city center of Irapuato include small stores often set up with migrant money or snack food items sold from a doorway (Buechler 2002).

Women's Participation in Irrigated Agriculture and Rural Livelihoods

This study points to the existence of a hidden economy of female farmers and water managers in small holder agriculture. In Guanajuato, as in other parts of Latin America, some women irrigate the fields they cultivate, either on their own or with the help of their children (usually sons), their brother or father-in-law, or less commonly, with the aid of their own brothers or father. While men also receive help from kin or fictive kin during irrigation, women are most likely to need this help when their husbands, fathers, or brothers migrate, take full-time, off-farm employment or when they become widows. The length of time women are the principal water managers for agriculture varies and depends to a large degree on labor availability within the household and within the network of kin and fictive kin relations. I focus here on the effect of male migration on women engaged in agricultural production with groundwater.

The few studies on male migration and female participation in agricultural water management in Latin America have focused mainly on surface water irrigation systems. These studies show that male migration forces women to take on additional agricultural tasks, including water management. As Ineke van der Pol has noted for various provinces of Cusco, Peru:

Each year more men migrate to other areas to find work. Agricultural production falls primarily on women. The distribution of water is decided in the community assemblies. The men usually stay until the planting and first irrigation. The second and third irrigation is the women's responsibility. That is, men are less and less involved in water management. (translation mine 1992)

Women's increasing participation in water management for irrigated agriculture because of male long or short term migration has also been documented for Ecuador (Ahlers and Smits 1991; Arroyo and Boelens 1997b; Krol 1997; Phillips 1987 cited in Ahlers 2000a, 209). In Licto, Ecuador, "increasingly, women participate in work that had been reserved for men; in a lot of communities they are the ones who irrigate, etc. Depending on the family and the community, some men return on the weekends, others once a month, once a season or once a year or even less frequently" (translation mine; Arroyo and Boelens 1997b, 10).

Even when it is of short duration, migration is often during critical periods in the agricultural season, which means that the agricultural work done by women, girls, and boys, intensifies and broadens to include traditional male activities such as irrigation and pesticide application.

Male migration has meant that in addition to irrigating flowers for personal use and for commercial sale, Nahuatl women in Hueyapan, Morelos state, Mexico, who do not usually have legal access to land or to water, must now irrigate and produce crops that men historically cultivated such as vegetables, fruits, corn, and beans (Carmona Quiróz 2001). Some of these women cultivate crops on land belonging to their husband, father, or mother-in-law, and others farm land that belongs to a brother who has migrated. Landless women work land that is rented by a male member of the household, who negotiates the terms of what is usually a verbal agreement with the landowner, but the male relative may play a very minor role after that.

At the institutional level, women are not well integrated into decision-making entities at the local or at higher levels, often because as nonland titleholders, they are ineligible for formal membership in the surface water irrigation users' associations *(módulos)*. Even when they are members of the water users' associations as titleholders (usually as widows), their participation is limited because meeting times often conflict with their home and field responsibilities and also because they experience male resistance in areas such as the administration of the irrigation system (Ahlers 2000b; Arroyo and Boelens 1997b; Brunt 1992; Krol 1997; Monsalvo Velásquez et al. 2000). The result is that they have little decision-making power over surface water management at the level of the basin, district, or local water user association.

Preliminary findings from this study near Irapuato suggest that women seem to have more control over what time they irrigate if the well user group they belong to is small and less control if the group of well users is large. If they are renters, the amount of control a woman has over the timing of the irrigations depends on her relationship with the well owner and with the well group members. Some women say that the reason that they hire a male irrigator (whom they supervise) is so that he can negotiate with the well owner and with the other well users over timings of irrigations. The irrigation schedule also depends on the location of the plot of land with respect to the well, as those closest to the well get the best irrigation schedule, and these users are usually the well owners—mostly men.

For women, daytime is preferable for water delivery to their fields for several reasons. The distance to the fields and the danger this implies for women at night is often cited. Some fields are almost an hour's walk (while others are only a few minutes away). Less often directly expressed is the issue of childcare. If a woman has small children, a night irrigation schedule infringes upon her capacity to care for her children as well as on having a child accompany her to the fields, especially when she has become head of household because of migration. To accomplish this, she must have at least two older children, one to care for the younger children at home and the other to accompany her. The accompanying child is ideally male so fellow community members view her as being chaperoned in the fields for what is often an all-night stay. Women's reputations are at risk if they irrigate at night because the fields are viewed as possible venues for sexual liaisons. This restriction on the public space that women are allowed to occupy to be accepted socially has been addressed in depth in the literature on South Asia. For example, what Bina Agarwal has noted in India is applicable to many areas of rural Mexico as well. She explains: "even in the absence of veiling or any explicit gender segregation of space, a preoccupation with the purity and chastity of women and the family's social status tends to define appropriate female behavior in ways which restrict women socially and, in indirect ways, also physically" (1994, 310).

This type of restriction has economic repercussions because women must often hire others to do the work for them, necessitating expenditures that men do not have to make. Money is particularly scarce in the home community, especially when a household member is trying to cross the border illegally rather than as a contracted laborer, has just arrived or begun work, or during economic downturns in the receiving country. The amount of money a migrant can send also frequently depends on the weather because rains curtail his usual employment in agriculture, in gardens, on golf courses, or in tourist-oriented businesses (field interviews with *ejido* women and male migrants, 1998–2002).

In Guanajuato, the increase in women's participation in agricultural activities is due not only to male migration but also to less available income for hiring field labor. As in the rest of Mexico, no longer does just one member of a household migrate to other areas in Mexico or to the United States; often more than one household member must go. This creates a labor shortage within the household and in the community at large, and, as will be argued later, causes alterations in the gender division of labor in groundwater management.

Groundwater Irrigated Agriculture, Male Migration, and Female Water Managers in the Bajío

The gendered division of labor in agriculture is undergoing major alterations due to labor shortages resulting from male migration. The total number of *ejidatarias* (women who have title to the land due to the death of their husbands) in the *ejido* studied is seventeen out of sixty-three. *Ejidatarias* here and in the rest of Mexico have less land than their male counterparts.[1] However, the number of women actually working land owned by their father, husband, brother, in-law, or another person in the *ejido* who rents them land varies greatly depending on the time of year and the duration of male migration.

Women's work in the area studied is traditionally mainly weeding and spreading fertilizer for all crops and harvesting of corn and sometimes strawberries. When men migrate, women often begin to take a much more active role in water management. For example, they hire and supervise a male irrigator, or they irrigate themselves.[2] With the growing problem of lack of water in the dams, groundwater has become an increasingly prized resource as it can be accessed year-round. For higher-value crops, such as strawberries, which require constant and considerable amounts of water, and for any crop grown in the dry season, groundwater is needed. Whether the wells are government wells shared between many users or private wells utilized by a group of farmers, falling water tables mean there may be less water available for each user and the timings of the irrigations may be carefully controlled. Wells must often be deepened, which is a costly undertaking. In the study area, there are only nine wells in a community of 400 households. Most must gain access to groundwater by renting land with access to a well.

Strawberries allow for a steady income as opposed to wheat, sorghum, or corn, which only provide earnings after several months. This income from strawberries is necessary for household expenses that include food, clothes, medicines, and children's school items. Women are responsible for covering these expenses either alone or together with remittances sent by their husbands. As one woman who worked land with access to well water rented by her migrant husband stated emphatically: "it is from there that we maintain ourselves, it's where we get money to eat" (Buechler 2000, 58).

The stories of particular women interviewed in this *ejido* who farm alone for most or all of the year due to male migration provide a clearer picture of the changes in gender divisions of labor and the challenges and obstacles women face.

For the past seven years, Guadalupe[3] from the midreach *ejido* has been cultivating strawberries and corn five hours a day on the quarter hectare of land her husband rents. Her husband migrates to Canada for at least four months each year as a contracted laborer. Each year they rent a different parcel of land that she irrigates when her turn comes during the day. However, as there are many members in the well group, land far from the well is irrigated at night, and this year her rented land is far away. Only when her husband is able to rent land nearer to the well can she irrigate during the day. She has five children: four sons and a two-year-old daughter. Three of her four sons, ages ten, thirteen, and sixteen, work with her in the fields after school each day and the eldest occasionally irrigates. Her brother-in-law also occasionally irrigates for pay. Her fourth son, age seventeen, has recently left school to begin working in a water purifying plant nearby the *ejido*. The household needed this income, explained Guadalupe, and she could not work in the packing plant located on the *ejido* because of its rotating schedule, which meant that every other week she would have to work a night shift, and with a young child, night work was impossible. Her oldest son will try to get a contract as an agricultural laborer to go to the United States when he turns eighteen.

The resulting labor scarcity caused by two household members working off the farm, one nearby and one in Canada, translates into an increased workload for Guadalupe, who must now work one more hour per day in the fields. She plants the strawberries each year, and this year she also planted corn. Her father taught her everything about cultivating strawberries, including how to irrigate them. He was landless but rented land in the same *ejido* to grow strawberries. She said that her main problem is the lack of water, and with a worried look she explained:

The water flows slowly because the well doesn't have much water. Like this time . . . well, we suffered a lot because since there are many plots of land that are irrigated with the same well there isn't enough water sometimes. Then when one doesn't need it anymore, the water comes. Since the well isn't very big it doesn't give much water. They give water, but too late. The strawberries were finished early in the season because there wasn't enough water. You see, if . . . if they aren't irrigated throughout the season more pests attack them. The pests keep building up on them and they finish sooner.

For Guadalupe, the hardest tasks involved in cultivating strawberries were planting and fumigating. When asked specifically whether she considered irrigating to be difficult, she responded that it was not, as she had observed this activity since she was a child. She indicated that irrigating at night was a problem for her as a woman. She said that the owner of the land that they are renting this year also plants strawberries on land that is contiguous to the land she rents from him. He likes to irrigate during the day and then passes the water along to the land she uses. She cannot control the timings of the delivery of the water in terms of the time of day or the day of the week. Only her sons or brother-in-law, because they are men, can irrigate the fields at night when the landowner is finished with the water. Guadalupe is not part of the well-user society *(sociedad de pozo)* because only landowners with land close to the well are allowed to become members. Nor is she part of the Water User Association of the *módulo* Irapuato as it is composed only of land titleholders.

Guadalupe's sister Kati rented land in past years to plant strawberries. Her husband has lived for two and a half years in the United States in Washington state, where he works in a flower greenhouse and has only been able to return for two months. Kati said that the remittances he sends her depend on the weather because he works for an hourly wage and cannot work when it rains or snows. The quarter hectare of land she rented and planted in strawberries was far from her house and this meant, "at night one doesn't go there." However, she was able to arrange with the well group that she could irrigate two times a week during the day. This she did for one year. The second year she planted the strawberries twice, but both times she lost the plants because they became infested with pests. She agreed with her sister, that the hardest task is fumigating because "the machine is heavy and sometimes people faint from the chemicals or they get a headache." Her seven- and her nine-year-old daughters both worked in the fields with her for three hours a day, picking strawberries and weeding.

Kati irrigated the land herself or hired an irrigator, explaining that she had to wait until the landowner had finished irrigating before she attended to her crop. However, she negotiated informally with other well group members to allow her to irrigate during the day, twice a week for two hours. She did this by going to the houses of the president and two other men in the well-user group and explaining her situation. Once the president agreed, the others agreed as well. She explained that irrigating requires "neither a lot nor a little" of water, which she learned by watching hired irrigators in strawberry fields where she had worked since she quit school at twelve. When she hired an irrigator, she sometimes picked the strawberries as he was irrigating. But, she said, often the irrigation was at night so she would "have to go [early in the morning] to see if it went well or not, before the water dried up."

Because her crop failed twice, Kati no longer rents any land. This experience "took away my will to plant strawberries." She now works as a day laborer for others who plant strawberries. If she works from 6:00 a.m. to 10:00 a.m., she earns forty pesos (about US$4.21) and if she works from 6:00 a.m. to 12:00 noon then she earns fifty pesos (about US$5.26) for weeding, planting, and picking. She also helps her sister cultivate corn on the land they rent with access to groundwater, which provides corn for her family's tortillas.

Lucha and her mother-in-law rent a quarter hectare of land with access to a well each year because Lucha's father-in-law had to sell his land before his death. She explained that although the strawberry plants and inputs are expensive, they provide her with an income every four days throughout the year except from September through November. She must buy all the inputs and then the landowner sells the strawberries and retains 30 percent of the profits. Lucha learned how to cultivate strawberries as a child on her family's land. Her husband used to go to Canada on contract for five months of the year but has been going illegally to the United States for more indefinite periods of time—working, ironically, on strawberry plantations in California and sending remittances. His sister and brothers-in-law are also in the United States. Before his trips, her husband usually helps plant the strawberries and then Lucha does the rest with her young boys and mother-in-law and with her sister-in-law who comes with her children from Texas to spend summer vacations with their grandmother.

Lucha hires a male irrigator to water the strawberries every four nights during the dry season, checking on the fields only in the morning, because she believes that it is dangerous to go to the remote fields at night. Like most rural Mexican women, she does not know how to drive (nor does her household have a pick-up truck), so she orders the fertilizer from a relative of her husband with a pick-up truck, whose family also rents land to plant strawberries (Buechler 2000, 54–55).

Mari plants strawberries and corn on her mother-in-law's land with well access primarily to help support her mother-in-law and her own family. She began to grow sorghum on an additional hectare when her brother-in-law left for the United States. Mari's husband, who has been in the northeastern United States for several years and visits only every two or three years for a few months, has been sending remittances which she has used to build a small house. Mari and her sons, ages fourteen and twelve, and her daughter, age eleven, go to the fields every day while her seven-year-old son takes care of his five-year-old sister. Mari's fourteen-year-old son buys the inputs and irrigates the land. He is considering making the sacrifice of going to the United States so that his father can finally return to the *ejido* and be with the rest of his children and his wife.

For Mari, the work in the fields is in addition to all the other types of work she performs every day. Aside from the household chores and taking care of her five children, she works in the vegetable packing plant located in the *ejido*. She has had this job for ten years largely to get health insurance for her kids, with brief interludes after the births of her two youngest children until they could walk.

Twenty-five-year-old Lili lost her father when she was just eleven. Her mother, as a widow, was given title to the land, but she has worked predominantly in the house rather than the fields. Lili has worked together with her brothers on their land, and they have their own well, cultivating strawberries, sorghum, corn, and wheat. Lili works in the strawberry fields from 6:00 a.m. until 10:30 a.m. twice a week, and three times a week to weed the sorghum or wheat fields from 10:00 a.m. to 2:00 or 3:00 p.m. She says that if she ever had to, she would know how to irrigate because she has watched her brothers or a hired irrigator do this many times.

Silvia rents a quarter of an acre of land with access to a well to cultivate strawberries, corn, and sorghum. She herself usually irrigates, which she learned from hired irrigators after her husband left nine years ago to work as a contracted laborer in Canadian greenhouses for three to eight months every year, and only occasionally hires a male irrigator for 100 pesos (US$10.53). She revealed a keen sense of water management, including the importance of not wasting water. Her husband's length of stay in Canada depends on the amount of work there is for him, and he earns about Can$500–600 a month if the weather and the crop is good, or if conditions are bad, Can$300 a month; however what she received depended on the exchange rate, which fluctuated. The eldest of Silvia's six children, a son, migrated to the United States at fifteen years and stayed there for three years, coming back for only a short while, then returning to the United States where he has married and now has a child. Now that he has a family, he cannot send back remittances. Silvia's unmarried sister lives with her and helps her in the house and in the fields, and Silvia has the help of her sixteen- and her thirteen-year-old daughters and her nine-year-old son. Her sixteen-year-old daughter now drives their pick-up after learning from her father, and Silvia told me proudly that she herself had just begun to drive.

Silvia explained that it was only after she married that she began to work in agriculture. She said with a smile that she loves to work in the fields. She also exclaimed: "I became accustomed to spend what I earn. Others just wait for the money from their husbands." Silvia used to sell the strawberries on the roadside near the city for an hour a day, but the "authorities" do not want fruit vendors there, so she must sell to middle persons and now earns less. The cost of inputs such as fertilizer and pesticides has risen, further reducing her income. She mitigates her risk by selling homemade sandwiches and hamburgers as well as soft drinks to school children and truckers from a stand close to the road.

Her daughters and son work from 5:00 to 8:00 p.m. every day except for Saturdays and holidays when they work from 7:00 a.m. to 3:00 p.m. However, she said that she and the children work for longer hours in the fields during the annual cyclical fall of the price of the strawberries but that when her husband is there, her daughters do not go to the fields.

The case of Celina shows the tenuous access women have to land and water. Celina's husband has one acre of land with access only to canal water, but because water was not being delivered, her husband decided to work his father's one and a half hectares of land with access to a group well and one and a half hectares of land with access to a canal. He planted the green tomatoes used in Mexican salsas but then left for a year to work in a factory in Atlanta, Georgia. Celina then planted sorghum, wheat, and corn with about two weeks' help a season from her two brothers. She weeded and applied fertilizer and hired one brother to irrigate for 150 pesos. However, she had a disagreement with her father-in-law over the amount of pesticides to apply, maintaining that she had followed her husband's instructions. The result was that her father-in-law took the land from her, and she now only farms her husband's one hectare of land irrigated with water from the canal. But this land is mostly rainfed and only cultivable in the short rainy season because there is rarely water in the dams for the winter crop. She has two cows, and for the fodder and other agricultural inputs, she pays for transportation since she cannot drive. She continues to farm with the help of her two landless brothers, and she had to sell her pick-up truck because her husband, in his second trip to the United States, couldn't find work and was unable to send them money. Her twelve- and her fifteen-year-old daughters are studying, but the elder must now drop out of school due to lack of funds. Her eighteen-year-old son works at an industrial park nearby.

Women's increased participation in the fields has not been recognized by the men in the *ejido* nor by many of the women. The male well users in this *ejido* state that women "only do a lot in the fields when their husbands are gone," and they do not seem to appreciate how long these absences usually are. Most men interviewed cannot name the women in their *ejido* who farm alone. The membership systems for the well user societies or groups and the Water User Associations require land titles, which effectively bars women from having any voice in groundwater management. The women who farm by themselves know the other women who farm alone, and some are related to one another. When their husbands return, they usually continue to work in the fields and also take up additional income-generating activities they stopped when their husbands left. Their husbands take over the decision-making, but because they migrate again after a short period of time, this is soon shared again between the husband (by means of letters and phone calls) and the wife who works daily in the fields.

In the COTAS, the role of women as representatives or as replacement representatives is more common for domestic water use than for agriculture. The role of one of the three hired personnel, the manager, seems to be important in influencing the level of female participation.[4] In one of the COTAS, the manager took extra care to encourage the participation of women at the general assembly by going to the PROGRESA (Programa de Educación, Salud y Alimentacion, a welfare program for low-income households with young children) meeting attended by many women and by announcing the meeting by loudspeaker in the local plazas. However, another manager told us that only 5 percent of the 100 people who attended the last general assembly were women. The assemblies in the COTAS he manages are announced through the board members who distribute the letters through the user associations. This manager insisted that was the only efficient way to do it. Therefore, because few women can be part of the associations, not many would find out about these assemblies.

Women play important roles in water management in Guanajuato with less help from household members and relatives than ever before. They irrigate by themselves or supervise male irrigators despite attitudes in and outside of their communities that this is not women's work. They know how to manage water due to their vast experience with agricultural work. Even though they often manage water alone, women continue to be viewed as mere helpers to a male farmer.

Though some of the women irrigate by themselves, others hire male irrigators, just as male farmers do. Of the women who irrigate, not one considered irrigating to be a strenuous task, mentioning instead applying pesticides or weeding as more physically taxing. This runs counter to arguments made in this and other areas of Latin America, such as Ecuador and Peru, that irrigation is a man's job and that women do not have the physical strength for it.

The income that women (and men) earn through agriculture in arid and semiarid areas is highly dependent upon access to and control over a steady supply of irrigation water in the long dry season and also during dry spells in the rainy season. Wells supply a more reliable quantity of water as it can be accessed when needed. As water managers, women face some of the same problems as men, such as the reduction in the water tables limiting the availability of groundwater in the wells.[5] If there is a shortage of water, their crops can be damaged and their incomes reduced. Another problem shared by all farmers is that the prices of agricultural inputs are rising faster than the prices of their crops. These factors contribute to male migration. Consequently, women are taking charge of irrigated agriculture just when the conditions for farming are becoming more and more adverse.

Women face serious barriers to their participation in water management based on their gender, including the lack of legal access to land and water, lack of social acceptance as irrigators especially at night, lack of driving skills, and related social constraints. Although well user group dynamics are predicated upon a notion of equity, more in-depth studies are needed to ascertain whether members have greater power than others in determining when they receive the water, and to examine more closely the power of renters to influence the order of irrigation turns. Gender and class (landless vs. landed, larger vs. smaller landowners) are important factors influencing groundwater management decisions. The timing of irrigation turns is more important for women than for men because they must balance household responsibilities and childcare with work in the fields. Cultural prohibitions against women's occupation of public space are reflected in the fact that women are not taught to drive and in the barriers against women's direct negotiations with men. Women are beginning to drive and their daughters are sometimes demanding that they be taught how to drive. The prohibition against the occupation of public space also includes the fields at night, which is precisely when they must often be irrigated.

Public space is also an issue for women in terms of participation in arenas such as the COTAS in which few women participate in the general assemblies and practically none are elected to the governing boards, which are composed of mostly large and medium-sized farmers. The few women who own land, tend to have smaller amounts of land than men. Their age and health may limit some female landowners' attendance at meetings so they send their sons instead. The multiple demands placed on their time in the home, in the fields and in other income-generating activities also limit their participation. However, most women who own land (who are mainly widows) do attend meetings that take place within their own ejido. They take their attendance very seriously, even though only a few speak at these meetings because of social and cultural barriers. For most women, the lack of attendance is simply because of barriers based on land ownership.

The general lack of awareness of women's importance in water management has meant that power relations based on gender within the *ejido* assemblies or other community institutions have not seemed to change. A new generation of women is coming of age in the *ejidos*, however, and these women are better educated, which means they are more likely to be more vocal (field interviews with teenage girls 1998–2002).

As Scott, Wester, and Garcés (1999) have explained, for surface water institutions there is also no intermediate institution between the *sociedades de pozo* at the well-user level and the COTAS at the level of the region. Adding another level with an office located close to the users would facilitate the participation of greater numbers of groundwater users in management and might open the door for greater female participation. If an intermediate level were established with quotas for female leadership based on water use rather than on landowning status, more women might be able to participate. Action research with the Commission for Water in each state is needed to draw attention to women's important roles in groundwater irrigation. This should be combined with gender training for water managers in governmental and nongovernmental institutions. Thus far, NGOs have not taken an active role in promoting women as water managers in the Bajío. NGOs as well as governmental institutions must begin to prioritize gender issues related to women's need for groundwater access and control.

Specific task forces need to be set up to address the particular needs of women who own land; have access to land through husbands, relatives, or in-laws; or rent land with access to groundwater for irrigation. These task forces need to interview women, and then draft a list of needs to convert into recommendations and plans. As a first step, women who take charge of groundwater management for agriculture as a result of male migration must be made visible to their communities and to decision-making bodies related to water management.

12 Toward a Broader Perspective

The preceding chapters have built a picture of the water sector in Latin America under stress, as it is in most regions of the world. Top-down management has failed to consider the community impacts of national policies and has ignored effective local forms of organization. This has led to rejection, confrontation, and conflict as seen in Bolivia and Argentina, and at the regional and local levels, fragmented management has contributed to inadequate water services and systems (Global Water Partnership 2000, 9).

Dávila-Poblete and Rico (chapter three) described how over the past ten years, as water has come to be seen as a crisis issue worldwide, all Latin American governments have nominally signed on to global water policies that encourage them to reframe their water sectors according to a common set of principles, most notably those defined in Dublin in 1992. As this book shows, however, signing and implementing are two vastly different steps, especially in the contexts of economic crises and poorly funded public sectors.

The eight case studies in this book provide evidence of the tremendous resourcefulness of women at the local level and the increasingly public roles women play in community water management. From the fields in Irapuato (Mexico), Llullucha (Peru), and Carchi (Ecuador), where women are eminently capable but where their husbands and communities do not explicitly recognize their capabilities, to small towns like La Purificación Tepetitla (Mexico) where residents have developed highly effective, autonomous water governance mechanisms, to the streets of Tucumán (Argentina) and Cochabamba (Bolivia) where women protested and helped defeat national plans for water privatization, we see women's influence on water management. These case studies all show that women's activities with water are significant to their households and to community well being, and that great variation exists in women's power in relation to water.

In this concluding chapter, we build an argument that effective and equitable water management must include women, and we spell out exactly what including women means. We discuss the threads of analysis that arise from the three case study sections of the book: neoliberal policies and their social impact, technology transfer and social organization, and participation and cultural change.[1] And we suggest how to pragmatically convert participatory concepts into practice and implement water management with a gender equity perspective. Finally, we provide four overarching conclusions that suggest the imperative of change in contemporary water policy and planning.

Neoliberal Policies and Their Social Impact

Part two of the book focused on the globalization process and its relationship to neoliberal policies, the effects of those policies in the water sector in Argentina and Bolivia, and the response of women. During the 1980s and 1990s, most Latin American governments embraced neoliberal policies, encouraged by the positive results that such policies had yielded in Southeast Asia as well as closer to home, in Chile. These policies meant that municipal water and sanitation services that had generally been managed by decentralized state or local government agencies were given in concession, sold, or transferred to the private sector, either to foreign-owned water agencies or subsidiaries of multinational corporations. Irrigation infrastructure and water rights were transferred or given under concession to water user organizations, promoting stakeholder participation. Thus, to varying degrees across Latin America, the management of the water sector as well as the infrastructure itself has been or is being passed from public to private hands.

The concession of municipal water services from the public to the private sector has significant social repercussions, because the logic of the two sectors is inherently different. When private enterprises provide water services, they are supply-driven because they usually provide services to those already with the infrastructure who can afford to pay. In contrast, municipal or government water services are demand driven because their goal is to provide water services to the greatest possible number of homes. Although government agencies cannot ignore the need to balance their budgets, coverage remains a primary goal. In most cases of privatization, only the best infrastructure is privatized, and the state is left with deteriorated facilities that need costly repairs. In addition, the public sector usually is left with the responsibility for the poor, who tend to be excluded from the privatized services as service fees increase.

The neoliberal model has created a significant conflict of interest for the state. On one hand, it is obliged (and often pressured) by its citizens to implement policies that respond to the needs of the population, while on the other, the need to conform to neoliberal policies that shrink the state forces it to privatize and/or commercialize the water sector. These are fundamentally incompatible situations because increased privatization or commercialization does not meet the needs of the population.

The tension between the objectives of the public and private sectors, and the tensions between the welfare functions of the state and neoliberal policies play themselves out in the social costs associated with privatization and can be devastating as demonstrated in both Tucumán, Argentina, and Cochabamba, Bolivia. Peredo, Bustamante, and Udaeta (in chapter five) point out that both before water service privatization in Cochabamba and again immediately after, tariffs increased with no corresponding improvements in water services. This has happened in cities across Latin America. The justification for these rising tariffs is that as rates increase people will use water more efficiently. Most people, however, tend to stop or delay payments rather than significantly change the way they use water, leading to a vicious cycle of reduced water sector income leading in turn to a reduced ability to maintain or extend services.

The case study of Tucumán provides another dimension of privatization. Giarracca and Del Pozo (in chapter six) explain that because many households had contributed to the construction of water infrastructure through cash payments and/or manual labor, privatization meant the transfer to the private sector of a good that contained significant community investment.[2] Though communities will allow the public sector to manage collective goods, it is another thing altogether to turn over the ownership of the infrastructure they helped build to the private sector. This is why the protests that swept Tucumán were not only about water tariffs but also distinctly about the ownership of the infrastructure (as was also the case in Cochabamba).

Once water has been established as an economic good, water markets are created, which is what has happened in Chile and which is under consideration in several other Latin American countries. In Ahlers' discussion of Mexican water markets in chapter four, she shows that when these policies are examined at the local level, their impact is threefold. First, market mechanisms and trade tend to dominate policy frameworks. Second, neoliberal policies are implemented in a "one size fits all" manner, without the nuances needed to make them practicable in each different local context. Third, the responsibility for resource management tends to shift from the state to distinct stakeholder groups, particularly those in the private sector.

In Tucumán and Cochabamba, once water services were privatized, market mechanisms determined subsequent policy. Privately owned water companies immediately increased tariffs before they took even one step to improve water services. This was most dramatic in Cochabamba, where half the population was not connected to the municipal water system, and the company announced no plans for service improvements. The intensity of the popular response, with a notably active participation by women, forced the government to cancel the contract with a multinational company, just as occurred in Tucumán where women organized the "Stop Payment" campaign.

In both cases, the "common people," with no access to the trappings of the cutting-edge, globalized world, were able to exert enough pressure that governments rescinded provincial and national laws despite the domestic and international repercussions this had for their administrations.

Why did this happen? Was the potential consequence of social unrest greater than the fallout from canceling the contract? Given that it is essential that Argentina and Bolivia demonstrate a stable investment climate or the international capital they seek will flow elsewhere, the political costs of repressing social unrest were clearly considered greater than the costs of giving in to the protestors' demands (which included international lawsuits for breach of contract). At the end of the day, the protests in Tucumán and Cochabamba point out the inherent weaknesses and contradictions in the neoliberal model itself.

The participation of women in the mobilizations in both Tucumán and Cochabamba was crucial. In both regions, women were centrally involved in organizing the demonstrations and protests, not only assuming positions of leadership but also mobilizing the elderly, men, other women, youths, and children. These two experiences demonstrate that when economic policies or legal decrees directly affect women, they take an active role and exercise leadership and develop unique strategies.

These case studies prove that even in today's globalized, neoliberal world, social movements play an important role. The social impact of water privatization was severe enough that top-down policies were met by bottom-up responses, and the local prevailed over the global.

Technology Transfer and Social Organization

Two case studies examine the gender implications of technology transfer, considering the incorporation of a gender perspective in water management projects sponsored by NGOs and/or development agencies in local communities.[3] Aguilar's chapter on the impacts of a joint Canadian/Costa Rican community water development project in Heredia province, Costa Rica, and Vera's chapter on the impacts of a soil conservation and irrigation project in Llullucha, Peru, have two overarching features in common: (1) In neither case did the external project teams take gender into consideration during project planning, and (2) by the end of both projects, both teams concluded that a gender perspective was *essential* to success. Nevertheless, how the project teams got from their starting positions to their conclusions differed significantly.

In Costa Rica, the project team began with a simple plan to test a manual water pump in rural communities. Once it was underway, the project expanded to include multiple water and sanitation related components. The most important lessons the project team learned were not technical but rather focused on the social aspects of technology transfer. One of the first challenges was to decide who would participate and how that participation was defined (this was years before participation had become a common feature of development projects). The project team, which included engineers and an anthropologist, men and women, departed from the prevailing norm of community participation as meaning community labor and focused attention on the heterogeneity of the community. This observation—that communities are not homogeneous—proved critical for the project's eventual success.

Of the many heterogeneities that constitute a community, the most important one for this particular project was gender. The project team understood very early on that for the project to work, both women and men would have to be involved in central and equitable ways. Equitable participation did not mean that everyone did the same thing but that barriers creating gender differentiated participation had to be dismantled or bypassed effectively. The team recognized the unequal relations between men and women in the communities and developed strategies to foster the construction of more equitable relationships that took into consideration gendered roles and responsibilities within households and communities.

The project Vera describes in Llullucha, Peru, also benefited greatly from the long amount of time the regional implementing agency was involved (five years), which permitted community women to engineer their inclusion even though the project was set up to exclude them completely. The Llullucha project team's number one lesson was the importance of community participation in technology transfer, which is what they discovered when after two years, they found that the community's priority was not soil conservation at all but irrigation water. However, even then, the definition of whom to consult was not inclusive and only included the male farmers because the agency defined participants as communal landholders, and in Llullucha, these were only the men. When community women protested the new irrigation project because the diversion of water dried up water for domestic animals and washing clothes, the project leaders had to go back to the drawing board to redesign the project once again.

Once the water project was redesigned to provide water both for the fields and for household needs, the implementing agency continued to identify community participants by only one criterion, land ownership, and remained blind to the fact that *both* men and women were engaged in farming even though the women could not own land. However, the project team was not alone in excluding women as participants; the cultural norms of the village dictated that men were farmers and women helpers. The women self-identified as helpers, arguing that while they could in fact carry out all the farming work, they did not have the technical language to talk about it.

The fact that language use distinguished the women from the men, and not the ability to do the work, provides a telling example of how power is socially constructed. This is further embedded in the productive/reproductive split that has women in charge of the work that is necessary to reproduce the worker: cooking, cleaning, providing water for bathing, washing clothes, and caring for the sick. However, the women were aware of the irrigation project and its benefits, and they organized to acquire a piece of land to farm collectively. This land immediately entitled the women to irrigation water and then they were eligible to participate in the project. Vera calls this remarkable process *active resistance*. Eventually, when the regional development agency found that women were far more reliable participants in credit programs than men were, the agency decided to extend loans to women in other communities.

Despite the multiple experiences the project team had in Llullucha that showed the limitation of including only the men as participants, the team did not fully comprehend the situation until they worked with the SNV

Netherlands Development Organization's gender assessment project. During that project the team came to recognize that their assumptions were severely flawed: they had assumed that their work was completely separate from gender relations and would have no impact on them, that technology transfer was a completely technical process, and that any benefits to the community would be equitably shared. The gender assessment highlighted that men and women had different priorities regarding water because of their different roles and responsibilities, and that a successful water project had to take into account all dimensions of water use in a given community. The outcome of the project in Llullucha strengthened the policy of the SNV Netherlands Development Organization to include a gender perspective in all stages of project work. Thus the actions of a group of poor women in a remote Andean community shaped the parameters for future regional projects as well as for projects worldwide.

These two cases of technology transfer in Costa Rica and Peru lead to some very significant conclusions. First and foremost, technology transfer is much more effective when project members recognize that it is intricately linked to social organization. There is a persistent and pernicious tendency to consider technology transfer the domain of men with an underlying and unquestioned assumption that women do not have the interest, ability, knowledge, or skills to deal with new technology. Nevertheless, these two case studies show just the contrary and reveal how water sector projects intersect with gender, household, and community dynamics. To carry out the projects without recognizing and exploring those intersections could only result in less effective outcomes. Second, a participatory approach is not in and of itself gender neutral. Gender has to be explicitly incorporated or the participatory approach can exclude women all together, even in cases where there are immediate and compelling reasons to include them.

These experiences in Costa Rica and Peru demonstrate that technology transfer is a catalyst for social change, sometimes intentionally and sometimes not. Social organization is not static; it evolves over time and in response to internal and external stimuli. Gender dynamics are one aspect of social organization and they, too, change. These cases show the ripple effect that even small projects can have. When technology transfer leads to social change it is not just in one direction. The community, the project team, and the sponsoring agency may all change, as the project affects the community and in turn community dynamics affect the project. Though the lessons learned in Peru and Costa Rica took many years, each new project does not have to start at the beginning again. Their experiences provide guidelines for implementing a gender perspective in the technology transfer process.

Participation and Cultural Change

The eight case studies demonstrate the heterogeneity of Latin American women's participation in water management for household use and for irrigation. These studies also highlight the structural obstacles stemming from the dominant gender system that women have to face when they embrace active participation. The cases reflect women's autonomy and their ability to make decisions in the process of becoming social actors and show how women's participation leads to social demands that in cumulative fashion result in a process of cultural change.

In its broadest sense, the participatory approach is part of the search for a more equitable distribution of the social benefits that can derive from development. It implies that citizenship must be fully exercised by both men and women, respecting the right of every citizen to be involved in matters that affect them. Participation is the best way to incorporate a diversity of interests, needs, and potential contributions throughout the decision-making process; it is also the best way to secure sustainable commitments from all social actors. The participatory approach assumes the real (not token) involvement of the public in all the steps of planning, implementing, and evaluating development strategies. In past decades, when totalitarian governments ruled many Latin American countries, participation of all kinds suffered a major setback, as it was often considered a suspicious activity and officially outlawed. In the 1990s, democratization strengthened civil society, and governments as well as development agencies expanded the use of the participatory approach as citizens' rights increased.

Decisions regarding water use and management are embedded in a complex matrix of social relations. This was acknowledged in Dublin, and the literature emphasizes the *lack* of participation as a limitation to sound water management. But the problem is more that participation is limited to groups with privileged access to decision making, such as private corporations.[4] Here we specifically examine what *real* citizens' participation could mean. From a gender perspective, participation plays a central role in achieving equity and is not conceived of in a pragmatic or instrumentalist form but as the right of both men and women to actively influence decision making and to have a say with real power in the processes that affect them.

In all the case studies, participation is important—from the community level to the regional level, to actions that have international influence. We focus here specifically on the different forms of women's participation that emerge in the studies by Ennis-McMillan in La Purificación Tepetitla, by Buechler in Irapuato—both in Mexico—and in the chapter by Bastidas on Carchi, in the Ecuadorian Andes. These case studies show how gradually, over the past few years, women have become more involved in water management outside the home, although historically men have assumed positions of authority and decision making and have administered water resources, especially where water is closely linked to productive activities and where irrigation water and household water are not separate systems. The studies by Ennis-McMillan, Bastidas, and Buechler link this change to several factors that are both internal (directly related to the women themselves) and external (related to both local and global economic and social processes).

We must first point to the fact that women's work outside the home involving water has increased. While it is true that women are primarily, if not exclusively, responsible for managing water within their households, they gradually have also become more responsible for water management outside the home. Their experiences with domestic water management are also useful for the public management of drinking water systems. Thus the case of La Purificación Tepetitla shows that it is more and more common for women to be elected to serve on the town's Drinking Water Committee. And in the Irapuato and Carchi cases, women have become more and more involved in the management of irrigation water. All three cases suggest that the greater participation of women not only means that they are exercising a right but also that they are assuming responsibilities they did not have before. However, as these cases also show, this in turn increases their workload because they are not relieved of chores they already had both inside and outside the home.

In recent decades, women have reached a higher level of formal education that contributes to their increasing participation at the same time as it validates their ability to assume decision-making positions in their communities. The study carried out in Carchi shows that when women have higher levels of education than the average for local men, and when they have a profession, it is easier for them to assume positions of leadership, to speak in public, and be heard. Furthermore, when women's informally obtained experience, abilities, and knowledge are acknowledged and valued, their participation in managing water systems is greater and the belief that irrigation work is an exclusively male activity is undermined. As the work carried out by women in managing water systems becomes more visible, women's roles in the decision-making processes of water management will grow, leading in turn to greater recognition of women's abilities and then to broader changes in gender relations.

Bastidas shows that in Carchi, women's participation in water management tends to increase significantly and gain greater social legitimacy where women are the heads of households, for example, when they are widowed, single, or separated, or daughters with elderly parents and no adult male siblings. Ennis-McMillan describes the same phenomenon in La Purificación Tepetitla. Women's participation in water management also significantly increases when men are absent due to migration. In Irapuato, Buechler shows that women assumed responsibility for water management in the fields when male relatives migrated, temporarily and sometimes permanently, changing socially assigned behaviors and roles. Women's tasks that were hidden or previously unacknowledged became visible, changing decision-making dynamics, though these changes were not as significant as could have been expected.[5]

The modernization process acts as an external factor that can lead to more active participation of both rural and urban women even though the relationship between gender and water differs in the countryside and the city. In the countryside, culturally based meanings of water coexist with modern infrastructure, and traditional water management practices are intertwined with modern water management. Historically set gender roles are challenged by modern phenomena such as male out-migration, waged labor opportunities for both men and women in rural agroindustry, expanded communication with the outside world, and better transportation. Although this encroachment of the modern has changed gender relationships, often increasing the spaces for women's participation, full modernization is resisted and the traditional can be fiercely defended when it comes to protecting the environment as well as maintaining the spiritual order of the world. In urban areas, where traditional perceptions and water management practices fade away, the intersection of gender and water stems mostly from the importance of water to women's roles in social reproduction. This has placed women on the front lines in responding to economic pressures (higher water rates) and political manipulations (inequitable water laws, privatization schemes that ignore local realities). Women have become protagonists of social movements over water services as seen in Tucumán and Cochabamba (see also Bennett 1995).

The blurring of the rural-urban dichotomy has occurred over the last twenty years with the growth of periurban areas such as La Purificación Tepetitla, where rural villages have been overtaken, or reached, by urban sprawl. In places such as La Puri, urban dwellers live side by side with villagers. Historically rooted water management practices evolve to meet the new context of the mixed population. At the same time, local women increasingly find waged income and their increased economic independence and higher levels of education lead to greater participation in their communities, including water management.

Among the obstacles to active participation in water management that women face, foremost is the relationship between gender inequities and social class inequities. In urban areas, higher-income groups have better water service, and neither women nor men tend to be involved in water management or in water-related social movements. It is in the lower-income neighborhoods that either receive poor water service or have no piped water, where women increasingly become involved. Until recently, in the countryside, class inequities stemmed mainly from land ownership. Today, access to water has become the most important factor in the class inequities stemming historically from land ownership. Buechler calls our attention to the differences between women who do not own land and have to rent it; those who own small parcels far from water wells; and men, who generally own their land and usually have bigger parcels. The women are disadvantaged from the start because land ownership with access to water is so often the prerequisite to participation in water user associations, which means their needs are not represented at the table. Ennis-McMillan shows that women from the low-income families in La Purificación had a harder time getting elected to the Drinking Water Committee and that their access to public institutions was more limited than men's. Sometimes these obstacles encourage greater participation in social movements, protests, and community mobilizations as happened in Tucumán and Cochabamba where a principal demand was for transparency in decision making and in the management of the local water systems.

Indispensable to the equitable distribution of opportunities for participation is the timely availability of information. Plenty of evidence in the case studies demonstrates that women are often not included in the distribution of information and therefore are prevented from participating. Cultural barriers often prevent women from attending water organization meetings: going to meetings may not be socially accepted practice for women, their husbands may not want them to participate, they may not have the legal rights required for attendance, or households may be registered only under the male head of household. All these circumstances contribute to keeping women ill informed and make them ineligible for decision-making positions in the water user associations. In this way their voices are lost.

Cultural phenomena are dynamic, and participation is not static. The participation of women takes place in a simultaneous context of cultural barriers and socioeconomic opportunities. Many times women's knowledge is not recognized by project staff, as in the Peruvian case, or by the women themselves. Sometimes women perpetuate their low self-esteem as they buy into the cultural code that water management is a "matter for men" and that women are only "helpers." However, as soon as someone asks their opinion, women generally begin to speak out and dare to make decisions. They begin to believe that, in spite of their real or apparent disadvantages, they have an important stake in the water management process. We must not ignore the situations that Buechler and Bastidas described where gender discrimination meant that in order not to lose their irrigation water, women heads of household had to hire men—whom they supervised—to negotiate on their behalf with other men on matters related to the water system, such as the irrigation schedule. To avoid gossip, women also had to ask their young sons to accompany them when they irrigated at night. Hiring male workers negatively affects their budgets because they have to pay for the services of an employee that a male head of household would not require.

The studies show that decisions are sometimes made in the name of women, assuming their compliance and shared interests with men. However, when they are consulted, women often express different priorities than those their closest male relatives or male politicians and bureaucrats mention. As one of the women interviewed in La Purificación said, "We all have our own ideas. Each person thinks differently, so it is good to include women." While different priorities can sometimes be accommodated, they can also lead to conflict. In Carchi, although men made decisions only after consulting the women, these discussions were not always without conflict. Many women interviewed said that they preferred to channel their energy toward other economic activities where they could control their own incomes. In the Irapuato case, water management is still carried out as if women don't irrigate, when in fact in some cases they do so regularly, even more so when the men are absent due to migration.

These cases also demonstrate that problems that exist at the national level regarding equitable water management are not always present at the community level. In La Purificación Tepetitla, historical principles of resource distribution served to equitably distribute water to all residents, avoiding the gender hierarchies that usually limit the participation of women in water management. This example obliges us to consider how the lessons learned from water management at the local level can be reproduced at a higher level. To achieve this, we must acknowledge the heterogeneity of circumstances in Latin America and begin community work without preconceived ideas of its needs, priorities, and social relationships. In fact, outsiders—engineers, politicians, and academics—may inadvertently create gender divisions due to their incorrect assumptions and thus create new obstacles for women (e.g., this happened in Llullucha). Because community participation in water management is so limited in urban areas, and outsiders almost inevitably come from more modernized (urban) locales, they are often blind to the degree to which women are already involved in water management in rural towns and in irrigation (as seen in Llullucha, Cochabamba, La Purificación Tepetitla, and Irapuato).

Integrated water resources management requires the creation of spaces that encourage open debate and make consensus possible. To create these spaces we must find pathways towards greater participation, which in turn will increase the power and status of disadvantaged groups. The examples of Carchis, Irapuato, and La Purificación Tepetitla show that both the water user associations and the grassroots organizations offer women, in both theory and in practice, an opportunity for more active participation. Likewise, they provide examples of how women's participation contributes to their community's social and economic development. As Buechler indicates, decentralization policies that transfer ground water management systems from the government to the users, such as those adopted in Mexico in the 1990s, open the possibility of creating new user organizations or strengthening existing organizations, and this in turn potentially sets the stage for more equitable participation of men and women at the local level.

At the same time, another obstacle for greater participation of women in decision-making processes is the dynamics of water associations themselves. Bastidas signals that even though no explicit rules limit women's participation in meetings, they are still considered a man's activity. The weakness of water user organizations in the Carchi area leads water users to resort to informal agreements that tend to favor male-to-male interactions and serve to further exclude women. Buechler notes that water user association meeting times in Irapuato and the form of invitations to meetings where irrigation system management is discussed often exclude women. In contrast, in La Purificación Tepetitla changes in the structure and operational dynamics of the local water committee gave women an opening to influence water management and to exercise communal authority in a legally acknowledged manner; today, women hold half of the management positions on the Drinking Water Committee.

Experience shows that participation cannot be mandated by decree; it is part of a profound cultural change that has to permeate all social actors. The participatory approach will never generate all its potential benefits if governments or those in charge of programs and projects only allow it when they need to comply with a legal requirement or when they have to implement the recommendations of international agencies. True participation implies embracing a process of community empowerment and adapting institutions so they can support and maintain such strategies in the long run.

The examples presented in this book show that women are at the center of important cultural changes. While change is slow, the testimonies presented in these studies let us glimpse shifts in women's perceptions of their roles and abilities, in men's perceptions regarding women's skills and abilities, and in the social discourse regarding both men and women. For example, in La Purificación Tepetitla all of those interviewed (men and women) said that they approved of the growing participation and involvement of women in civil positions in charge of managing water at the community level.

It is precisely in this participation, more than in the water policies, programs, and projects, where we can see the cultural change that is underway in Latin America regarding women's identities, their roles, and their exercise of citizenship. These transformations are happening in a process of multidirectional continuity where traditional norms and customs persist alongside new forms of action that redefine gender relations and the role of women in their communities.

Though for development professionals and policy-makers it can be a challenge to find ways to encourage women's participation (especially in Latin American countries where cultural tradition has established hierarchical gender relations), the studies presented in this book indicate that a good starting point is to look at what women are already doing on the ground, to identify their efforts at actively participating in water-related decisions, and to learn from how they have changed their traditional and historical roles and values. The evidence lets us see how the world is changing, not only as a result of the globalization of the economy but also by the globalization of certain values that bear upon gender relations and citizens' rights. These case studies challenge us to consider and strengthen this trend toward the greater participation of women in water management at the community level as a key strategy for truly equitable development.

Converting Concepts into Practice

The lessons learned from the case studies that can enhance water management practices fall into three overlapping categories: understanding the community, enabling participation, and fostering equitable water resource management.[6] Several of the case studies are key in demonstrating how crucial it is that water project teams understand the communities they work with, no matter what level the project operates on. It is essential to recognize the heterogeneity of communities, and to be explicit about the water needs, uses, and priorities of all subgroups. This means identifying all social actors involved with water in the community, their roles, responsibilities, and their social relations, paying close attention to gender differences. Project planners and technicians need to be open to "seeing"; in other words, they need to be open to reality instead of automatically imposing their predetermined understandings. The heterogeneity of social actors—and of their needs and priorities—was evident in Vera's case study in Llullucha, Peru, in Aguilar's case study in Heredia Province, Costa Rica, and in the study of the "Water War" in Cochabamba, Bolivia.

At the national and international level, it is also fundamental that policy makers and planners develop deeper understandings of the communities on whose behalf they design policies and projects. The case studies by Giarraca and Del Pozo in Tucumán, Argentina, and by Bustamante, Peredo, and Udaeta in Cochabamba, Bolivia, are examples of very significant misreadings and misunderstandings of community and water usage by transnational corporations, and by national and regional governments. As Ahlers points out, a one-size-fits-all water policy does not work. And as Vera suggests, water management is a social construct based on a panoply of intersecting social relations. The failure of the Compagnie Générale des Eaux in Tucumán and of Bechtel in Bolivia are directly attributable to their inability to understand the social relations of local communities, aided and abetted by national and regional governments who turned a blind eye to the realities of their own constituents vis-à-vis water.

While gaining an understanding of the community is the first step, the case studies presented in this book demonstrate that community participation does not happen automatically even when project leaders use a participatory approach. Two principal lessons emerge from the case studies. First, that planners must remember that communities are heterogeneous and so is community water use, and gender often differentiates the latter. Second, one has to go out of one's way to create the conditions for equitable and effective participation for all affected segments of the community. Even though this is time consuming, the benefits outweigh the costs.

Aguilar's discussion of her project in Costa Rica indicates that the primary reason that it was successful is because the project team took the time to understand the community. They were assiduous in developing decision-making processes, data collection methods, educational and training materials, training techniques and spaces, and clearly equitable divisions of project costs and benefits that engaged both the women and the men. The project team itself was heterogeneous in terms of gender and specialization, and they found that different spaces in the community opened up to them based on their own gender. Furthermore, the team modeled gender equity in its leadership, engaged in mutual respect and dialogue with each other and with the community and showed that men and women can do any kind of work in the water sector. The fact that women are as capable as men—or more capable—in all areas of household water management, including irrigation, is amply demonstrated by the work of Ennis-McMillan and by Buechler in Mexico, Bastidas in Ecuador, and by Vera's account of how the women of Llullucha successfully farmed collective land after they were excluded from the regional development irrigation project. Vera's case study shows that participatory methods can be used to exclude as well as to include. When a project team misunderstands community dynamics over water, then women can be left out even when there are compelling and vital reasons to include them. Participation has to be defined inclusively, but this can only be done when a project's designers understand not only who needs to participate and why, but what the relations of power are between the project participants and the role that water plays in those relations.

One of the most powerful examples of successful community participation in water management emerges in Ennis-McMillan's study of La Purificación Tepetitla, where the community has a longstanding water management system that was developed locally and relatively autonomously from any Mexican government or institutional structure. Water management in La Purificación Tepetitla appears to be the most equitable of any of the case studies. This system has been in place for decades, and continues to operate successfully to date, even as the number of female heads of household has exploded, adding women to the Drinking Water Committee. Community water management in La Purificación Tepetitla suggests that resource management designed with equity from the very start is inherently more stable than management designed with the implicit (and sometimes explicit) biases of most government and institutional resource management systems.

Reaching for Gender Equity in the Water Sector

Four overarching conclusions regarding water and gender emerge from this book. First, the elimination of gender biases is a key mechanism for increasing the effectiveness and reach of water sector investments. Water sector planning, technology transfer, and the participatory method are not gender neutral. They will be gender biased until the connections between gender and water are made explicit and addressed. Thus, equitable participation for men and women has to be an explicit goal, and has to be systematically enabled in all facets of water sector work. This means understanding, respecting, and addressing gender differentiation in roles, responsibilities, needs, and priorities. It means equitable access to resources, including land, water, credit, and training. It means taking into account all uses of water by all members of a community in the design phase of water investments. This does not imply that every project must address all water needs but rather that every project's goals and ramifications are explicit and realistic. Effective and equitable planning in the water sector takes a long time with deep preliminary research and evaluation of the community involved, whether it is a local community, a province, or an entire nation.

Second, equitable planning implies that heterogeneous and competing priorities for water usage be respected. An example of how this does *not* happen is found in the current prioritization of water for irrigation in the rural sector, which ignores the very real costs to health and productivity that stem from inadequate and poor quality household water supplies. Irrigation water and household water are equally important for family and community well being, but planning and investments fail to reflect that, prioritizing irrigation because it is in men's domain in the sphere of production.

Third, investments in the water sector alter power dynamics at all levels. For example, in Llullucha and in Heredia Province, community water projects altered women's roles and consequently affected gender relations. On a different level, in Tucumán, women were protagonists of the fight, moving on to other community leadership roles after their success in reversing the privatization of their region's water system. The Cochabamba Water War is a further example of the same process. Tucumán, Cochabamba, Heredia, and Llullucha reveal the many layers of power dynamics: between large investors and national governments, between national and local governments, between large investors and end users, between governments and end users, between project teams and communities, between husbands and wives, and so on. As water projects alter power dynamics, cultural and social change takes place, in turn altering the context in which the project is implemented.

Fourth, and finally, for gender biases in the water sector to be eliminated there must be an enabling environment. It is not enough to talk about what is needed; formal structures have to be created that move the process forward. These structures include not only new laws but also governments committed to the implementation of these laws, they require not only new financing decisions but the will to respect new investment priorities at the community and national levels, and they have to be built on a foundation of gender equity. A huge gap still exists between policy and what happens on the ground. The case studies, however, indicate that communities are not passive recipients of inequitable development decisions. Because water affects the everyday lives, health, and sustainability of individuals, families, and communities, they react when their water services are tampered with. And their reactions can undermine, subvert, or facilitate water investments. Water must be a catalyst for equitable development and steps must be taken to enable that. The costs of not doing so are simply far too great, and the proven benefits of equity are too important to ignore.

Notes

Chapter 1: Introduction

1. We define management in its broadest sense, including policy making, planning, and implementation at the national, state, and local levels.

2. Increasingly, water management problems have become linked to ecological and environmental concerns. At times, as Steve Mumme has suggested (personal communication, April 2003), the environment is an alternative discourse and pathway to mobilization over water resource problems for some communities. This is evident in the case study on Tucumán, Argentina (chapter six). The mobilizations that pressured the Tucumán government to rescind its privatization contract for the region's water management with a French multinational was boosted when the region's water came out of household faucets brown for a month because of excessive manganese in the water. In other regions, such as the Colorado River Delta in the Mexicali Valley, Mexico, environmental degradation has been conflated with water management. Though it is beyond the scope of this book to explore the environment-water-gender nexus, examples of these connections were found in some of our case studies.

Chapter 2: The Connection between Gender and Water Management

1. We define gender as the social construction of differentiated roles, rights, and responsibilities for women and men. Gender relations are the socially constructed relationships between men and women regarding household, work, and community. Gender roles, rights, responsibilities, and relations are context specific in that they are defined by a particular culture at a particular time. As such, they evolve and change over time, reflecting larger changes within the culture and society in which they exist (Levy 1992).

2. The dichotomy between water for health and hygiene and water for irrigation has been perpetuated for decades by the "basic needs" focus. Both uses of water are essential for good health and hygiene.

3. We must also distinguish between the *de jure* and *de facto* realities: one thing is the law, another its implementation. This is where culture becomes a variable that shapes and limits implementation not only of policy but also of legal frameworks.

4. Note that in urban areas, the right to water means the right to municipal water services. In rural areas, where municipal water services do not exist, the right to water means the right to irrigate as well as the right to use wells or nearby rivers or the irrigation canals for household water. Rural landowners may be deeded the right to the water that passes across their land or lies under it, while nonlandowners must rely on the right to seek access, which in the end is hardly a social right at all.

5. The sphere of reproduction refers to the place where all the domestic tasks necessary to "produce" and "reproduce" the worker for the sphere of production occur. Reproduction refers not only to biological reproduction but to social reproduction and includes all the household work necessary to keep all family members healthy, clean, fed, and rested so that they can attend school and/or work. Typically, the sphere of reproduction is the responsibility of women. Men's role in production refers to both the highly masculine world of water resource management and to the use of water as a production input, especially in the context of rural irrigation.

6. For irrigation examples of this ideology in Mexico, see Carmona Quiróz and Monsalvo Velázquez 1998; Ahlers 2000a; Brunt 1992. For the Andean countries, see Boelens and Zwarteveen 2002b.

209

7. For examples, see Ahlers 2000a; Ahlers 2000b; Buechler and Zapata Martelo 2000; Kloezen 2002; Monsalvo Velázquez et al. 2000; Vos 2002.

8. For examples, see Lynch 1991; Franke 1993; Vattuone et al. 1996; Tuijtelaars de Quiton et al. 1994; Bastidas 1999.

9. See, for instance, Jácome and Krol 1994; Arroyo and Boelens 1998; van der Pol 1992; Ahlers and Smits 1991; Monsalvo Velázquez et al. 2000.

10. For México, see Buechler and Zapata 2000; for the Andean countries, see Boelens and Zwarteveen 2002b.

11. See Zwarteveen and Meinzen-Dick (2001) for an elaboration of this point.

12. Monsalvo Velázquez et al. (2000) use the term *water culture* in a similar sense, referring to the professional norms, customs, priorities, and patterns of behavior that characterize the professional involvement with water.

13. For just one of many examples, see van der Pol 1992. Buechler (see chapter 11, this book) also cites women in rural Mexico who say that irrigation work is easy for them.

14. Personal communication from Rutgerd Boelens, 2001.

15. Ahlers (2000a) gives one example, but it is a common phenomenon across Latin America.

16. In rewarding and promoting certain types and styles of thinking and doing, the professional culture in the water world also creates strong obstructions against nonengineering professionals, such as those from the social sciences, not only in terms of identifying problems but also in terms of solving them.

Chapter 3: Global Water and Gender Policies: Latin American Challenges

This chapter was translated by Aníbal Yáñez-Chávez, Lawrence A. Herzog, and Vivienne Bennett, and edited by Linda Farthing and Vivienne Bennett.

1. With the spread of globalization, anti- and pro-movements have arisen. The antiglobalization movement has expressed its positions very visibly at world events in Washington, D.C., Seattle, Porto Alegre, and other cities worldwide.

2. Although changing notions of citizenship and human rights are not expressions of economic "determinism," the economic process of globalization frames them.

3. In many cases, the Chilean example of applying neoliberal principles to the water sector has served as a model. For more information on Chilean water markets, see Dourojeanni and Jouravlev 1999, 2001.

4. For example, the theme for the 2002 World Food Day (October 16) was "Water: Source of Food Security."

5. The Brundtland Commission was created to prepare for the Earth Summit in Rio de Janeiro. Its report went beyond viewing women simply as victims of environmental degradation and saw them instead as having knowledge and skills that make them effective administrators of natural resources.

6. Representatives from 172 governments, including 108 heads of state, participated in the Earth Summit.

7. Criticism of these programs has come not only from organizations within the United Nations but also from the Secretary General himself, who acknowledged that the goals had not been met and who urged worldwide cooperation to establish reachable goals for 2015.

8. The Dublin principles detailed in chapter one became known as the Dublin-Rio principles after the 1997 Earth Summit of Rio+5.

9. For example, Section II (18.1–18.90) of Agenda 21 addresses the protection of the quality and supply of freshwater resources and the application of integrated approaches to the development, management, and use of water resources, while Section III, "Global action for women towards sustainable and equitable development" (24.1–24.12), highlights the role women play in changing current consumption and production patterns and underscores that women's active involvement is required for the successful implementation of all the Earth Summit's resolutions.

10. The Johannesburg gathering made various buildings available for meetings on particular topics; the building devoted to water issues was called "Waterdome."

11. By *gender system*, we mean a system of socioculturally determined hierarchical social relationships that regulate the assignment of roles, access and control over resources, participation in decision-

making processes, and the power of men and women. This system is structurally based on the sexual division of labor and on the social and historical construction of differences between men and women, as well as on a set of norms and social conventions that affect the perceptions that people have of themselves and of their roles in the development of their communities and countries (Rico 1994a).

12. In Latin America, the application of a gender analysis to nontraditional issues is a recent development. To date there are not enough studies or statistics on, for example, how a gender approach could affect issues such as the debt, international trade, or the transnationalization of economies.

13. The infusion of gender issues across the agenda means that they are taken into account in the whole project cycle and in the cycle of public policy formulation.

14. The United Nations established INSTRAW in 1976 to fulfill commitments made at the First World Conference for Women, held in Mexico in 1975. In the 1990s, INSTRAW and UNICEF were the first organizations to develop methodologies and training to actively involve women and enable their decision-making power in water projects as a way to assure project sustainability (INSTRAW 1994; Whitaker 1992).

15. In 1983, the United Nations Development Programme launched the Promotion of the Role of Women in Water and Environmental Sanitation, known as PROWWESS, which in 1992 was included in the UNDP's Water and Sanitation Program with the World Bank.

16. The twelve areas of special concern in this document are: women and poverty, women's education and training, women and health, violence against women, women and armed conflicts, women and the economy, women in the exercise of power and decision making, institutional mechanisms for the advancement of women, women's human rights, women and the mass media, women and the environment, and female children.

17. In Latin America in recent years, there has been a growing discourse about developing methodologies that incorporate a gender focus and an intercultural perspective in irrigation projects in the Andean region (Claverías 2002) as well as in Mexico and Central America. However, the case studies in this book show the huge gap that persists between discourse and practice.

18. One interesting exception is the NGO Mujeres en Desarrollo Dominicana (MUDE, Women in Dominican Development) in the Dominican Republic, which for eight years has been carrying out drinking water and environmental sanitation projects with a gender approach in poor rural communities that are hard to reach and that have few concrete possibilities to receive state aid (communication from Adela Williams to the electronic conference on gender and water held in Latin America in February 2002).

19. At the governmental level, these include world summits, meetings between regional leaders, and meetings between leaders from different regions. Meetings among nongovernmental organizations include those held by sectoral and intersectoral groups, organizations of women, children, the elderly, and others.

20. While international financial agencies continue to insist that water resources be seen as a whole, at the national level most countries place drinking water and water for irrigation under the auspices of different ministries. This structural distinction between drinking water and irrigation water is detailed in chapter two.

Chapter 4: Gender Dimensions of Neoliberal Water Policy in Mexico and Bolivia

The research in Mexico was funded by the International Water Management Institute, and I would like to acknowledge the research assistance of Luz Elena Martinez, Silvana Pacheco, and Irene Portillo. The research in Bolivia was funded through the Mario Einaudi Center for International Studies at Cornell University, and I am especially grateful for the help and insights provide by Rocio Bustamante and Tom Kruse in Bolivia.

1. The policy document came out in 1993 as a result of experimenting with the Water Law in Chile and redesigning the Mexican Law during the 1980s and after consultation rounds with water sector specialists, NGO fora, the first 1992 Earth Summit in Rio and the 1992 Dublin Conference.

2. The Dublin principles for water are: (1) freshwater is finite and essential to sustain life, development, and environment; (2) management should be participatory; (3) women are central to providing, managing and safeguarding water; (4) water has an economic value and should be recognized as

an economic good. It explicitly specifies, though, that "Within this principle, it is vital to recognize first the basic right of all human beings to have access to clean water and sanitation at an affordable price."

3. For a detailed description of the new Water Law, see Ahlers 1999; Fortis and Ahlers 1999.

4. As soon as the law came into being, water markets became legal. In practice, however, water marketing unfolded at different paces across the country. In Sinaloa, a lively market emerged immediately; in the Comarca Lagunera, the market really took off in 1995–1996.

5. The average annual precipitation over the past ten years has been 220 mm, while the average evaporation is 2200 mm.

6. As the legal ramifications of selling rights were unclear for most users, farmers would speak of renting out their rights for one or more seasons. For the purpose of this chapter, I distinguish between permanent and temporary sales. After gaining more trust, however, many of the men conceded that they had effectively sold their rights permanently. In many cases, the contracts drawn up for these transactions were framed in such a way that the right was transferred permanently, without acquiescence of the original owner.

7. The groundwater in Irrigation district 011 is highly contaminated with arsenic.

8. The same day, the public water system of Cochabamba was sold to a private international consortium including the U.S. engineering firm Bechtel, supported by both the World Bank and the Inter American Development Bank (IDB).

9. For a more detailed discussion of gender, cosmovision, and irrigation, see Boelens and Zwarteveen (2002b).

Chapter 5: Women in the "Water War" in the Cochabamba Valleys

This chapter was translated by Anibal Yáñez-Chávez and edited by Linda Farthing. We thank the women of the Federation of Irrigators of the Department of Cochabamba (Federación Departamental de Regantes de Cochabamba, FEDECOR) for providing us with the testimonials and accounts of their participation in the Water War, particularly Carmen Peredo for her contributions and support in the organization of the November 2001 workshop on "Women in the 'Water War'" sponsored by FEDECOR, the Fundación Solón, the Centro de Investigación y Promoción del Campesinado (CIPCA), and the Centro Andino para la Gestión y Uso del Agua (Centro Agua) at the Universidad Mayor de San Simón in Cochabamba.

1. Equivalent to a U.S. state or Canadian province.

2. In Bolivia, drinking water supply and sewerage services are regulated by law (each law is numbered). Any changes to an existing law require its replacement with a different number. For this reason, Law 2066 replaced the initial Law 2029.

3. The neighborhood committees are based on residence in a particular zone or neighborhood and have an elected leadership. They form part of associations and confederations at a national level and are officially considered the basic units for planning and resource allocation purposes under the 1993 Law on Popular Participation. This law sought to increase public participation at the local level, in both rural and urban areas, and was created, along with the Law on Administrative Decentralization and the Law on Education Reform, to respond to social unrest and to address the long-unmet basic needs of the population.

4. *Campesinos,* translated as "peasants," are literally are people who live in the countryside. In Bolivia, the word *peasants* is commonly used as synonymous to indigenous. The vast majority of Bolivian *campesinos* are from Quechua, Aymara, or Guaraní ethnic groups.

5. The Misicuni Multiple Project (drinking water, irrigation, and electricity) has long been seen as a solution to the problem of the chronic water shortage. This project has become a great regional utopia and promises to execute it frequently figure in the speeches of local politicians.

6. The new tariff format agreed upon in the concession contract was a progressive structure that classified users into nine groups. The concessionaire was guaranteed a rate of return of at least 15 percent and no more than 17 percent. Tariffs had to be collected "in Bolivianos at the official dollar exchange rate as published by the Central Bank of Bolivia on the last day of the period for which service is being charged" (Appendix 5, Section 1.5 of the Aguas del Tunari contract). In addition, "the

dollar value of all tariffs . . . will be adjusted annually . . . taking into account cost inflation in dollars expressed as variations in the CPI (Consumer Price Index) of the United States of America" (Appendix 5, Section 1.5 of the Aguas del Tunari contract). To fulfill these requirements, tariffs were increased an average of 35 percent in January 2000.

7. When the first public request for bids to provide drinking water and sewerage services to the city of Cochabamba was declared unfilled the first time around, the government, instead of issuing a second request for bids, decided to make the initial terms more flexible and authorized direct negotiations with the Aguas del Tunari consortium (which had been established a few weeks earlier). During these direct negotiations, the consortium found itself in a position to impose its own terms and conditions on a government anxious under enormous pressure to privatize the water service. One example of the conditions the consortium imposed was that the consortium could demand an indemnity payment from the Water Superintendent if the contract was terminated, even if such termination was the consortium's fault (e.g., if it failed to meet its contractual obligations or violated the law). This condition was unheard of in such negotiations.

8. The Coordinadora comprised the Committee in Defense of Water, the Cochabamba Peasant Irrigators Federation, the Factory Workers Federation, the Teachers Federation, the Merchants Federation, the Peasant Federation, and professional organizations of engineers, lawyers, economists, and others.

9. Women in *polleras* are those wearing traditional indigenous dress.

10. The Cochabamba Civic Committee is an organization that brings together various departmental institutions interested in regional issues.

11. The Coordinadora carried out the Popular Poll on March 26, 2000. The questions asked were: (1) Do you accept the fee increase? (2) Should the contract with Aguas del Tunari be annulled? (3) Do you agree with how Law 2029 makes water private? Of the 46,276 people who voted, 99 percent said no to the first question, 96 percent said yes to the second, and 97 percent said no to the third.

12. This means superior or irresistible force, the Roman-law equivalent of an *act of God* (translator's note).

13. In Spanish, the word *coordinadora* is feminine and can mean either a "coordinating committee" or a "female coordinator." Thus, because the Coordinadora Departamental en Defensa del Agua y de la Vida was popularly abbreviated to "la Coordinadora" and because so many women were in the streets participating in the Water War, some people in Cochabamba mistakenly believed that "La Coordinadora" referred to a female coordinator who was in charge of the movement.

14. During the wars of independence, it was also women (the heroines of la Coronilla) who defended the city from the advances of the Spanish crown.

15. A *chichería* is where *chicha* is sold; *chicha* is a fermented alcoholic beverage made from maize that is a traditional drink of the Cochabamba valleys.

16. An expression of contempt in the Quechua language that literally means dirty barefoot Indian.

17. Coca leaves come from a plant indigenous to the Andes, sacred in Inca culture. Today, they are used in traditional rituals as an offering or to ask for the protection of *Pachamama* (Mother Earth). They are also chewed by laborers to increase their ability to withstand the rigors of excessive physical labor.

18. The term *usos y costumbres* (customary practices) refers to traditional customs and rights that govern behavior of a given ethnic group. The term is mainly, but not exclusively, used with regards to indigenous communities. It can also be used to describe behavior in rural towns and poor urban areas that have closer or more recent links to the traditional customs and philosophies of the prevailing ethnic group to which they belong.

Chapter 6: To Make Waves

This chapter was translated by Herzonia Yáñez-Chávez and Vivienne Bennett, with the collaboration of Norma Giarracca, and edited by Linda Farthing.

1. During 1996, with the conflict in full force, Dycasa drastically reduced its participation in the partnership leaving the Compagnie Générale des Eaux to deal with civil society and the provincial government in Tucumán.

2. *Piquetes* are demonstrations; *escraches* are public denunciations of certain subjects (former dictators, corrupt officials, etc.) in front of their places of residence; *cacerolazos* are demonstrations with people in the streets banging pots and pans.

3. Civil disobedience is a subcategory of a collective action. It has the following objectives: to be deliberative, autonomous, disruptive, and nonviolent and to question an institutional decision taken in the name of a "majority."

4. He won with more than 40 percent of the votes, therefore not representing the majority of the population.

5. The percent of the population supporting the Stop Payment campaign increased over time. While at its peak, 90 percent of the population supported the campaign; over most of the period in which the Stop Payment campaign took place, at least 70 percent of the population supported it.

6. A London *Observer* and BBC reporter explained: "[T]his happened [in Argentina] because they started out at the end of the 80s with orders from the IMF and World Bank to sell off all their public assets. . . . I mean, things we wouldn't dream of doing in the U.S., like selling off their water system which was sold off for a song to a company called Enron" (http://www.gregplast.com). (The reporter meant that the World Bank and IMF would never dream of doing in the United States what it does routinely elsewhere: insist on privatizations.)

7. They sent out questionnaires to the residents and then forwarded the responses to the company, with copies to the regulating agency (ERSACT).

8. The Compagnie Générale des Eaux, through its lawyers, threatened users in an attempt to collect what they owed. In November 2001, it demanded payment once again. This time, the user associations denounced that the company's demands were supported by the current governor who had withdrawn the province's lawsuit against the Compagnie Générale des Eaux.

9. Currently María Julia Alsogaray faces several corruption charges.

10. The women who began the struggle for human rights during the military dictatorship (1976–1983) were also considered "crazy." Today, these women are the Mothers from the Plaza de Mayo. Elsewhere in Argentina, women farmers who fought for their lands are frequently also described as "crazy" (see Giarracca and Teubal 2001).

11. The National Women's Conference is held every year and is sponsored by organizations that fight for women's rights. Usually, around 15,000 women attend, along with guests from other countries.

12. The southern region of the province of Buenos Aires granted the concession for its water services to the U.S.-based Azurix Corporation (a subsidiary of Enron) in 1995. By early 2002, Azurix too was forced to leave the country because of public protest in several cities (Bahía Blanca, Pehuajó, Carlos Casares, July 9) that erupted because of the poor quality of its service.

Chapter 7: Irrigation Management, the Participatory Approach, and Equity in an Andean Community

This chapter was translated by Herzonia Yáñez-Chávez and Vivienne Bennett and edited by Linda Farthing.

1. The Instituto de Manejo de Agua y Medio Ambiente (IMA, Institute for Water Management and the Environment) is a special project of the Cusco regional government. IMA participates in two watersheds (Huatanay and Mapacho) and is also active in several native communities in the jungle, in Pillcopata Cusco.

2. The role of SNV during the study was to supervise technical staff from the participating institutions so that their personnel could carry out the research using participatory methodologies with a gender perspective developed by SNV itself. To this end, SNV trained a team of engineers and sociologists from each of the participating institutions. At the same time, the sociologists and engineers helped SNV fine tune its methodology by providing feedback based on their knowledge of the regions, their communities, and their cultures. They also worked with the leadership of their own institutions to engender changes in their internal functioning leading to greater support of the SNV study. After the Llullucha project described in this chapter, IMA carried out similar projects in two other communities with the direct help of an SNV gender advisor. Through this work, IMA has been

asked to train the personnel of other institutions in the use of the participatory methodologies.

3. Llullucha is a small, Andean community in Paucartambo province in Cusco. It has only 30 families (with an average of 7 members per family); 23 percent of its population is illiterate, and 64 percent of those who cannot read or write are women. The community is located between 3,025 and 3,800 meters above sea level, on one side of the open but very steep valley of Quencomayo, only 1.5 kilometers from Paucartambo, the main political, administrative, and commercial center of the province. Paucartambo has a population of approximately 260 families (with an average of 6 members per family), and is located 118 kilometers from the city of Cusco, which can be reached by an unpaved road in approximately three or four hours.

4. Participatory Rural Appraisal "is a family of approaches and methods used to enable rural people to share, enhance, and analyze their knowledge of life and conditions, to plan, to act, and finally to monitor and evaluate. It has three foundations or pillars: (1) the behaviour and attitudes of outsiders, who facilitate, not dominate; (2) the methods, which shift the normal balance from closed to open, individual to group, from verbal to visual, and from measuring to comparing; and (3) partnership and sharing of information, experience, food and training, between insiders and outsiders, and between organizations" (Chambers 1997, 104). Household, as used in this study, is based on two concepts: the first defines household as a kinship-based group engaged in both production and consumption, with corporate ownership of certain resources and a degree of joint decision making among members (Cloud 1998, in Zwarteveen 1997b). To explain the intrahousehold resource allocation, the second concept is based on the bargaining model (Hart 1992, in Zwarteveen 1997b), which defines household as a political arena constituted by particularly dense bundles of rules, rights, and obligations governing relations between men and women, and between elders and younger members of a community.

5. Rapid Rural Appraisal can be described as a "semi-structured activity carried out in the field by a multi-disciplinary team and designed to acquire quickly new information" (Chambers 1997, 116).

6. Gender interface is defined as the encounters, confrontations, and/or discontinuities in the interests, power relationships, knowledge, and values between women and men, among women of different social status, and among men. In this analysis, the concept of symbolic boundary is important, as it makes explicit the position of a given social actor (those who have water rights or have land) vis-à-vis other social actors (those who have no rights to water or land). Women have to deconstruct and cross these symbolic boundaries if they claim water rights. They have to convince local authorities or other politically influential people of the legitimacy of their claim and their rights (Vera 1999). See also Arce and Long (1992) and Brunt (1992).

7. The TPAs were a package of technological proposals to improve and maximize production; they include soil conservation practices, agroecological practices, optimal water use practices (e.g., sprinkler irrigation), production of organic matter, improved storage facilities for storing seeds, and improved cattle corrals. By providing participants with economic incentives, all the TPAs were implemented.

8. As a result of the successes in Llullucha, IMA mainstreamed a gender perspective into other projects. Shortly after the Llullucha project ended, IMA requested that a gender advisor from SNV train a few IMA technicians so that they could be in charge of supervising pilot projects with a participatory approach from a gender perspective. Two years after the SNV gender advisor began training the IMA staff, other agencies began asking that these specialized IMA staff provide training courses for their personnel.

Chapter 8: Water as a Source of Equity and Empowerment in Costa Rica

This chapter was translated by Aníbal Yáñez-Chávez and edited by Linda Farthing.

1. The "Handpump Technology" project was a joint effort by Canada's International Development Research Centre (IDRC) and Costa Rica's Technology Foundation (Fundación Tecnológica, FUNDATEC) through the Department of Construction Engineering of the Costa Rica Institute of Technology (Instituto Tecnológico de Costa Rica, ITCR).

2. These communities are La Chaves, with a total of 87 families; El Palmar, with 113 families; and Ticari with 96 families. The total number of people in 1986 was 1,776 out of Costa Rica's total popu-

lation of 3 million inhabitants. On average, about 10 percent of the residents of the communities were immigrants from Nicaragua.

3. During this period, significant numbers of Nicaraguans migrated to Costa Rica, and the mass media spread the word that many of these people were infected with disease.

4. The term the project team used for the communal facilitators was *multiplicador comunal*. The English equivalent would be *community multiplier*, which is a term not easily understood. For this reason, we have chosen to use the term *communal facilitator*. However, it should be noted that the term in Spanish contains within it the concept of multiplying the benefits of the project by training community members to keep the project going and expanding over time.

Chapter 9: Women, Equity, and Household Water Management in the Valley of Mexico

I am deeply grateful to the residents of La Purificación Tepetitla for supporting my research efforts. For helpful comments on this chapter, I thank Vivienne Bennett, Jill Sweet, Sara Curran, Susan Walzer, Tim Karis, and Linda Farthing. Research funds were provided by the International Predissertation Fellowship Program from the Social Science Research Council and the American Council of Learned Societies with support from the Ford Foundation, the Inter-American Foundation, the Wenner-Gren Foundation for Anthropological Research, Michigan State University, and Skidmore College. This chapter was completed during a Visiting Research Fellowship at the Center for U.S.-Mexican Studies, University of San Diego. The views presented in this chapter are my own and not those of the individuals or institutions mentioned above.

1. The word *pueblo* means both the people and the community.

2. This chapter addresses water management in a periurban zone that includes agriculture with irrigation. La Purificación Tepetitla is part of a small-scale irrigation unit that includes a number of neighboring communities that have rights to portions of surface water flowing from mountain springs. In Mexico, privatization efforts have focused more attention on the large-scale irrigation districts and large-scale urban systems (see Whiteford and Melville 2002). La Purificación Tepetitla is representative of the situation of numerous smaller Mexican communities with small-scale irrigation and local household water systems.

3. For an overview of civil-religious hierarchies and *cargo* systems in Mexico and Central America, see Stephen and Dow 1990.

4. While wastewater and threats to water quality concern local residents, there is greater concern about the daily hardships associated with water quantity and distribution (see Ennis-McMillan 2001a).

5. For further discussion, see Ennis-McMillan 2001a, 2002.

6. Before 2000, the Drinking Water Committee consisted of seven positions; but the community voted in 2000 to expand the number of from seven to eighteen because of the community population growth.

7. For more on privatization issues, see Ennis-McMillan 2002.

Chapter 10: Women and Water in the Northern Ecuadorean Andes

1. In Carchi, Ecuador, the area of study, people use the word *mestizo* to refer to locals who do not self-define as either Indigenous or Afro-Ecuadorean.

2. *Paramos* are high altitude, cold regions above the treeline in tropical South America.

3. *Huasipungueros* were peasants who worked on the big haciendas. The landlord would give each *huasipunguero* and his family a plot of two or three hectares of land (sometimes more) for family consumption. In exchange, the *huasipunguero* had to work four or five days of the week on the haciendas. In some cases, in return for their labor, they could use a yoke of oxen to plough their fields and receive water turns during the weekends.

4. Each user group has its own president, and the presidents of the eleven user groups come together to form the main board of the Garrapatal Canal water-user association.

5. The term *family life cycle* is defined by the life stage of the heads of the households. The concept of family life cycle as used in this analysis does not imply that household development follows a pre-

determined pattern; that is, although many households have similarities, not every household will develop through identical life stages. Therefore, the different stages in the family life cycle used to group the households under study were defined inductively.

6. These are households of women who have children and are either widowed, divorced, or separated.

7. The water law of 1972 legally protects the use of water for these purposes.

8. Pimampiro is a community about two hours driving distance from the community of El Tambo.

9. The study area was based on a focus group of twenty-one women and a survey of sixty households.

10. The average exchange rate for 1997 was US$1 = S/. 3,210. (In 2000, when Ecuador dollarized the economy, the exchange rate was US$1= S/. 25,000.)

11. The total number of cases for this question was fifty-four. For obvious reasons, this number excluded the female heads of household.

Chapter 11: Women at the Helm of Irrigated Agriculture in Mexico

This research, undertaken between 1998 and 2002, was funded by the International Water Management Institute. The author gratefully acknowledges this generous support.

1. In 1998, 53 percent of those women who received new land titles given as part of the counter reforms to Article 27 of the Constitution were given less than five hectares of land (Valenzuela and Robles 1996, 40–41 in Deere and León 2001, 368–69). Sixty-eight percent of the women were more than fifty years old and 36 percent more than sixty-five years old compared with 54 percent and 23 percent for men. Furthermore, 25 percent of the *ejidatarias* were the sole income earners for their households, and the majority worked their land (Robles et al 2000, 64 in Deere and León 2001, 369).

2. Many men in the Bajío also hire irrigators, which is considered to be a specialized job.

3. All names are fictitious to protect the interviewees' anonymity.

4. The other two people paid by the state are the administrator and the technician.

5. The Rural Energy Law, passed on December 2002, with the goal of increasing Mexican farmers' competitiveness in the North American Free Trade Agreement, would have had significant negative impacts on groundwater overdraft if it had reduced energy prices as envisioned. However, the government has raised the prices of electricity and diesel. A program was initiated in 2003, however, to offer diesel credits for low-income farmers.

Chapter 12: Toward a Broader Perspective

1. We chose the themes for the three case study sections because they address overarching issues in contemporary policy development as well as in water policy and in gender policy. Needless to say, however, there are many points of intersection across the eight case studies. While each case study was placed in the section of the book that it most "spoke to," each touches on numerous themes.

2. In almost all Latin American countries, the Inter-American Development Bank and other institutions that loaned funds for the construction and expansion of water systems encouraged the involvement of water users, either through a fee or via manual labor for the construction of the infrastructure, as a way to increase the recoverability of costs.

3. One question we asked the case study authors to consider was whether any outsiders (NGOs, consultants, government bureaucrats from outside the case study area) were important to the success or failure of incorporating gender into water management in a given case study (or of allowing women to take part in water management). If yes, we asked who they were, what they did or did not do that made a difference, and why.

4. Chapters five and six provide examples of private enterprises that were able to direct water management policies to their best interests.

5. Decision making for water management in Irapuato took place in the COTAS and WUAs that were not accessible to women. And at the household level, the fact that male migration was temporary, so that the men kept returning periodically to their homes, limited the extent of permanent changes in women's roles in the decision-making process.

6. It was not the intent of this book to provide a manual or handbook for project work. Such material is the purview of development agencies, and several agencies are already deeply involved in ongoing publication of such guidelines and principles. For example, handbooks have been created by the SNV Netherlands Development Organization (1997) and the Swedish International Development Agency (no date). See also the work of Agualtiplano (www.agualtiplano.net).

Bibliography

Agarwal, Bina. 1994. *A Field of One's Own: Gender and Land Rights in South Asia*. Cambridge, England: Cambridge University Press.

Aguilar, Lorena, Ivania Ayales, and Guiselle Rodríguez. 1997. Género y figura no son hasta la sepultura: Guía para la construcción de relaciones de equidad en iniciativas de desarrollo sostenible. San José, Costa Rica: Unión Mundial para la Naturaleza (UICN, World Conservation Union).

Aguilar, Lorena, and Elías Rosales. 1988. *Guía Sanitaria en busca de una buena salud*. San José, Costa Rica: Centro de Capacitación para el Desarrollo-CECADE.

———. 1997a. *La bomba manual UNIMADE. Módulo 3*. San José: Fundación Tecnológica de Costa Rica (FUNDATEC) and Editorial Absoluto.

———. 1997b. *Protección sanitaria para pozos con ferrocemento*. San José: Fundación Tecnológica de Costa Rica (FUNDATEC) and Editorial Absoluto.

Aguilar, Lorena, Elías Rosales, and H. Navarro. 1986–1989. *Informes proyecto "Tecnología de bombas manuales (Costa Rica)."* San José: Instituto Tecnológico de Costa Rica.

———. 1989–1990. *Estrategias participativas para el abastecimiento de agua*. San José: Instituto Tecnológico de Costa Rica.

Aguilar, Luis. 1993. *Problemas públicos y agenda de gobierno*. Mexico City: Miguel Angel Porrúa Grupo Editorial.

Ahlers, Rhodante 1999. "Dynamic or Dynamite: Water Marketing in the Comarca Lagunera, Mexico." Paper presented at the conference Environment of Greater Mexico: History, Culture, Economy, and Politics. University of California, San Diego, La Jolla, March 5–6.

———. 2000a. "Gender Relations in Irrigation Districts in Mexico." In *Gender and Water Management in Latin America*, edited by Cecilia Tortajada, 203–16. New Delhi: Oxford University Press.

———. 2000b. "Relaciones de Género y Mercados de Agua en la Comarca Lagunera." In *"Anduve detrás de todo a la corre y corre . . .": Género y Manejo del Agua y Tierra en Comunidades Rurales de México*, edited by Stephanie Buechler and Emma Zapata, 157–75. International Water Management Institute Serie Latinoamericana, no. 14. Montecillo, Mexico: International Water Management Institute and Colegio de Postgraduados.

———. 2002a. "From Tied Hands to Empty Hands: The Catch 22 of Entitlement. A Debate on Gender, Power and Water Rights." Paper prepared for the 2002 Conference on Feminist Economics, Occidental College, Los Angeles, California. July 12–14.

———. 2002b. "Moving in or Staying Out: Gender Dimensions of Water Markets in a Mexican Irrigation District." In *Managing a Sacred Gift: The Privatization of Water Rights in Mexico*, edited by R. Melville and S. Whiteford, 65–86. Transformation of Rural Mexico Series. La Jolla, Calif.: Center for U.S.-Mexican Studies, UCSD.

Ahlers, Rhodante, and E. Rymshaw. 1998. "La política en la practica: Mercados de agua en cuatro distritos de riego en México." In *III Seminario Internacional Transferencia de los Sistemas de Riego*, edited by E. P. Vélez, A. E. Garcia, J. E. R. Panta, and E. M. Saenz, 195–202. Montecillo, Mexico: Colegio de Postgraduados.

Ahlers, Rhodante, and Annet Smits. 1991. Ya mismo: Verschillende aspekten van waterproblematiek voor boeren en boerinnen. MSc thesis, Wageningen Agricultural University, Wageningen, The Netherlands.

Alberti, Pilar Manzanares, Edith Carmona, and Emma Zapata Martelo. 2000. "Género, Irrigación y Cultura del Agua en el Distrito de Riego 011 Alto Rio Lerma, Guanajuato, Mexico." In *Género y*

Manejo del Agua y Tierra en Comunidades Rurales de México, edited by Stephanie Buechler and Emma Zapata, 133–56. International Water Management Institute Serie Latinoamericana, no. 14. Mexico City: International Water Management Institute and Colegio de Postgraduados.

Aldana Martínez, Gerardo. 1994. *San Pablo Ixayoc: Un caso de proletarización incompleta.* Colección Tepetlaostoc, no. 4. Mexico City: Universidad Iberoamericana.

Appendini, Kirsten. 1998. "Changing Agrarian Institutions: Interpreting the Contradictions." In *The Transformation of Rural Mexico: Reforming the Ejido Sector*, eddited by Wayne Cornelius and David Myhre, 25–38. La Jolla: Center for U.S.-Mexican Studies, University of California, San Diego.

Aranda, Josefina. 2000. "Políticas Públicas y Mujeres Campesinas." In *Tiempo de Crisis, Tiempo de Mujeres*, edited by Josefina Aranda, Carlota Botey, and Rosario Robles, 51–93. Oaxaca, Mexico: Universidad Autónoma Benito Juárez de Oaxaca, Centro de Estudios de la Cuestión Agraria Mexicana, A.C.

Arce, Alberto, and Norman Long. 1992. "The Dynamic of Knowledge. Interface between Bureaucrats and Peasants." In *Battlefield of Knowledge: The Interlocking of Theory and Practice in Social Research and Development*, edited by Norman Long and Anita Long, 211–25. London: Routledge.

Arizpe, Lourdes, and Carlota Botey. 1987. "Mexican Agricultural Development Policy and Its Impact on Rural Women." In *Rural Women and State Policy: Feminist Perspectives on Latin American Agricultural Development*, edited by Carmen Diana Deere and M. León, 67–83. Boulder, Colo.: Westview Press.

Arrona, Pilar Esquivel. 1999. "Sufre El Campo Descapitalización." A.M. *Irapuato*. Sept. 18. p. 1, col. 1, 2 and p. 5, col. 1–4.

Arroyo, Aline, and Rutgerd Boelens. 1997a. *Mujer campesina e intervención en el riego andino: Sistemas de riego y relaciones de género, caso Licto, Ecuador.* Quito, Ecuador: CAMAREN (Sistema de Capacitación en el Manejo de Recursos Naturales Renovables), Riego Comunitario Andino, CESA (Central Ecuatoriana de Servicios Agrícolas), SNV (Stichting Nederlandse Vrijwilligers).

———. 1997b. "Riego Andino y Equidad de Género. El Caso de Licto, Ecuador." Paper presented at the Forty-ninth International Congress of Americanists, in the session "Aguas que Fluyen, Aguas que Gotean." Quito, July 7–11.

———. 1998. "Andean Irrigation and Gender Equity." In *Searching for Equity: Conceptions of Justice and Equity in Peasant Irrigation*, edited by Rutgerd Boelens and Gloria Dávila, 396–418. Assen, The Netherlands: Van Gorcum.

Asmal, Kader. 1999. "Water and Sustainable Development: Cities in Crisis." Keynote Address, Stockholm Water Symposium, Stockholm, August 9.

Assies, Willem. 2001a. David Fights Goliath in Cochabamba: Water Rights, Neoliberalism and the Renovation of Social Protest in Bolivia. Working Paper. Zamora: El Colegio de Michoacán.

———. 2001b. David vs. Goliat en Cochabamba: Los derechos del agua, el neoliberalismo y la renovación de la propuesta social en Bolivia. *T'inkazos* 4 (8): 106–34

Ayad, Mohamed, Bernard Barrère, and James Otto. 1997. "Demographic and Socio-economic Characteristics of Households." *DHS Comparative Studies* 26: iii–75.

Bakker, Karen. 2002. "From State to Market? Water *Mercantalización* in Spain." *Environment and Planning A* 34: 767–90.

Barrig, Maruja. 2001. "Latin American Feminism: Gains, Losses and Hard Times." *NACLA* 34 (5): 29–31.

Barrón, Antonieta Pérez, and José Manuel Hernández Juárez. 2000. "Los Nómadas del Nuevo Milenio." *Cuadernos Agrarios* 19–20: 150–68.

Bastidas, Elena P. 1999. Gender Issues and Women's Participation in Irrigated Agriculture: The Case of Two Private Irrigation Canals in Carchi, Ecuador. International Water Management Institute (IWMI) Research Report, no. 31. Colombo, Sri Lanka: IWMI.

———. 2001. Assessing Potential Response to Changes in the Livelihood System of Diverse, Limited-Resource Farm Households in Carchi, Ecuador: Modeling Livelihood Strategies Using Participatory Methods and Linear Programming. Ph.D. diss., University of Florida, Gainesville.

Batuone, Maria, Emma Yep, and Ilda Segura. 1996. Mirando el riego con enfoque de género. Estudio de casos de seis instituciones de desarrollo: IMA, CADEP-José María Arguedas, IMAR-Norte,

ITDG-Sicuani, Desco-Chincha y Ideas Piura. Lima: SNV (Stichting Nederlandse Vrijwilligers) Peru.

Bauer, Carl J. 1998. *Against the Current: Privatization, Water Markets and the State in Chile.* Natural Resources Management and Policy Series, no. 14. Norwell, Mass.: Kluwer Academic Publishers.

Bauman, Zygmunt. 2001. *La globalización. Consecuencias humanas.* Mexico City: Fondo de Cultura Económica.

Benda-Beckmann, Keebet von. 1996. "Development, Law and Gender-Skewing: An Examination of the Impact of Development on the Sociolegal Position of Indonesian Women With Special Reference to Minangkabau." *Journal of Legal Pluralism* 30/31: 87–120.

Benería, Lourdes. 1999. "Globalization, Gender and the Davos Man." *Feminist Economics* 5 (3): 61–83.

Bennett, Vivienne. 1995a. Gender, Class, and Water: Women and the Politics of Water Service in Monterrey, Mexico. *Latin American Perspectives* 22 (2): 76–99.

———. 1995b. *The Politics of Water: Urban Protest, Gender, and Power in Monterrey, Mexico.* Pittsburgh: University of Pittsburgh Press.

Bhalla, Ajit, and Frédéric Lapeyre. 1997. "Social Exclusion: Towards an Analytical and Operational Framework." *Development and Change* 28: 413–33.

Boelens, Rutgerd. 1998. "Gestión colectiva y construction social de sistemas de riego campesino. Una introducción conceptual." In *Buscando la equidad. Concepciones sobre justicia y equidad en el riego campesino,* edited by Rutgerd Boelens and Gloria Dávila, 87–106. Assen, The Netherlands: Van Gorcum.

Boelens, Rutgerd, and Gloria Dávila, eds. 1998. *Searching for Equity: Conceptions of Justice and Equity in Peasant Irrigation.* Assen, The Netherlands: Van Gorcum.

Boelens, Rutgerd, and Bernita Doornbos. 2002. "The Battlefield of Water Rights. Rule-making and Empowerment in the Area of Conflicting Normative Frameworks—Irrigation Development in Ceceles, Ecuador." In *Water Rights and Empowerment,* edited by Rutgerd Boelens and Paul Hoogendam, 217–40. Assen, The Netherlands: Van Gorcum and Comp.

Boelens, Rutgerd, and Paul Hoogendam, eds. 2002. *Water Rights and Empowerment.* Assen, The Netherlands: Van Gorcum.

Boelens Rutgerd, and Margreet Zwarteveen. 2002a. "Contenidos de género de los derechos de agua en el riego Andino: Discursos y compra de discursos." Draft chapter for *Water Rights and Empowerment,* edited by Rutgerd Boelens and Paul Hoogendam. Assen, The Netherlands: Van Gorcum.

———. 2002b. "Gender dimensions of water control in Andean irrigation." In *Water Rights and Empowerment,* edited by Rutgerd Boelens and Paul Hoogendam, 75–109. Assen, The Netherlands: Van Gorcum and Comp.

Bolivia Press, 2000. Special Edition No. 1, Boletín electrónico quincenal del Centro de Documentación e Información Bolivia (CEDIB).

Bolivia Press, 2000. Special Issue April 7, Boletín electrónico quincenal del Centro de Documentación e Información Bolivia (CEDIB).

Bond, Patrick. 2000. "Economic Growth, Ecological Modernization or Environmental Justice? Conflicting Discourses in Post Apartheid South Africa. Capitalism." *Nature and Socialism* 11 (1): 33–59.

Boserup, Ester. 1970. *Women's Role in Economic Development.* London: Allen & Unwin.

Bravo, Loreto, and María Nieves Rico. 2001. *Hacia la institucionalización del enfoque de género en las políticas económico-laborales en América Latina.* Serie Seminarios y Conferencias, no. 20. LC/L.1667-P. Santiago, Chile: CEPAL.

Bribiesca Casterjón, José Luis. 1960. "El Agua Potable en la República Mexicana (séptima y última parte [seventh and final part])." *Ingeniería Hidráulica Mexicana* 14 (1): 107–25.

Briscoe, John. 1997. "Managing Water as an Economic Good: Role for Reforms." Keynote paper presented at the International Commission on Irrigation and Drainage Conference, Oxford, England.

Brunt, Dorien. 1992. *Mastering the Struggle: Gender, Actors and Agrarian Change in a Mexican Ejido.* CEDLA Latin America Studies 64. Amsterdam: CEDLA.

Brydom, Lynne, and Sylvia Chant. 1989. *Women in the Third World: Gender Issues in Rural and Urban Areas.* New Brunswick, N.J.: Rutgers University Press.

Buechler, Stephanie. 2000. "El Trabajo de las Mujeres, Niños, Niñas y Hombres en Parcelas Irrigadas de Guanajuato en Épocas de Crisis." In *Género y Manejo del Agua y Tierra en Comunidades Rurales de México*, edited by Stephanie Buechler and Emma Zapata, 41–70. International Water Management Institute Serie Latinoamericana, no. 14. Mexico City: International Water Management Institute and Colegio de Postgraduados.

———. 2001. "Water and Guanajuato's Ejido Agriculture: Resource Access, Exclusion and Multiple Livelihood Strategies." Ph.D. diss., Binghamton University, Binghamton, N.Y.

———. 2002. "Irrigated Agriculture on Mexican *Ejidos:* Complementarities with Off-farm and Non-farm Economic Strategies." In *Managing a Sacred Gift: Water Management Strategies in Mexico*, edited by Scott Whiteford and Roberto Melville, 125–42. La Jolla: Center for U.S.-Mexican Studies, University of California, San Diego.

Buechler, Stephanie, and Emma Zapata Martelo, eds. 2000. *"Anduve detrás de todo a la corre y corre . . .": Género y Manejo del Agua y Tierra en Comunidades Rurales de México*. International Water Management Institute Serie Latinoamericana, no. 14. Montecillo, Mexico: International Water Management Institute and Colegio de Postgraduados.

Buechler, Steven, and F. Kurt Cylke. 1997. "The Centrality of Social Movements." In *Social Movements: Perspectives and Issues*, edited by Steven Buechler and F. Kurt Cylke, 1–5. Mountain View, Calif.: Mayfield Publishing Company.

Bustamante, Rocio. 2000. "El difícil camino de la formulación de una nueva Ley de Aguas para Bolivia." Conference presented to the Seminario Taller del Foro Público, Cochabamba, Bolivia, February 23–24.

———. 1998. "Normas de manejo del espacio y gestion campesina de riego: El caso de San Pedro de Condo-Oruro." Internal document: Cochabamba, Bolivia.

Bustelo, Eduardo S. 2001. "Expansion of Citizenship and Democratic Construction," In *The Poverty of Rights: Human Rights and the Eradication of Poverty*, edited by Willem van Genugten and Camilo Perez-Bustillo, 3–28. London: Zed Books.

Canadian Council for International Cooperation (CCIC)/MATCH International Centre. 1994. *Dos mitades forman una unidad*. San José, Costa Rica: Unión Mundial para la Naturaleza (UICN, World Conservation Union). [Translation of CCIC-MATCH. *Two Halves Make A Whole: Balancing Gender Relations In Development*. Ottawa: CCIC-MATCH, August 1991.]

Cancian, Frank. 1965. Economics and Prestige in a Mayan Community: The Religious Cargo System in Zinacantán. Stanford, Calif.: Stanford University Press.

———. 1990. "The Zinacantán Cargo Waiting Lists as a Reflection of Social, Political, and Economic Changes, 1952–1987." In *Class, Politics, and Popular Religion in Mexico and Central America*, edited by Lynn Stephen and James Dow, 63–76. Washington, D.C.: American Anthropological Association.

Carmona Quiróz, Edith, and Gabriela Monsalvo Velázquez. 1998. "Las mujeres y el riego: Dos experiencias pioneras en la investigación." *Taller de los resultados de los estudios realizados en el Distrito 011 "Alto Río Lerma,"* Valle de Santiago, Guanajuato, Mexico.

Carmona Quiróz, Edith L. 1999. "Mercados de Agua Subterránea en Cortazar, Distrito 011, Guanajuato." Consultancy report. International Water Management Institute.

———. 2001. "El Oro Blanco de Hueyapan, Lugar Donde Nace el Agua. La Organización de Mujeres y Hombres en la Pequeña Irrigación." Paper presented as part of "Gender and Water in Rural Areas" panel at the Asociación Mexicana de Estudios Rurales (AMER) conference, Zacatecas, Mexico, June.

Carney, Judith. 1988. "Struggles over Crop Rights and Labor within Contract Farming Households in a Gambian Irrigated Rice Project." *Journal of Peasant Studies* 15: 334–49.

Carrasco, Pedro. 1961. "The Civil-Religious Hierarchy in Mesoamerican Communities: Pre-Spanish Background and Colonial Development." *American Anthropologist* 63 (3): 483–97.

CEAG (Comisión Estatal del Agua de Guanajuato). 2000a. Map of Groundwater tables in Guanajuato state entitled: "El Agua Subterránea en el Estado de Guanajuato." Guanajuato, Guanajuato, Mexico: CEAG.

———. 2000b. *Aqua Forum: Memorias del Expoagua, 2000*. Guanjuato, Guanajuato, Mexico: CEAG.

————. 2001. "Estudios Hidrogeloógicos y Modelos Matemáticos de los Acuíferos del Estado de Guanajuato." 2001. Guanajuato, Mexico: Comisión Estatal del Agua de Guanajuato.

Cebada Contreras, María del Carmen P. 1995. "Los Emigrantes Guanajuatenses en Estados Unidos y Mercado de Trabajo." *Cuadernos del CICSUG* 5.

CEDIB. 2000. "Una guerra mas allá del agua" February–April 2000, compilation of articles published in Bolivia Press, Centro de Documentación e Información Bolivia (CEDIB), Cochabamba, Bolivia.

Centro Nacional para el Desarrollo de la Mujer y la Familia (CMF). 1995. *Plan para la igualdad de oportunidades entre mujeres y hombres, 1996–1998.* Colección Documentos, no. 11. San José, Costa Rica.

CEPAL (Comisión Económica para América Latina y el Caribe). 1998. *Recomendaciones de las reuniones internacionales sobre el agua: De Mar del Plata a París,* LC/R, 1865. Santiago, Chile: Comisión Económica para América Latina y el Caribe October.

————. 2002. *Globalización y Desarrollo.* Brasilia: Comisión Económica para América Latina (CEPAL), May.

CEPAL (Comisión Económica para América Latina y el Caribe), Programa de las Naciones Unidas para el Desarrollo (PNUD), and Programa de las Naciones Unidas para el Medio Ambiente (PNUMA). 2002. *América Latina y el Caribe hacia la cumbre mundial sobre el desarrollo sostenible. Conferencia regional preparatoria.* Rio de Janeiro, Brazil, October 23–24, 2001. Serie Seminarios y Conferencias, no. 22. Santiago, Chile: CEPAL.

CGIAB (Comisión para la Gestión Integral del Agua en Bolivia). 2001a. *Estado de situación de aguas en Bolivia. Primera Parte: Le Ley de 1906.* Todo Sobre el Agua 3: 1–8.

————. 2001b. *Las Leyes Sectorales y el Recurso Agua.* Presented during the national consultations. Cochabamba, July 2001.

Chambers, Robert. 1997. *Whose Reality Counts? Putting the First Last.* London: Intermediate Technology Publications.

CGIAC. 2000. "La gestión integral del agua en Cochabamba." Synthesis of the electronic discussion forum organized by CGIAC and CONDESAN, Cochabamba, Bolivia, February 28–April 15.

Chance, John K. 1990. "Changes in Twentieth-Century Mesoamerican Cargo Systems." In *Class, Politics, and Popular Religion in Mexico and Central America,* edited by Lynn Stephen and James Dow, 27–42. Washington, D.C.: American Anthropological Association.

Chance, John K., and William B. Taylor. 1985. "Cofradías and Cargos: An Historical Perspective on the Mesoamerican Civil-Religious Hierarchy." *American Ethnologist* 12 (1): 1–26.

Chaney, Elsa, and García Castro, Mary, eds. 1993. Muchacha, cachifa, criada, empreada, empregadinha, sirvienta y . . . más nada. Trabajadoras del hogar en América Latina y el Caribe. Caracas, Venezuela: Editorial Nueva Sociedad.

Chico Goerne, Francisco Javier. 2001. "Agua y Participación Social." *Memorias del Expoagua, Aqua Forum,* no. 25, Centro de Estudios del Agua de Guanajuato (CEAG).

Chomsky, Noam, and Heinz Dieterich. 1996. *La sociedad global. Educación, mercado y democracia.* Mexico City: Editorial Planeta.

Cirelli, Claudia. 1996. "Abasto de agua a las ciudades: la perspectiva de las zonas abastecedoras—el caso de San Felipe y Santiago, Alto Lerma." In *Apropiación y usos del agua: Nuevas líneas de investigación,* edited by Roberto Melville and Francisco Peña, 65–80. Chapingo, Mexico: Universidad Autónoma Chapingo.

Claverías, Ricardo. 2002. *Género e interculturalidad en los proyectos de riego. Metodología para la sistematización.* Lima, Peru: Centro de Investigación, Eduación y Desarrollo-Agualtiplano.

Cleaver, Francis, and Diane Elson. 1995. *Women and Water Resources: Continued Marginalization and New Policies.* International Institute for Environment and Development (IIED) Gatekeeper Series, no. 49. London: IIED.

Colombo, Ariel. 2001. "Justificación de la desobediencia civil." Photocopy.

Comisión Brundtland. 1998. *Nuestro futuro común.* Madrid: Alianza Editorial.

Comision Nacional de Agua. 1994. Proyecto de Reglamento del Distritio 017: Región Lagunera, Coahuila y Durango. Mexico: Ciudad Lerdo.

Comisión Bruntland. (1998). *Nuestro futuro común.* Madrid: Alianza Editorial.

Congreso Mundial de la Mujer para un Planeta Sano. 1991. *Agenda de acción de la mujer 21.* San José, Costa Rica: Fundación Arias para la Paz y el Progreso Humano.

Coordinación Nacional de Mujeres de Organizaciones Civiles por un Milenio Feminista and Red de Mujer y Medio Ambiente. 2000, February. *Informe Alternativo Preliminar "Pekín+5."* Unpublished paper.

Cosgrove, W. J., and F. R. Rijsberman. 2000. *World Water Vision: Making Water Everybody's Business.* London: World Water Council, Earthscan.

Cox, Stephen, and Sheldon Annis. 1988. "Community Participation in Rural Water Supply." In *Direct to the Poor: Grassroots Development in Latin America,* edited by Sheldon Annis and Peter Hakim, 65–72. Boulder, Colo.: Lynne Rienner Publishers.

Cruz, Alejandro, and Gilbert Levine. 1998. "El Uso de las Aguas Subterráneas en el distrito 017, Región Lagunera." *Serie latinoamericana,* No. 3. IWMI, Mexico.

Dávila-Poblete, Sonia. 1998. "Mexico's Two Principal Hydro-Agricultural Policies from a Gender Perspective." In *Gender Analysis and Reform of Irrigation Management: Concepts, Cases, and Gaps in Knowledge,* edited by Douglas Merrey and Shirish Baviskar, 87–103. Colombo, Sri Lanka: International Water Management for Irrigation.

————. 1999. "¿Quién tendrá que pagar la cuenta?" In *Población y Medio Ambiente: Descifrando el Rompecabezas,* edited by Haydea Izazola, 303–25. Mexico City: El Colegio de México, Sociedad Mexicana de Demografía,

————. 2000. "Women and Agenda 21 in Mexico." In *Women and Water Management: The Latin American Experience,* edited by Cecilia Tortajada, 184–202. New Delhi: Oxford University Press.

————. 2001. "Las Políticas del Agua y la Participación de Las Mujeres." Keynote Address, Primer Encuentro Sobre Mujer y Agua, Instituto de la Mujer de Gunajuato, Comisión Estatal de Aguas de Guanajuato. Guanjuato, Mexico: Aquaforum, Comisión Estatal de Aguas de Guanajuato.

Deere, Carmen Diana, and Magdalena León. 1982. *Women in Andean Agriculture: Peasant Production and Rural Wage Employment in Colombia and Peru.* Geneva: International Labour Office.

————. 1987. *Rural Women and State Policy: Feminist Perpectives on Latin American Agricultural Development.* Boulder, Colo.: Westview Press.

————. 1997. "Gender, Land, Water: From Reform to Counterreform in Latin America." In *Gender Analysis and Reform of Irrigation Management: Concepts, Cases and Gaps in Knowledge,* edited by Douglas Merrey and Shirish Baviskar, 134–54. Proceedings of the Workshop on Gender and Water, September 15–19, Habarana, Sri Lanka. Colombo, Sri Lanka: International Water Management Institute.

————. 2000. *Género, Propiedad y Empoderamiento: Tierra, Estado y Mercado en América Latina.* Bogota, Colombia: TM Editores, UN Facultad de Ciencias Humanas.

————. 2001. *Empowering Women: Land and Property Rights in Latin America.* Pittsburgh: University of Pittsburgh Press.

de Janvry, Alain, Elisabeth Sadoulet, Benjamin Davis, and Gustavo Gordillo. 1999. "Reformas del Sector Ejidal: De la Reforma Agraria al Desarrollo Rural." In *Reformando la Reforma Agraria Mexicana,* edited by Laura Randall. México, D.F.: Universidad Autónoma Metropolitana, El Atajo Ediciones.

Della Porta, Donatella, and Mario Diani. 1999. *Social Movements.* Oxford, England: Basil Blackwell Publishers.

de la Fuente, Manuel. 2000. *La guerra por el agua en Cochabamba: Crónica de una dolorosa victoria.* Serie Documentos de Reflexión Académica, no. 15, Facultad de Ciencias Económicas y sociología (FACES).

Democracy Center. 2002. Bechtel vs. Bolivia: Bechtel's Legal Action against Bolivia. http://www. democracyctr.org/bechtel/bechtellegalaction.htm, accessed October 21, 2002.

Deere, Carmen Diana, and Magdalena León. 1982. *Women in Andean Agriculture: Peasant Production and Rural Wage Employment in Colombia and Peru.* Geneva: International Labour Office.

————. 1987. *Rural Women and State Policy. Feminist Perpectives on Latin American Agricultural Development.* Boulder, Colo.: Westview Press.

————. 1997. "Gender, Land, Water: From Reform to Counterreform in Latin America." In *Gender Analysis and Reform of Irrigation Management: Concepts, Cases and Gaps in Knowledge*, edited by Douglas Merrey and Shirish Baviskar, 134–54. Proceedings of the Workshop on Gender and Water, September 15–19, Habarana, Sri Lanka. Colombo, Sri Lanka: International Water Management Institute.

————. 2000. *Género, Propiedad y Empoderamiento: Tierra, Estado y Mercado en América Latina*. Bogota, Colombia: TM Editores, UN Facultad de Ciencias Humanas.

————. 2001. *Empowering Women: Land and Property Rights in Latin America*. Pittsburgh: University of Pittsburgh Press.

de Janvry, Alain, Elisabeth Sadoulet, Benjamin Davis, and Gustavo Gordillo. 1999. "Reformas del Sector Ejidal: De la Reforma Agraria al Desarrollo Rural." In *Reformando la Reforma Agraria Mexicana*, edited by Laura Randall. Mexico City: Universidad Autónoma Metropolitana, El Atajo Ediciones.

Della Porta, Donatella, and Mario Diani. 1999. *Social Movements*. Oxford, England: Basil Blackwell Publishers.

Democracy Center. 2002. Bechtel vs. Bolivia: Bechtel's Legal Action against Bolivia. http://www.democracyctr.org/bechtel/bechtellegalaction.htm, accessed October 21, 2002.

DeWalt, Billie R. 1975. "Changes in the Cargo System of Mesoamerica." *Anthropological Quarterly* 48 (2): 87–105.

Dey, Jenny. 1981. "Gambian Women: Unequal Partners in Rice Development Projects?" *Journal of Development Studies* 7 (3): 109–22.

Díaz, Heliodoro Cisneros, Diego E. Platas Rosado, and Aurelio León Merino. 1996. "Asociación en Participación entre Empresarios y Pequeños Agricultores." In *Actores del Desarrollo Rural—Visiones para el Análisis*, edited by Emma Zapata Martelo and Martha Mercado González. Montecillo, Mexico: Colegio de Postgraduados, Programa de Estudios del Desarrollo Rural, Edo. de México, México.

Dibbits, Ineke, Elisabeth Peredo, and Ruth Volgger. 1995. *Trenzando ilusiones: Reflexiones y propuestas de mujeres que trabajan con mujeres*. La Paz, Bolivia: Edited by Tahipamu.

Dourojeanni, Axel, and Andrei Jouravlev.1999. *El Código de Aguas en Chile: Entre la ideología y la realidad*. Serie Recursos Naturales e Infraestructura, no. 3. Santiago de Chile: Comisión Económica para América Latina y el Caribe (CEPAL).

————. 2001. *Crisis de gobernabilidad en la gestión del agua*. Serie Recursos Naturales e Infraestructura, no. 35. Santiago de Chile: Comisión Económica para América Latina y el Caribe (CEPAL).

Durand, Jorge, Douglas S. Massey, and Rene M. Zenteno. 2001. "Mexican Immigration to the United States: Continuities and Change." *Latin American Research Review* 36 (1): 107–27.

ECLAC (Economic Commission for Latin America and the Caribbean). 1991. *Sustainable Development: Changing Production Patterns, Social Equity, and the Environment*. LC/G.1648. Santiago, Chile: ECLAC.

————. 1994. *Regional Programme of Action for the Women of Latin America and the Caribbean, 1995–2001*. LC/G.1855. Santiago, Chile: ECLAC.

————. 1998a. "Report of the Seventh Session of the Regional Conference on the Integration of Women into the Economic and Social Development of Latin America and the Caribbean, Santiago de Chile, November 19–21, 1997." LC/G2016 (crm.7/7). Santiago, Chile: ECLAC.

————. 1998b. *The Institutionality of Gender Equity in the State: A Diagnosis for Latin America and the Caribbean*. LC/R.1837. Santiago: ECLAC.

————. 2000a. "Report of the Eighth Session of the Regional Conference on Women in Latin America and the Caribbean, Lima, Peru, February 8–10, 2000." LC/G.2087 (crm.8/6). Santiago, Chile: ECLAC.

————. 2000b. *Servicios urbanos y equidad en América Latina: Un panorama con base en algunos casos*. Santiago, Chile: Sustainable Development and Human Settlements Division, ECLAC, September.

————. 2002. *Globalization and Development*. LC/G.2157. Santiago, Chile: ECLAC.

Elmendorf, Mary. 1981. *Women, Water and the Decade: Water and Sanitation for Health Project*. Technical Report 6 (OTD 35). Washington, D.C.: Agency for International Development.

Enge, Kjell I., and Scott Whiteford. (1989). *The Keepers of Water and Earth*. Austin: University of Texas Press.

Ennis-McMillan, Michael C. 1998. *Drinking Water Politics in Rural Mexico: Negotiating Power, Justice, and Social Suffering*. Ph.D. diss., Michigan State University. Ann Arbor, Mich.

———. 2001a. "Suffering from Water: Social Origins of Bodily Distress in a Mexican Community." *Medical Anthropology Quarterly* 15 (3): 368–90.

———. 2001b. *La Purificación Tepetitla: agua potable y cambio social en el somontano*. Translated by Carmen Viqueira Landa and Andrea Ruiz. Colección Tepetlaostoc, no. 7. Mexico City: Universidad Iberoamericana and Archivo Histórico del Agua.

———. 2002. "A Paradoxical Privatization: Challenges to Community-Managed Drinking Water Systems in the Valley of Mexico." In *Protecting a Sacred Gift: Water and Social Change in Mexico*, edited by Scott Whiteford and Roberto Melville, 27–48. La Jolla: Center for U.S.-Mexican Studies, University of California, San Diego.

Escobar, Arturo. 1992. "Culture, Economics, and Politics in Latin American Social Movements Theory and Research." In *The Making of Social Movements in Latin America: Identity, Strategy, and Democracy*, edited by Arturo Escobar and Sonia E. Alvarez, 62–85. Boulder, Colo.: Westview Press.

———. 1995. *Encountering Development: The Making and Unmaking of the Third World*. Princeton, N.J.: Princeton University Press.

Escobar, Arturo, and Sonia E. Alvarez. 1992. "Introduction: Theory and Protest in Latin America Today. " In *The Making of Social Movements in Latin America: Identity, Strategy, and Democracy*, edited by Arturo Escobar and Sonia E. Alvarez, 1–15. Boulder, Colo.: Westview Press.

Escobar, Agustín Latapí, Frank D. Bean, and Sidney Weintraub. 1999. *La Dinámica de la Emigración Mexicana*. Mexico City: CIESAS.

FAO (Food and Agriculture Organization of the United Nations). 1998. *Rural Women and Food Security: Current Situation and Perspectives*. Rome: FAO.

FEDECOR (Federación Departamental de Cochabamba de Organizaciones de Riego). 1998. "Propuesta a ser considerada para la elaboración del ante proyecto del recurso hídrico." (Proposal in Response to the Draft Water Law.) Cochabamba, Bolivia, August 21.

Feldstein, Hilary, and Susan Poats, eds. 1989. *Working Together: Gender Analysis in Agriculture*. Case Studies, vol. 1. West Hartford, Conn.: Kumarian Press.

Feldstein, Hilary, and Susan Poats. 1990. "Conceptual Framework for Gender Analysis in Farming Systems Research and Extension." In *Working Together: Gender Analysis in Agriculture*. Case Studies, vol. 1, edited by H. Feldstein and S. Poats, 7–37. West Hartford, Conn.: Kumarian Press.

FIRA (Fideicomisos Institutidos en Relación con la Agricultura). 1997. "El Mercado de Derechos de Agua en el Sector Rural de Mexico." *Boletín Informativo* 24 (291). FIRA (Mexico).

Flores, María de los Angeles. 1995. "El abasto y desalojo del agua en la Zona Metropolitana de la Ciudad de México (ZMCM)." In *Agua, Salud y Derechos Humanos*,edited edited by Iván Restrepo, 399–409. Mexico City: Comisión Nacional de Derechos Humanos.

Flórez, Margarita, and Pablo Solón. 2001. "La guerra del agua: La Estrategia del manejo." *Integrado de los Recursos Hídricos del BID, y la participación ciudadana en el caso de Bolivia*. http://www.funsolon.org/FUNDACION/FS.html.

Foley, Michael. 1995. "Privatizing the Countryside: The Mexican Peasant Movement and Neoliberal Reform." *Latin American Perspectives* 22: 59–76.

Fortis, Manuel, and Rhodante Ahlers. 1999. "Naturaleza y extension del mercado de agua en el D. R. 017 de la Comarca Lagunera, Mexico." International Water Management Institute (IWMI) Serie Latinoamericana, no. 10. Mexico: IWMI.

Fracchia, Myriam Figueiredo. 1999. "La Identidad Social de la Mujer en el Distrito de Riego el Carrizo, Sinaloa y Su Desarrollo en el Uso y Manejo de los Recursos Naturales en Sistemas de Alta Productividad." In *Género, Sustentabilidad y Cambio Social en el México Rural*, edited by Verónica Vázquez García. Colegio de Postgraduados, Montecillo: Edo. de México, México.

Franke, J. 1993. "Mujer y Riego." 1993. Unpublished discussion paper. Cayambe, Ecuador: IEDECA. 1993.

Fundación Solón. 2000, April. *Modificaciones a la Ley de Agua Potable y Alcantarillado*. Tunupa, Bolivia, 3–12.

Gandarillas, Humberto. 1997. "Riego en Bolivia." In *Cuestión agraria boliviana: Presente y futuro*, edited by Academia Nacional de Ciencias de Bolivia, Secretaria Ejecutiva PL 480, Titulo III, 143–91. La Paz: Academia Nacional de Ciencias de Bolivia.García de la Cruz, José Manuel, and Ángeles Sánchez Díez. 2002. "Maastricht y Washington: Dos experiencias diferentes." *Política y Cultura. América Latina: estudios críticos de la ideología dominante*17 (Spring) 25–44.

García Lascuráin, María. 1995. "Calidad de vida y consumo de agua en la periferia metropolitana: del tambo a la llave de agua." In *Agua, Salud y Derechos Humanos*, edited by Iván Restrepo, 123–62. Mexico City: Comisión Nacional de Derechos Humanos.

Gelles, Paul. 2000. *Water and Power in Highland Peru: The Cultural Politics of Irrigation and Development*. New Brunswick, N.J.: Rutgers University Press.

Gerben, Gerbrandy, and Paul Hoogendam. 1998. *Aguas y Acequias*. Bolivia: Plural editors/CID.

———. 2002. "Materialising Rights: Hydraulic Property in the Extension and Rehabilitation of Two Irrigation Systems in Bolivia." In *Water Rights and Empowerment*, edited by Rutgerd Boelens and Paul Hoogendam, 36–50. Assen, The Netherlands: Van Gorcum and Comp.

Giarracca, Norma, ed. 2001. *La protesta social en la Argentina*. Buenos Aires: Alianza Editorial.

Giarracca, Norma, and M. Teubal. 2001. "Crisis and Protest in Argentina: The Movimiento Mujeres Agropecuarias en Lucha." *Latin American Perspectives* 28 (6): 38–53.

Gill, S. 2001. "Constitutionalizing Inequality." Paper presented at the Global Tensions Conference, Cornell University, Ithaca, N.Y., March 9–10.

Gleick, Peter H. 1996. "Basic Water Requirements for Human Activities: Meeting Basic Needs." *Water International* 21: 83–92.

Global Water Partnership Technical Advisory Committee. 2000. *Integrated Water Resources Management*. Technical Advisory Committee Background Papers, no. 4 (March). Stockholm: Global Water Partnership.

Gómez Sahagún, Lucila. 1992. *San Miguel Tlaixpan: Cultivo tradicional de la flor*. Colección Tepetlaostoc, no. 1. Mexico City: Universidad Iberoamericana.

González, Humberto, and Margarita Calleja Pinedo. 1999. "La Construcción de Cadenas Internacionales de Frutas y Hortalizas: Vínculos e Interdependencia Entre Texas y México." In *Agricultura de Exportación en Tiempos de Globalización-El Caso de las Hortalizas, Frutas y Flores*, edited by Hubert C. Grammont, Manuel Angel Gómez Cruz, Humberto González and Rita Schwentesius Rindermann. Mexico City: IIS/UNAM, CIESTAAM, CIESAS OCCIDENTE, Plaza y Valdés.

González, Rodrigo, José. 1993. *Santa Catarina del Monte: Bosques y hongos*. Colección Tepetlaostoc, no. 3. Mexico City: Universidad Iberoamericana.

Goonatilake, Susantha. 1984. *Aborted Discovery: Science and Creativity in the Third World*. London: Zed Books.

Gorriz, Cecilia. M., Ashok Subramanian, and José Simas. 1995. *Irrigation Management Transfer in Mexico: Process and Progress*. World Bank Technical Paper, no. 292. Washington, D.C.: The World Bank.

Garcés Restrepo, Carlos, Sam Johnson III, Gil Levine, and Christopher Scott. 1997."Mexico Irrigation Sector Profile." Texcoco, Mexico: IWMI.

Green, Cathy, and Sally Baden. 1995. "Integrated Water Resources Management: A Gender Perspective." *IDS Bulletin* 26 (1): 92–100.

Gros Espiell, Hector. 2001. "Poverty and Social Justice in Latin America: Economic and Social Rights and the Material Conditions Necessary to Render Them Effective." In *The Poverty of Rights: Human Rights and the Eradication of Poverty*, edited by Willem van Genugten and Camilo Perez-Bustillo, 129–40. London: Zed Books.

Gutierrez, Zulema, and Cardona Silvia. 1998. *La dinamica campesina en la gestión del agua: La flexibilidad en las relaciones de género en el riego*. Cochabamba, Bolivia: Programa de Riego Andino y de los Valles (PEIRAV).

Guzmán, Virginia. 2001. *The Institutionality of Gender in the State: New Analytical Perspectives*. Serie Mujer y Desarrollo, no. 32 (September). LC/L.1511-P. Santiago, Chile: ECLAC.

————. 2002. *Las relaciones de género en un mundo global*. Serie Mujer y Desarrollo, no. 38 (April). Santiago, Chile: CEPAL.

Harding, Sandra. 1991. *Whose Science? Whose Knowledge?* Ithaca, N.Y.: Cornell University Press.

Hart, Gillian. 1992. "Household Production Reconsidered: Gender, Labor Conflict, and Technological Change in Malaysia's Muda Region." *World Development* 20: 809–23.

Hendriks, Jan. 2002. "Water Rights and Strengthening Users' Organisations: The Art of Negotiating. Challenges for Institutions Assisting Community Irrigation in the Andes." In *Water Rights and Empowerment*, edited by Rutgerd Boelens and Paul Hoogendam, 52–74. Assen, The Netherlands: Van Gorcum and Comp.

Herrera Toledo, Cesar. 1997. "National Water Master Planning in Mexico." In *National Water Master Plans for Developing Countries*, edited by Asit K. Biswas, César Herrera Toledo, Héctor Garduño Velasco, and Cecilia Tortajada Quiroz, 8–53. New Delhi: Oxford University Press.

Hildebrand, Peter. 1976. *A Multi-disciplinary Methodology for Generating New Technology for Small, Traditional Farmers*. Instituto de Ciencia y Tecnología Agrícolas (ICTA), Sector Público Agrícola, Guatemala.

Holden, P., and M. Thobani. 1996. *Tradable Water Rights: A Property Rights Approach to Resolving Water Shortages and Promoting Investment*. Washington, D.C.: The World Bank.

Ibarra Mendívil, Jorge Luis. 1996. "Recent Changes in the Mexican Constitution and Their Impact on the Agrarian Reform." In *Reforming Mexico's Agrarian Reform*, edited by L. Randell, 49–62. New York: M. E. Sharpe.

Illo, Jean. 1988. *Irrigation in the Philippines: Impact on Women and Their Households*. Bankgkok: The Population Council.

INEGI (Instituto Nacional de Estadística, Geográfica e Informática). (1991). *Guanajuato: Datos por Ejido y Comunidad Agraria*. Censo Estatal Agropequaria,. Aguascalientes, Aguascalientes: INEGI.

————. 1993. "Cuaderno Estadístico Municipal." Aguascalientes, Aguascalientes: INEGI.

————. 1995a. "Guanajuato: Conteo de Población y Vivienda Resultados Definitivos." Aguascalientes, Aguascalientes: INEGI.

————. 1995b. *La Purificación: Abolengo Nacido de la Tierra*. Mexico City: INEGI.

————. 1997a. "Cuaderno Estadistica Municipal de Pueblo Nuevo." Aguascalientes, Aguascalientes: INEGI, 1997.

————. 1997b. "La Migración en México." Aguascalientes, Aguascalientes: INEGI.

————. 2000. *Estadísticas del Medio Ambiente del Distrito Federal y Zona Metropolitana 2000*. Available online at http: //www.inegi.gob.mx/difusion/espanol/acercamexico/facermex.html. Accessed March 1, 2002.

Instituto Nacional de Estadística, Geografia e Informática (INEGI) y SEMARNAP. 1997. *Estado del Medioambiente Mexicano*. Aguascalientes, Aguascalientes: INEGI.

INSTRAW (International Research and Training Institute for The Advancement of Women). 1994. Women, Water Supply and Sanitation Training Seminar. Guyana, Santo Domingo: INSTRAW.

Jackson, Cecile. 1993. "Doing What Comes Naturally? Women and Environment in Development." *World Development* 21 (12): 1947–63.

————. 1998. "Gender, Irrigation, and Environment: Arguing for Agency." *Agriculture and Human Values* 15 (4): 313–24.

————. 2002. "Disciplining Gender?" *World Development* 30 (3): 497–509.

Jacome, Rosario, and Marjon Krol. 1994. Nosotros también surequamos, cantereamos y regamos: Relaciones de género en el Proyecto Pungales. Riobamba, Ecuador: CESA.

Jarman, Julie. 1997. "Water Supply and Sanitation." In *A City For All: Valuing Difference and Working With Diversity*, edited by Jo Beall, 182–93. London: Zed Books.

Jelín, Elizabeth. 1990. "Citizenship and Identity: Final Reflections." In *Women and Social Change in Latin America*, edited by Elizabeth Jelín, 184–207. London: Zed Books.

Johannesburg Summit. 2002. "UN Secretary-General Names Five Key Areas Where Johannesburg Summit Can Make a Real Difference." Available online at http://www.johannesburgsummit.org/html/whats_new/feature_story10.html. Accessed October 22, 2002.

Johnson, Pamela, and Naomi Krogman. 1993. "Gender-related Factors Influencing the Viability of Irrigation Projects in Lesotho." *Journal of Asian and African Studies* 28: 4.

Jones, Christine. 1986. "Intra-household Bargaining in Response to the Introduction of New Crops: A case-study from North Cameroon." In *Understanding Africa's Rural Households and Farming Systems*, edited by J. L. Moock, 105–23. Boulder, Colo.: Westview Press.

Kabeer, Naila. 1997. *Reversed Realities: Gender Hierarchies in Development Thought*. London: Verso.

———. 2000. *The Power to Choose*. London: Verso.

Kahrl, William. 1982. *Water and Power: The Conflict Over Los Angeles' Water Supply in the Owens Valley*. Berkeley: University of California Press.

Kasperson, Jeanne X., Roger E. Kasperson, and B. L. Turner II. 1996. "Regions at Risk: Exploring Environmental Criticality." *Environment* 38 (10): 4–15, 26–29.

Kauffer Michel, Edith Francoise, and Antonino García García. 2003. "Mujeres en los Comités de Agua del Estado de Chiapas: Elementos para entender una participación con segregación genérica." In *Género y Medio Ambiente*, edited by Esperanza Tunon Pablos, 295–321. Chiapas, Mexico: ECOSUR. SEMARNAT, Plaza y Valdés.

Kloezen, Wim. 2002. "Accounting for Water. Institutional Viability and Impacts of Market-oriented Irrigation Interventions in Central Mexico." Ph.D. diss., Wageningen University, Wageningen, The Netherlands.

Kloezen, Wim, Carlos Garcés Restrepo, and Sam H. Johnson III. 1997. "Impact Assessment of Irrigation Management Transfer in the Alto Río Lerma Irrigation District, Mexico." Colombo, Sri Lanka: International Water Management Institute (IWMI).

———. 1998. "Nuevas Experiencias Productivas y Nuevas Formas de Organización Flexible de Trabajo en la Agricultura Mexicana." Mexico City: Procuraduría Agraria.

Kohl, Benjamin. 2002. "Stabilizing Neoliberalism in Bolivia: Privatization and Participation." *Political Geography*, 21 (4) 449–472.

Krol, Marjon. 1994. "Irrigatie is mannenwerk. Genderverhoudingen in een kleinschalig irrigatieprojekt in de Ecuadoriaanse Andes." MSc thesis, Wageningen Agricultural University, Wageningen, The Netherlands.

———. 1997. "Gender and Water Rights in Pungales, Eduador." Paper prepared for the lecture series "Irrigation and Development," Wageningen University, Wageningen, The Netherlands. Mimeograph.

La Gaceta. 1998. Provincial newspaper, Tucumán, Argentina.

Lane Rodríguez, Marci. 1994. "Estudio preliminar sobre la reconstrucción del sistema de riego en la región de Texcoco en 1920–1930 y 1991." In *Sistemas hidráulicos, modernización de la agricultura y migración*, edited by Carmen Viqueira Landa and Lydia Medina Mora, 137–88. Zinacantepec, Estado de México: El Colegio Mexiquense and Universidad Iberoamericana.

Lansing, J. and Leslie Kish. 1957. "Family Life Cycle as an Independent Variable." *American Sociological Review* 22 (5): 512–19.

Latapí, Agustín Escobar, Frank D. Bean, and Sidney Weintraub. 1999. *La Dinámica de la Emigración Mexicana*. México, D.F.: CIESAS.

Lara, Sara María Flores, ed. 1995. *El Rostro Femenino del Mercado de Trabajo Rural en América Latina*. Caracas: UNRISD and Nueva Sociedad.

Lebrecque, Marie France. 1998. "Women and Gendered Production in Rural Yucatan: Some Local Features of Globalization." *Urban Anthropology* 27 (2): 233–62.

Le Goulven, Patrick, Thierry Ruf, and Hugo Ribadeneira. 1989. "Traditional Irrigation in the Andes of Ecuador: Research and Planning." Proceedings of the VII Afro-Asian Regional Conference, International Commission on Irrigation and Drainage (ICID), Tokyo. New York: Tavistock Publications.

Ledo, Carmen. 1994. *Problemática del agua en la ciudad de Cochabamba*. Cochabamba: Centro de Estudios de Población.

———. 1997. "Ciudad de Cochabamba, el agua potable como componente de la desigualdad social y de su estructura urbana interna." *Búsqueda* 7 (11). FACES—Universidad Mayor de San Simon.

Lee, Terence R., and Andrei S. Jouravlev. 1998. *Prices, Property and Markets in Water Allocation*. Serie Medio Ambiente y Desarrollo LC/L.1097/I. Santiago, Chile: ECLA.

Levy, Caren. 1992. "Gender and the Environment: The Challenge of Cross-cutting Issues in Development Policy and Planning." *Environment and Urbanization* 4 (1): 134–49.

Lipschutz, Ronnie, and Judith Mayer. 1996. *Global Civil Society and Global Environmental Governance: The Politics of Nature from Place to Planet.* Albany: State University of New York Press.

Loftus, Alex, and David McDonald. 2001. "Sueños líquidos: Una ecología política de la privatización del servicio de agua en Buenos Aires." *Realidad Económica* 183 (October–November), 75–101.

Long, Norman, and Anita Long. 1992. "From Paradigm Lost to Paradigm Regained? The Case of an Actor-Oriented Sociology of Development." In *Battlefield of Knowledge: The Interlocking of Theory and Practices in Social Research and Development,* edited by Norman Long and Anita Long, 16–43. London: Routledge.

Lynch, Barbara D. 1991. "Women and Irrigation in Highland Peru." *Society and Natural Resources* 4: 37–52.

———. 1993. "The Bureacratic Tradition and Women's Invisibility in Irrigation." In *Proceedings of the 24th Chacmool Conference,* 333–42. Calgary, Alberta: University of Calgary, Archeological Association.

Marañón, Boris Pimentel. 1999. "La gestión del agua subterránea en Guanajuato: La experiencia de los COTAS." *Estudios Agrarios* 5 (12): 153–74.

Marsh, Robin, and David Runsten. 1998. "The Organic Produce Niche Market: Can Mexican Smallholders be Stakeholders?" In *The Transformation of Rural Mexico: Reforming the Ejido Sector,* edited by Wayne A. Cornelius and David Myhre, 277–306. La Jolla: Center for U.S.-Mexican Studies, University of California, San Diego.

Mathews, Holly F. 1985. "'We are Mayordomo': A Reinterpretation of Women's Roles in the Mexican Cargo System." *American Ethnologist* 17: 285–301.

Mattos Crespo, Roger. 1999. *Informe sobre la situación del recurso hídrico.* Ministerio de Desarrollo Sostenible y Planificación, La Paz, Bolivia.

McAfee, Kathy. 1999. "Selling Nature to Save It? Biodiversity and Green Developmentalism." *Environment and Planning D: Society and Space* 17: 133–54.

McMichael, Philip. 1996. *Development and Social Change: A Global Perspective.* Thousand Oaks, Calif.: Pine Forge Press.

Meinzen-Dick, Ruth, and Margareet Zwarteveen. 1997. "Gendered Participation in Water Management: Issues and Illustrations from Water Users' Associations in South Asia." Paper prepared for the Workshop on Women and Water, IIMI, Sri Lanka, September.

Melucci, Alberto. 1992. "Frontier Land: Collective Action Between Actors and Systems." In *Studying Collective Action,* edited by Mario Diani and Ron Eyerman 238–259. London: Sage Publications.

Melville, Roberto. 1996a. "Política Hidráulica Mexicana: Oportunidades para la investigación." In *Apropiación y usos del agua: nuevas líneas de investigación,* edited by Roberto Melville and Francisco Peña, 17–29. Estado de México: Universidad Autónoma Chapingo.

———. 1996b. "El abasto de agua a las grandes ciudades y la agricultura de riego." In *Apropiación y usos del agua: nuevas líneas de investigación,* edited by Roberto Melville and Francisco Peña, 53–64. Estado de México: Universidad Autónoma Chapingo.

Melville, Roberto, and Claudia Cirelli. 2000. "La crisis del agua: Sus dimensiones ecológica, cultural y política." *Memoria* 134 (April): 26–30.

Mohanty, Chandra T. 1991. "Under Western Eyes: Feminist Scholarship and Colonial Discourses." In *Third World Women and the Politics of Feminism,* edited by C. T. Mohanty, A. Russo and L. Torres, 51–80. Indianapolis: Indiana University Press.

Mollinga, Peter P. 1998. "On the Waterfront: Water Distribution, Technologies and Agrarian Change in a South Indian Canal Irrigation System." Ph.D. diss., Wageningen Agricultural University, Wageningen, The Netherlands.

Monsalvo Velázquez, Gabriela. "Sostenibilidad Institucional de Las Asociaciones de Riego en México." México, D.F., México: Instituto Internacional del Manejo del Agua (IWMI), Serie Latinoamericana: No. 8, 1999.

Monsalvo Vélazquez, Gabriela. 1997. La razón de la costumbre versus la costumbre de la razón: Mecanismos consuetudinarios de organización y participación de usuarios (as) en comunidades del Distrito de Riego 011 "Alto Río Lerma," Guanajuato, México. MSc Thesis, Colegio de Posgraduados, Montecillo, Mexico.

Monsalvo Velázquez, Gabriela, and Emma Zapata. 2000. "Participación y Toma de Decisiones de

Usuarios y Usuarias en Dos Comunidades del Distrito de Riego 011: Alto Río Lerma, Guanajuato, México." In *Género y Manejo del Agua y Tierra en Comunidades Rurales de México*, edited by Stephanie Buechler and Emma Zapata, 11–40. International Water Management Institute Serie Latinoamericana, no. 14. Mexico City and Montecillo, Mexico: International Water Management Institute and Colegio de Postgraduados.

Monsalvo Velázquez, Gabriela, Emma Zapata Martelo, and Pilar Alberti Manzanares. 2000. "Género, irrigación y cultura del agua en el distrito de riego 011 Alto Río Lerma, Guanajuato, México." In *Género y Manejo del Agua y Tierra en Comunidades Rurales de México*, edited by Stephanie Buechler and Emma Zapata, 101–132. International Water Management Institute Serie Latinoamericana, no. 14. Mexico City and Montecillo, Mexico: International Water Management Institute and Colegio de Postgraduados.

Morgan, Lynn M. 1993. *Community Participation in Health: The Politics of Primary Care in Costa Rica*. Cambridge, England: Cambridge University Press.

Moser, Caroline, and Karen Levy. 1986. *A Theory and Methodology of Gender Planning: Meeting Women's Practical and Strategic Needs*. DPU Gender Working Paper, no. 11. University College, London.

Muller, Pierre, and Yves Surel. 1998. *L'analyse des politiques publiques*. Paris: Editorial Montcheretien.

Mummert, Gail. "In Fields Not Their Own: Commercial Agriculture in Ario de Rayón, Michoacán." In *Resource Management, Production, and Marketing in Rural Mexico*, edited by Rodríguez Gómez and Richard Snyder. La Jolla: Center for U.S.-Mexican Studies, University of California, San Diego.

Muñoz, Patricia Ríos. 2000. "Balance de las Políticas de Recortes y Controles de Ernesto Zedillo." *La Jornada*, November 27.

Myhre, David. 1998. "The Achilles' Heel of the Reforms: The Rural Finance System." In *The Transformation of Rural Mexico: Reforming the Ejido Sector*, edited by Wayne A. Cornelius and David Myhre, 39–65. La Jolla: Center for U.S.-Mexican Studies, University of California, San Diego.

Netherlands Development Assistance. 1997. *Rights of Women to the Natural Resources Land and Water*. Women and Development Working Paper, no. 2. The Hague: Department of Rural and Urban Development, Women and Development Division, Netherlands Development Assistance, Development Cooperation Information Department, Ministry of Foreign Affairs.

Nuijten, Monique. 1998. "In the Name of the Land: Organization, Transnationalism, and the Culture of the State in a Mexican Ejido. " Ph.D. diss., Wageningen Agricultural University, Wageningen, The Netherlands.

Nuñez, Guillermo. 1997. *Manejo integral sostenible de la cuenca del Río "El Angel."* Perfil del Proyecto "Carchi-Condesan," Mesa de Concertación, CONDESAN, Quito, Ecuador.

Pacheco Bonfíl, Silvana. 1999. *Diferencias genéricas en al accesso y uso del agua para el riego en dos ejidos de la Comarca Lagunera*. Monticello: Colegio de Postgraduados.

———. 2000. "Diferencias Económicas y de Género en el Acceso al Agua para el Riego en la Comarca Lagunera: Dos Estudios de Caso." In *Género y Manejo del Agua y Tierra en Comunidades Rurales de México*, edited by Stephanie Buechler and Emma Zapata, 71–100. International Water Management Institute Serie Latinoamericana, no. 14. Mexico City and Montecillo, Mexico: International Water Management Institute and Colegio de Postgraduados.

Palerm Viqueira, Jacinta. 1993. *Santa María Tecuanulco: Floricultores y músicos*. Colección Tepetlaostoc, no. 2. Mexico City: Universidad Iberoamericana.

———. 1995. "Sistemas hidráulicos y organización social: La polémica y los sistemas de riego del Acolhuacan septentrional." *Mexican Studies/Estudios Mexicanos* 11 (2): 163–78.

Parker, Ian. 1992. *Discourse Dynamics. Critical Analysis for Social and Individual Psychology*. London: Routledge.

Peredo, Elizabeth. 2001. "Memoria sobre Género y Etnicidad" (draft). *Memoria de Seminario sobre la problemática de género y etnicidad en la sociedad boliviana*. Fundación Solón, La Paz, June 27.

Peredo Beltrán, Elizabeth. 2002. "La Guerra del Agua de Cochabamba en la Mirada de las Mujeres." *Defendamos los Bienes Comunes* 1 (1): 12.

Pérez Lizaur, Marisol. 1973. *Población y sociedad: Cuatro comunidades del Acolhuacan*. Mexico City: Secretaría de Educación Pública.

Postel, Sandra. 1997. *Last Oasis: Facing Water Scarcity.* The World Watch Environmental Alert Series. New York: Norton and Company, Inc.

Pradhan, Rajendra, and Ujjwal Pradhan. 2000. "Negotiating Access and Rights: Disputes over Rights to an Irrigation Water Source in Nepal." In *Negotiating Water Rights*, edited by B. Bruns and R. Meinzen-Dick, 200–221. London: International Food Policy Research Institute/Intermediate Technology Publications.

PRONAR. 2000. *Inventario Nacional de Sistemas de Riego.* Cochabamba, Bolivia: Ministerio de Agricultura Gandaria y Desarollo Rural.

Ramirez, Miguel D. 1995. "The Political Economy of Privatisation in Mexico, 1983–92." *Organization* 2 (1): 87–116.

Rap, Edwin, Philippus Wester, and Luz Nereida-Perez Prado. 1999. The articulation of irrigation reforms and the reconstitution of the hydraulic bureacracy in Mexico. Paper presented at the Conference "The Politics of Irrigation Reforms," December 11–14. Hyderabad, India: INPIM, GOI and WUR.

Rap, Edwin, Philippus Wester, and Luz Nereida Pérez-Prado. 2004. "The Politics of Creating Commitment: Irrigation Reforms and the Reconstitution of the Hydraulic Bureaucracy in Mexico." In *The Politics of Irrigation Reform. Contested Policy Formulation and Implementation in Asia, Africa and Latin America*, edited by Peter P. Mollinga and Alex Bolding, 57–94. Aldershot, UK: Ashgate.

Reisner, Marc. 1987. *Cadillac Desert: The American West and Its Disappearing Water.* New York: Penguin Books.

Restrepo, Iván. 1995. "La crisis del agua en México." In *Agua, Salud y Derechos Humanos*, edited by Iván Restrepo, 9–17. Mexico City: Comisión Nacional de Derechos Humanos.

Rico, María Nieves. 1994a. *Development and Gender Equity: An Uncompleted Task.* Serie Mujer y Desarrollo, no. 13. Social Development Division, Women and Development Unit, ECLAC. Santiago, Chile: ECLAC.

———. 1994b. "Género y medio ambiente, nuevos desafíos para el desarrollo." In *Población y Ambiente. Interrelaciones que afectan el desarrollo andino*, edited by Cesar Quiroz and Eloisa Tréllez, chapter 3. Lima, Peru: CALEIDOS, FNUAP.

———. 1998a. *Gender, the Environment and the Sustainability of Development.* Serie Mujer y Desarrollo, no. 25 (October). LC/L.1144. Santiago, Chile: ECLAC.

———. 1998b. "Women in Water-related Processes in Latin America: Current Situation and Research and Policy Proposals." *International Journal of Water Resources Development* 14 (4) pages 461–71.

Rickson, Sarah T. 1997. "Outstanding in their Field: Women in Agriculture." *Current Sociology* 45 (2): 91–133.

Ringler, Claudia, Mark Rosegrant, and Michael S. Paisner. 2000. *Irrigation and Water Resources in Latin America and the Caribbean: Challenges and Strategies.* EPTD (Environment and Production Technology Division). Discussion Paper, no. 64. Washington, D.C.: International Food Policy Research Institute.

Rionda, Luis Miguel. 2000. "Migración Internacional." Paper presented at the Second Conference on Population and Development, State Population Program for Guanajuato, Guanajuato City, May 3–4.

Ríos, Monica, and Jorge Quiroz. 1995. "The Market of Water Rights in Chile: Major Issues." *World Bank Technical Paper 285.* Washington, D.C.: The World Bank.

Robles, Rosario. 2000. "El Ajuste Invisible." In *Tiempo de Crisis, Tiempo de Mujeres*, edited by Josefina Aranda, Carlota Botey, and Rosario Robles, 22–50. Oaxaca: Centro de Estudios de la Cuestión Agraria Mexicana A.C., Universidad Autónoma Benito Juárez de Oaxaca.

Rodda, Annabel. 1991. *Women and the Environment.* London: Zed Books Ltd.

Rodríguez Rojo, Alma Rosa. 1995. *San Juan Tezontla: Lucha por el agua.* Colección Tepetlaostoc, no. 6. Mexico City: Universidad Iberoamericana.

Rosegrant, Mark, and Hans Binswanger. 1994. "Markets in Tradable Water Rights: Potential for Efficiency Gains in Developing Country Water Resource Allocation." *World Development* 22: 1613–25.

Rosegrant, Mark, and Renato Gazmuri. 1996. "Establishing Tradable Water Rights: Implementation of the Mexican Water Law." *Irrigation and Drainage Systems* 10: 263–279.

Rubio Vega, Blanca. 1997. "La Crisis Agrícola en los Noventa y la Feminización Rural en México." In *Desarrollo Rural y Género—Estratégias de Sobrevivencia de Mujeres Campesinas e Indígenas ante la Crisis Económica*, edited by Pilar Alberti Manzanares and Emma Zapata Martelo.

Rus, Jan, and Robert Wasserstrom. 1980. "Civil-Religious Hierarchies in Central Chiapas: A Critical Perspective." *American Ethnologist* 7 (3): 466–78.

Safa, Helen I. 1990. "Women's Social Movements in Latin America." *Gender and Society* 4 (3): 354–69.

Salazar, Cecilia. 2000. *Politización desde abajo (las mujeres en la participación popular)*. La Paz, Bolivia: Coordinadora de la Mujer, Universidad Mayor de San Andrés, Post Grado en Ciencias del Desarrollo (CIDES-UMSA), Viceministerio de Planificación Estratégica y Participación Popular.

Sandoval, Ricardo Minero. 2002. "Los COTAS de Guanajuato en el Contexto del Manejo del Agua en México." *Aqua Forum*, no. 26. Centro de Estudios del Agua de Guanajuato (CEAG).

Schaefer-Davis, Susan. 1996. "Implementing Gender Policy in the Water and Sanitation Sector." *Natural Resources Forum* 20 (3): 189–98.

Scheper-Hughes, Nancy. 1992. *Death without Weeping: The Violence of Everyday Life in Brazil*. Berkeley: University of California Press.

Scott, Christopher, Philippus Wester, and Carlos Garcés. 1999. "Institutional Responses to Groundwater Depletion: The Aquifer Management Councils in the State of Guanajuato, México." Paper presented at the International Symposium on Integrated Water Management in Agriculture, Gómez Palacio, Durango, Mexico, June 16–18.

Secretaría de Estado de la Mujer (SEM). 2000. *Plan Nacional de Equidad de Género. Acciones coordinadas desde el Estado para el desarrollo de la mujer*. Santo Domingo: SEM.

Serageldin, Ismael. 1995. *Toward Sustainable Management of Water Resources*. Washington, D.C.: The World Bank.

SIDA (Swedish International Development Cooperation Agency). n.d. *A Gender Perspective in the Water Resources Management Sector: Handbook for Mainstreaming*. Department for Natural Resources and the Environment Publications on Water Resources, no. 6. Stockholm: SIDA.

Simbolon, Ineke. J. 1997. "Understanding Women and Land Rights in the Context of Legal Pluralism: The Case of Toba-Batak, Indonesia." In *Gender and Land Use: Diversity in Environmental Practises*, edited by Mirjam de Bruijn, Ineke van Halsema, and Heleen van den Hombergh, 69–86. Amsterdam: Thela Publishers.

Sitarz, Daniel. 1993. *Agenda 21: The Earth Summit Strategy to Save Our Planet*. Boulder, Colo.: Earthpress.

Sokolovsky, Jay. 1995. *San Jerónimo Amanalco: Un pueblo en transición*. Colección Tepetlaostoc, no. 5. Mexico City: Universidad Iberoamericana.

Solís de Alba, Ana Alicia. 2002. *El movimiento sindical pintado de magneta: Productividad, sexismo y neocorporativismo*. Mexico City: Editorial Itaca.

Sotomayor, Jorge, and C. Garcés. 1996. *Perfil de Riego de la República del Ecuador*. Quito: International Irrigation Management Institute.

Sotomayor, Jorge, Wim Kloezen, Carlos Garcés-Restrepo, and Elena P. Bastidas. 1999. *Manejo del agua en las acequias privadas garrapatal y el tambo en la provincia del Carhi, Ecuador*. International Water Management Institute Serie Latinoamericana, no. 4. Mexico City: International Water Management Institute.

Spiertz, Joep, and Melanie G. Wiber. 1996. "The Role of Law in Natural Resource Management." *Recht der Werkelijkheid*. The Hague: VUGA.

Stacey, Judith. 1998. "Can There Be a Feminist Ethnography?" *Women's Studies International Forum* (11) 1.

Stephen, Lynn. 1990. "The Politics of Ritual: The Mexican State and Zapotec Autonomy, 1926 to 1989. " In *Class, Politics, and Popular Religion in Mexico and Central America*, edited by Lynn Stephen and James Dow, 43–60. Washington, D.C.: American Anthropological Association.

———. 1991. *Zapotec Women*. Austin: University of Texas Press.

———. 1992. "Women in Mexico's Popular Movements: Survival Strategies against Ecological and Economic Impoverishment." *Latin American Perspectives* 19 (1): 73–96.

Stephen, Lynn, and James Dow. 1990. "Introduction: Popular Religion in Mexico and Central America." In *Class, Politics, and Popular Religion in Mexico and Central America*, edited by Lynn

Stephen and James Dow, 1–24. Washington, D.C.: American Anthropological Association.

Stratford, Elaine. 1995. "Gender and Environment: Some Preliminary Questions About Women and Water in the South Australian Context." *Gender, Place and Culture* 2 (2): 209–15.

Swedish International Development Cooperation Agency (SIDA). n.d. *A Gender Perspective in the Water Resources Management Sector: Handbook for Mainstreaming*. Department for Natural Resources and the Environment, Publications on Water Resources, no. 6. Stockholm: SIDA.

Swyngedouw, Eric. 1999. "Modernity and Hybridity: Nature, Regeneracionismo, and the Production of the Spanish Waterscape 1890–1930." *Annals of the Association of American Geographers* 89 (3): 443–65.

Tarrow, Sidney. 1997. "Cycles of Protest." In *Social Movements: Perspectives and Issues*, edited by Steven Buechler and F. Kurt Cylke, 263–86. Mountain View, California: Mayfield Publishing Company.

Thomas-Slayter, Barbara, Andrea Lee Esser, and M. Dale Shields. 1993. *Tools of Gender Analysis: a Guide to Field Methods for Bringing Gender into Sustainable Resource Management*. Worcester, Mass.: ECOGEN, International Development Program, Clark University.

Thomas-Slayter, Barbara, Rachel Polestico, Andrea Lee Esser, and Octavia Taylor. 1995. "The SEGA Approach." In *A Manual for Socio-Economic and Gender Analysis: Responding to the Development Challenge*, edited by Barbara Thomas-Slayter, 25–44. Worcester, Mass.: ECOGEN-Clark University.

Thorpe, Andy. 1997. "Structural Adjustment and the Agrarian Sector in Latin America." In *The 'Market Panacea': Agrarian Transformation in Developing Countries and Former Socialist Economies*, edited by M. Spoor, 15–28. London: Intermediate Technology.

Tortajada, Cecilia, ed. 2000. *Women and Water Management: The Latin American Experience*. Oxford: Oxford University Press.

Tovar, Marcela. 1998. *Estrategia para la inclusión de la equidad de género en el Departamento Nacional de Planeación*. Consultancy report for the Unidades de Planificación Regional y Urbana y Desarrollo Territorial, Bogota, Colombia.

Townsend, Janet, Emma Zapata, Jo Rowlands, Pilar Alberti, and Marta Mercado. 1999. *Women and Power: Fighting Patriarchy and Poverty*. London: Zed Books.

Tuijtelaars de Quitón, Christiane, Maria Esther Pozo, Rosse Mary Antezana Iriarte, and Roxana Saavedra Crespo. 1994. *Mujer y riego en Punata, aspectos de género: Situación de uso, acceso y control sobre el agua para riego en Punata*. Cochabamba, Bolivia: PEIRAV.

United Nations. 1979. *Convention on the Elimination of All Forms of Discrimination against Women*. Geneva: United Nations.

———. 1986. *The Nairobi Forward-Looking Strategies for the Advancement of Women*. New York: United Nations.

———. 1992a. *The Dublin Statement and Report of the Conference*. International Conference on Water and the Environment: Development Issues for the Twenty-first Century, Dublin, Ireland, January 26–31. New York: United Nations.

———. 1992b. *Report of the United Nations Conference on Environment and Development*. A/CONF.151/26. New York: United Nations.

———. 1992c. Agenda 21 press report.

———. 1995. *Report of the Fourth World Conference on Women*. A/CONF.177/20. New York: United Nations.

———. 2000. *Resolution adopted by the General Assembly. Further actions and initiatives to implement the Beijing Declaration and Platform for Action*. A/res/s-23/3, New York, November.

———. 2001. *State of the World's Children*. New York: UNICEF.

———. 2002. *Earth Summit Agenda 21*. United Nations Division for Sustainable Development. Available online at http://www.un.org/esa/sustdev/agenda21text.htm. Accessed December 5, 2002.

UNESCO (United Nations Economic and Social Council). 2002. "Rio de Janeiro Platform for Action on the Road to Johannesburg, 2002." Commission on Sustainable Development acting as the preparatory committee for the World Summit on Sustainable Development, second preparatory session, January 28–February 8. E/CN.17/2002/PC.2/5/Add.2. Available online at http://www

.johannesburgsummit.org/html/documents/un_docs/pc2doc5add2e_rio_dejaneiro.pdf Accessed June 3, 2004.

Uphoff, Norman. 1986. *Improving International Irrigation Management with Farmer Participation: Getting the Process Right*. Studies in Water Policy and Management, no. 11. London: Westview Press.

Vallejo, Ivette. 1997. *Documento general sobre la cuenca del Río El Angel. Proyecto: Población, uso de la tierra, consumo de agua y medioambiente. Una exploración comparativa de las interrelaciones, competencias, conflictos y alternativas al norte del Ecuador*. Quito: Programa de Sociedades Andinas y Desarrollo Sustentable (DESU-FLACSO).

van der Pol, Ineke. 1992. *Claro, hay que pelear el agua. Roles de género en las actividades de riego*. Lima: Netherlands Development Organization (Stichting Nederlandse Vrijwilliges, SNV).

van Genugten, Willem, and Camilo Perez-Bustillo, eds. 2001. *The Poverty of Rights: Human Rights and the Eradication of Poverty*. London: Zed Books.

Van Koppen, Barbara. 1997. "Water Rights and Poverty Alleviation. Inclusion and Exclusion of Resource-poor Women and Men as Right Holders in Externally Supported Irrigation Development." Paper for the workshop on Women and Water, IIMI (international Irrigation Management Institute). Sri Lanka. Department of Irrigation and Soil and Water Conservation. Wageningen Agricultural University, Wageningen, The Netherlands.

———. 1998. "Poverty, Gender and Targeted Irrigation Development." Paper presented at the Water and Politics Seminar, Department of Irrigation and Soil and Water Conservation, Wageningen Agricultural University, Wageningen, The Netherlands.

van Wijk-Sijbesma, Christine. 1998. *Gender in Water Resource Management, Water Supply and Sanitation: Roles and Realities Revisited by* Technical Paper, no. 33. The Hague: International Water and Sanitation Centre.

Vargas, María. 1998. "Latin America and the Caribbean." In *Rural Women and Food Security: Current Situation and Perspectives*, edited by the Food and Agriculture Organization of the United Nations (FAO), 96–115. Rome, Italy: FAO.

Vargas, Sergio, Gabriela Monsalvo Velázquez, and Phillipus Wester. 2000. "Cambios Socioeconómicos y Diferenciación Productiva en los Distritos de Riego en la Cuenca Lerma-Chapala, México." In *Asignación, Manejo y Productividad de los Recursos Hídricos en Cuencas*, eds. Christopher Scott, Phillipus Wester, and Boris Marañón, 77–92. Mexico City: Serie Latinoamericana no. 19. International Water Management Institute, 2000.

Vattuone, María Elena, Emma Yep, and Hilda Segura. 1996. *Mirando el riego con enfoque de genero*. Lima, Peru: SNV.

Vera, Juana. 1993. *Sistematización de experiencia de capacitación a especialistas campesinos en la Escuela de riego campesino, Cabanaconde*. Arequipa, Peru: Dirección de Capacitación y Sistematización de la Cooperativa Peruana–Alemana de Seguridad Alimentaria (COPASA).

———. 1996. *Normatividad legal y local para el uso de recursos naturales. Estudio de caso de tres comunidades campesinas de Paruro*. Cuzco, Peru: IMA (Instituto de Manejo de Agua)-Cuzco.

———. 1999. "Engendering the Debate of Irrigation Development. Gender Interface and Irrigation System Concepts as Starting Points. A Mexican Case from Quiringuicharo in Michoacán." M.Sc. Thesis, Wageningen Agricultural University, Wageningen, The Netherlands.

Whiteford, Scott, Francisco A. Bernal, Heliodoro Díaz Cisneros, and Esteban Valtierra-Pacheco. 1998. "Arid-Land *Ejidos:* Bound by the Past, Marginalized by the Future." In *The Transformation of Rural Mexico: Reforming the Ejido Sector*, edited by Wayne Cornelius and David Myhre, 381–89. La Jolla: Center for U.S.-Mexican Studies, University of California, San Diego 1998.

Villalobos, Raul, M. Choque, E. Llerena, M. de la Riva, and M. Condori. 1993. *Rol de la Mujer en Sistemas de Riego*. Puno, Peru: Instituto de Investigaciones para el Desarrollo Social del Antiplano-UNA.

Villarreal, Magdalena. 1994. "Wielding and Yielding: Power, Subordination and Gender Identity in the Context of a Mexican Development Project." Ph.D. diss., Wageningen Agricultural University, Wageningen, The Netherlands.

Viqueira Landa, Carmen. 1994. "La aplicación de la teoría del despotismo oriental a Mesoamérica." In

Regadíos y estructuras de poder, edited by J. Romero and C. Giménez, 53–71. Alicante, Spain: Instituto de Cultura Juan Gil-Albert.

Vos, Jeroen. 2002. "Metric Matters: The Performance and Organisation of Volumetric Water Control in Large-Scale Irrigation in the North Coast of Peru." Ph.D. diss., Wageningen University, Wageningen, The Netherlands.

Wester, Philippus, Boris Marañon Pimentel, and Christopher Scott. 1999. "Institutional Responses to Groundwater Depletion: The Aquifer Management Councils in the State of Guanajuato, Mexico." Paper presented at the International Symposium on Integrated Water Management in Agriculture, June 16–18, 1999. Gómez Palacio, Mexico.

Whitaker, Helen. 1992. *Promoción de la participación de la Comunidad en los proyectos de abastecimiento de agua: Una guía para trabajar con la mujer*. Tegucigalpa, Guatemala: UNICEF.

Whitaker, Morris D. 1990. *El Rol de la Agricultura en el Desarrollo Económico del Ecuador*. Quito: IDEA.

Whiteford, Linda M. 1997. "The Ethnoecology of Dengue Fever." *Medical Anthropology Quarterly* 11 (2): 202–23.

Whiteford, Scott, and Roberto Melville, eds. 2002. *Protecting a Sacred Gift: Water and Social Change in Mexico*. La Jolla: Center for U.S.-Mexican Studies, University of California, San Diego.

Wieringa, Susan. 1994. "Women's Interest and Empowerment: Gender Planning Considered." *Development and Change* 25 (4): 829–48.

Wilcox-Young, Linda. 1987. "Internationalization of the Labor Process in Agriculture: A Case Study of Agroindustrial Development in Mexico's El Bajío." Ph.D. diss., University of California, Berkeley.

Wilcox-Young, Linda. 1993. "Labour Demand and Agroindustrial Development: The Evidence from Mexico." *The Journal of Development Studies* 30 (1): 168–89.

WMO/IDB (World Meteorological Organization and Inter-American Development Bank). 1996. *Water resources assessment and management strategies in Latin America and the Caribbean*. Proceedings of the WMO/IDB Conference, San José, Costa Rica, May 6–11.

Wolf, Eric R. 1957. "Closed Corporate Peasant Communities in Mesoamerica and Central Java." *Southwestern Journal of Anthropology* 13 (1): 1–18.

———. 1986. "Vicissitudes of the Closed Corporate Peasant Community." *American Ethnologist* 13: 325–29.

Wolf, Eric R., and Angel Palerm. 1955. "Irrigation in the Old Acolhua Domain, Mexico." *Southwestern Journal of Anthropology* 11: 265–81.

———. 1993. *Water Resources Management*. World Bank Policy Paper, no. 12335. Washington, D.C.

———. 1999a. *World Bank Policy Matrix Through 2001*. Washington, D.C.

———. 1999b. *Bolivia Regulatory Reform and Privatization Technical Assistance Project*. Available online at http://www.wds.worldbank.org/servlet/WDSContentServer/WDSP/IB/1998/05/14/000009265_3980929101532/Rendered/PDF/multiopage.pdf. Accessed on October 12, 2003.

———. 1999c. *Bolivia Public Expenditures Review*. Report 19232. BO. Washington, D.C.: World Bank.

———. 2001. *Engendering Development: Through Gender Equality in Rights, Resources, and Voice*. New York: Oxford University Press and World Bank.

World Water Council. 2000a. *Final Report*. World Water Council's Second World Water Forum and Ministerial Conference: From Vision to Action, The Hague, The Netherlands, March 17–22. The Hague: Water Management Unit, Ministry of Foreign Affairs.

———. 2000b. *Second Announcement: The Third World Water Forum (What Will Happen in Kyoto, Shiga and Osaka)*. Brochure prepared by the Secretariat of the Third World Water Forum. Tokyo, Japan.

———. 2000c. *World Water Council: The International Water Policy Think Tank*. Brochure prepared by World Water Council Secretariat. Marseille, France.

World Water Vision. 1999. "Mainstreaming Gender in Water Resources Management: Why and How." Background paper for the World Vision Process, UNESCO, Paris.

www.earthsummit2002.org. Available online at http://www.johannesburgsummit.org/html/whats_new/feature_story39.htm. Accessed on June 2, 2004.

Young, Robert. 1986. "Why Are There So Few Transactions among Water Users?" *American Journal of Agricultural Economics* 68 (5): 1144–51.

Zwarteveen, Margreet. 1994. *Gender Issues, Water Issues: A Gender Perspective to Irrigation Management.* International Irrigation Management Institute (IWMI) Working Paper, no. 32. Colombo, Sri Lanka: IWMI.

Zwarteveen, Margreet. 1997a. "A Plot of One's Own: Gender Relations and Irrigated Land Allocation Policies in Burkina Faso." International Irrigation Management Institute Research Report, no. 10. Colombo, Sri Lanka: IWMI.

———. 1997b. "Gender Issues, Water Issues. A Gender Perspective to Irrigation Management." Working Paper, no. 32. International Irrigation Management Institute (IIMI). DGIS, DADIDA.

———. 1997c. "Water: From Basic Need to Commodity. A Discussion on Gender and Water Rights in the Context of Irrigation." *World Development* 25 (8): 1335–5.

———. 1998. "Identifying Gender Aspects of New Irrigation Management Policies." *Agriculture and Human Values* 15: 310–12.

Zwarteveen, Margreet, and Ruth Meinzen-Dick. 2001. "Gender and Property Rights in the Commons: Examples of Water Rights in South Asia." *Agriculture and Human Values* 18: 11–25.

Zwarteveen, Margreet, and Nita Neupane. 1996. *Free Riders or Victims: Women's Nonparticipation in Irrigation Management in Nepal's Chhattis Mauja Irrigation Scheme.* International Irrigation Management Institute (IIMI) Research Report, no. 7. Colombo, Sri Lanka: IIMI.

Contributors

Lorena Aguilar is a senior gender advisor at *Unión Mundial para la Naturaleza*, and regional coordinator of their Mesoamerican unit. She has a master's degree in anthropology from the University of Kansas. She has worked for nine years in development projects and the design of public policy in Central America, specializing in applying social and gender factors to natural resources conservation and management. She is an international consultant in the area of water, gender, environmental health, and community participation.

Rhodante Ahlers is a doctoral candidate at Cornell University where she is working on privatization of water resources and social justice in the context of both rural and urban planning. She has done research on gender and irrigation policy and development in Mexico, Ecuador, Bolivia, Cambodia, Bhutan, and Sri Lanka.

Elena P. Bastidas is Courtesy Assistant Professor of International Programs, Institute of Food and Agricultural Sciences (IFAS) at the University of Florida. She received her Ph.D. in food and resource economics at the University of Florida in 2001. Elena coordinates University of Florida's Ecuador Summer Abroad Program, where she is the instructor for the Gender, Environment, Agriculture, and Participation (GEAP) summer course. Her research has focused on social aspects of natural resource management, farming systems, and gender analysis.

Vivienne Bennett is associate professor of Latin American studies and chair of the Liberal Studies Department at California State University, San Marcos. Her publications include *The Politics of Water: Urban Protest, Gender and Power in Monterrey, Mexico* (University of Pittsburgh Press, 1995) and numerous articles and book chapters on urban social movements in Mexico as well as on issues of water resource management in Mexico. She has presented her work widely in the United States, Europe, and Mexico.

Stephanie Buechler has a master's degree in public affairs and a Ph.D. in sociology. She is currently a postdoctoral scientist at the International Water Management Institute (IWMI) in Hyderabad, India. She has conducted research, published, and produced videos on livelihood strategies among women, men, and children in the United States, Honduras, Bolivia, Mexico, and India. Her work in Mexico and India with IWMI has focused on urban, periurban, and rural access to water, including wastewater, and gender, class, and caste issues.

Rocío Bustamante de Romero is an attorney as well as a researcher at the Andean Center for Water Management and Water Use (Centro Agua) at the Universidad Mayor de

San Simón, Cochabamba, Bolivia. In addition to her J.D. degree, she has a master's degree in the management of agricultural knowledge systems and social research from Wageningen Agricultural University, The Netherlands. Her fields of specialization and publication include water legislation (including customary laws and rights) and water policy issues in the Andean region.

Sonia Dávila-Poblete is a technical advisor for the Global Water Partnership (GWP). She is Bolivian and has a master's degree and Ph.D. in sociology. Her areas of specialization are organizational processes, water and sustainable development policies and gender. She has various publications about water and sustainable development policies from a gender perspective, as well as on the organizational aspects of the hydroagricultural sector, among other topics.

Norma Del Pozo was a leader of the protests against the privatization of the water system in Tucumán, Argentina. She has worked in popular education and was in charge of the education program of the Liga de Cooperativas Cañeras de Tucumán (Federation of Sugar Cane Peasants of Tucumán).

Michael C. Ennis-McMillan is associate professor of anthropology at Skidmore College, Saratoga Springs, New York. He is author of *La Purificación Tepetitla: Agua potable y cambio social en el somontano* (2001). His areas of interest include medical anthropology, environmental anthropology, and grassroots development in Latin America. Since 1993, he has been studying the political, cultural, and environmental aspects of installing and managing piped water systems in the Valley of Mexico.

Norma Giarracca is a researcher and associate professor in the sociology department of the University of Buenos Aires. She is chair of the Grupo de Estudios Rurales of the Instituto de Investigaciones "Gino Germani" and the former chair of the Grupo de Trabajo de Desarrollo Rural of CLACSO (Latin American Social Sciences Council). She has written extensively on social protests in Argentina and on Latin America rural issues with special reference to Mexico and Tucumán, Argentina. Recent books edited include *¿Una Nueva Ruralidad en América Latina?* and *La Protesta Social en la Argentina*.

Elizabeth Peredo, a social psychologist, is the director of the Women, Identity and Work Division, in the Fundación Solón, La Paz, Bolivia—an NGO promoting gender and human rights equity for women in household, community, and labor union contexts, as well as human rights in trade and water issues. She is the author of multiple books and articles on gender, class, and ethnic identities and human rights in multicultural societies. She has also written and directed documentaries on women's issues and coordinated campaigns to promote human rights of indigenous women in Bolivia.

María Nieves Rico is social affairs officer for the Women and Development Unit of the Economic Commission for Latin America and the Caribbean (United Nations), based in Chile. She is an Argentine anthropologist with a master's degree in development sociology from the Universidad Complutense de Madrid, where she is also a Ph.D. candidate. Her areas of specialization are gender, development, and public policy. She has authored various publications about sustainable development, poverty, and gender policies in Latin America and the Caribbean, among other topics.

Juana Vera Delgado is an agronomist with a master's degree in Management of Agricultural Knowledge Systems and Social Research from Wageningen Agricultural University of The Netherlands, where she is currently a doctoral candidate. She specializes in gender and irrigation management, sustainable agriculture and gender policies, gender and rural development. She has extensive experience as a rural development promoter in the Peruvian Andes as well as in Bolivia. She was a technical advisor in gender and rural development for the Netherlands Development Agency in Peru.

María Esther Udaeta, a sociologist, works at the Centro de Investigación y Promoción del Campesinado (CIPCA, Center for Research and Promotion of Peasantry) in La Paz: one of the first NGOs in Bolivia to have worked with indigenous communities at the national level. She also runs the National Roundtable on Water, bringing together fourteen NGOs that focus on water issues in Bolivia. She is experienced in developing projects that incorporate and promote community participation and decentralized management with a gender perspective.

Margreet Zwarteveen is a lecturer and researcher with the Irrigation and Water Engineering Group at the Department of Environmental Sciences at Wageningen University, The Netherlands. She holds an MS.c. in irrigation and development studies, and is finalizing her Ph.D. on gender and irrigation management at the same university. She has been involved in research in Sri Lanka, Bangladesh, Nepal, and West Africa. She has published widely on gender, irrigation development, and water resources management.

Index

active resistance, 8, 121, 195

Agenda 21, 37, 38, 46, 210n9 (chap. 3). *See also* United Nations Conference on Environment and Development

agrarian reform: in Bolivia, 68; in Ecuador, 157; in Mexico, 61–62, 67–68

Agua del Aconquija: formation of, 91; operation in Tucumán, 95–99; proposals to replace, 99–101. *See also* Compagnie Générale des Eaux

Aguas del Tunari: contract terms of, 78, 80–81, 212n6 (chap. 5), 213n7; opposition to, 79, 81, 88, 213n11

Alsogaray, María Julia, 101, 214n9

Angel River. *See* El Angel River

Appropriate Productive Technologies. *See* Tecnologías Productivas Apropiades (TPAs)

Argentina: economic crises in, 101, 105; human rights in, 94, 214n10; military in, 94–95, 214n10; N 23.696 (law to reform public administration), 95–96; neoliberalism in, 51, 92, 100, 105, 191; privatization in, 96, 99, 105, 190, 214n6; social unrest in, 92, 94, 105, 193; and UN Conference on Water, 35; water user associations in, 95, 99; and the World Bank, 96, 214n6. *See also* Monteros; Tucumán

Asociación en Defensa de los Usuarios y Consumidores de Tucumán (Association in Defense of Users and Consumers of Tucumán, ADEUCOT), 97, 100–4, 106

Association in Defense of Users and Consumers of Tucumán. *See* Asociación en Defensa de los Usuarios y Consumidores de Tucumán (ADEUCOT)

Bajío, the, 19, 170, 175, 188, 217n2 (chap. 11)

Banzer, Hugo, 66–67, 78, 81

Basin Advisory Boards (Mexico), 174. *See also*

Basin Commissions and Committees (Mexico)

Basin Commissions and Committees (Mexico), 175. *See also* Basin Advisory Boards (Mexico)

Bechtel, 67, 78, 204, 212n8

Beijing Platform for Action, 43–44. *See also* Fourth World Conference on Women

Bolivia: agrarian reform in, 68; *campesinos* in, 76, 78–79, 82, 85, 212n4; customary laws and practices in, 68, 88–89; indigenous peoples in, 67–68, 75, 89; irrigators' associations in, 68, 78, 88–89; Neighborhood Committees, 74–75, 212n3; neoliberalism in, 8, 51, 66, 68–70, 191; privatization in, 56, 66–70; social movements in, 72, 79, 200; *usos y costumbres* in, 66–68, 70, 88; water commercialization in, 56, 66, 68–69, 96; water commodification in, 8, 54, 80; Water Law in, 54, 66–68; water legislation in, 32, 66, 212n2; and the World Bank, 54, 66, 78, 86. *See also* Cochabamba; Law 2029; Law 2066; Water War

Brazil, 3. *See also* United Nations Conference on Environment and Development

Brundtland Commission, 34, 210n5

Buenos Aires, 92, 94, 105–6, 214n12

Bussi, Antonio Domingo, 94–95

campesinos: in Bolivia, 76, 78–79, 82, 85, 212n4 (chap. 5); defined, 212n4 (chap. 5); in Mexico, 137, 141, 153. *See also* indigenous peoples; peasants

Canada, 54; and Handpump Technology project, 194, 215n1; migration from Mexico to, 170, 181, 183–84

Carchi: described, 156–57; *mestizo* in, 156, 216n1 (chap. 10); water management in, 8, 190, 198–99, 201–3; water user associations in, 157, 202–3. *See also* Ecuador

243